NAVIGATING A RESTLESS SEA
Mobilizing Innovation in Your Community

Cover image generated by StableDiffusion with the prompt: "Create a vertical book cover for a book called 'Navigating a Restless Sea' with dangerous looking ocean waves matching style of the Great Wave off Kanagawa by Katsushika Hokusai that include boats."

Text copyright © 2024 Peter J. Denning and Todd W. Lyons
All rights reserved.
Printed in the United States of America.
No part of this book may be reproduced, or stored in a retrieval system, or transmitted in any form or by any means, electronic, mechanical, photocopying, recording, or otherwise, without express written permission of the publisher.

ISBN-13: 978-1-962984-30-0 print edition
ISBN-10: 978-1-962984-31-7 e-book edition

Waterside Productions
2055 Oxford Ave
Cardiff, CA 92007
www.waterside.com

PETER DEDICATES TO

Dorothy, my wife and partner for over 50 years

Anne, Diana, and Ava, my next generation

My numerous students, who brought this to work into their lives

TODD DEDICATES TO

Kristi, my wife who encourages me and keeps me grounded

Grace, Eleanor and Jordan who keep my eyes on the future

Our students and fellow travelers who strive valiantly every day

NAVIGATING A RESTLESS SEA

Mobilizing Innovation in Your Community

Peter J. Denning and Todd W. Lyons

Foreword by Ron Kaufman

Waterside Productions

CONTENTS

Foreword by Ron Kaufman
Preface
Acknowledgements
Prolog

Part I – The Basic Practices of Innovation
    1   Awakening 1
    2   Beginning 27
    3   Skilling 39
    4   Leading 47
    5   Navigating 61

Part II – Navigating Social Space
    6   Conversations 81
    7   Worlds 99
    8   Coordination 115
    9   Declarations 125
    10   Assessments 139
    11   Moods 155
    12   Trust 171
    13   Power 189
    14   Resistance 201

Part III – Bringing It into the World
    15   Embodying 221
    16   Executing 243
    17   Mobilizing 255
    18   Becoming 273
    19   Measuring 285
    20   Machines 299
    21   Mastery 315
    22   Epilog 331

Appendices
    A1   Key Distinctions 335
    A2   Summary of the Eight Practices 344
    A3   Self-assessment Tools 348
    A4   Domains of Concerns 350
    A5   Compilation of Somatic Exercises 354
    A6   Horizons of Innovation 357
    A7   Taxonomy of Innovation Models 362

FOREWORD
Ron Kaufman

What is the difference between an idea, an invention, and a successful innovation?

New ideas arise in a certain kind of thinking. Some emerge new and full of sparkling imagination. Others are the same as or close to ideas we've had before. Some ideas erupt spontaneously while others must be deliberately pursued. Many ideas are commonplace, *"Let's have ice cream!"*, while others can change the way we see the world, *"I wonder if gravity bends light?"*

New ideas may surface in moments of calm and quiet reflection. Others appear in enthusiastic conversations. Ideas may be inspired by nature, music, architecture, art, food, history, culture, tradition, or any other ingredient of life that arouses your imagination. Some ideas will drift away as easily as a pleasant and passing summer breeze. Others take the world by storm. Ideas can be a dime a dozen, yet an idea whose time has come may be worth a fortune.

In classrooms, laboratories, and brainstorming sessions, we are asked to "generate lots of new ideas" and told, "No idea is a bad idea," which may not be a good idea. Some ideas are truly bad as serious accidents and catastrophes across history attest. This is not to say that a wide range of creative ideas is inappropriate or unwanted, even those that appear difficult, dangerous, impossible, or absurd. Rather, it is to remind idea generators to remain emotionally curious and intellectually open as their ideas are questioned and challenged, changed, refined, elevated, evaluated, and potentially improved.

In the context of innovation leadership, an improved idea is not just a better idea. An improved idea is when more people bring more attention, time, energy, and resources to push that idea toward the possibility of tangible reality. This is when ideas gain traction and begin to demonstrate workability. Hunches and concepts are tried and tested. Patents yield prototypes, and possibilities show their real-world potential. Start-ups launch, investors lurk, and skunkworks churn out variations that may – or may not – ever see the light of day.

I distinguish a good idea (for example, 3D additive printing) from a working invention (commercially available 3D printers) and a genuine innovation (3D printers routinely building parts on ships).

An effective invention demonstrates the workability of an idea. This is not the same as a successful innovation.

Countless inventions emerge only to fail in the field, flop in the market, or be rejected by a community and soon forgotten. A working prototype is not a successful commercial product. A patent is not the same as an embraced and established new practice.

In this extraordinary book, co-authors Peter Denning and Todd Lyons reveal that *successful innovation exists only when an existing or emerging community embraces and adopts a new practice.* Successful innovation is when some new way of living, working, playing, or fighting becomes the accepted way of getting those things done. Innovation is not a process leading to adoption, *it is the adoption.*

Authors Peter Denning and Todd Lyons are brilliantly suited to write and share this book because they have been navigating for decades in a restless sea churning with good and bad ideas, working and failed inventions, and struggling and occasionally successful innovations.

Peter Denning's passion for ideas and experimentation was revealed as a teenager when he solved linear equations with pinball machine parts, long before lines of code were being written for advanced computer chips. Across his many years at MIT, Princeton,

Purdue, George Mason, NASA, and the Naval Postgraduate School (NPS), Peter has witnessed and helped shape our era's epic journey through conceptual and technical breakthroughs, prolific papers and books, and by participating in endless conversations, bold experiments, numerous inventions, and fewer – yet precious – successful innovations. Peter knows what truly changes the world is not the new technologies we create. It is when these technologies are coupled with new behaviors that we enable our communities to grow, adapt, and thrive. He has been there, and he has done that. To put this in metaphor, Peter didn't just get the t-shirt; he designed it, printed it, and – through his teaching and his writings today – distributes it with enthusiasm to thousands.

Todd Lyons works alongside Peter as his co-author, co-creator, and instructor of Innovation Leadership at NPS. For 30 years as an active US Marine, Todd guided, implemented, analyzed, assessed, and recommended more new ideas than most of us would imagine in a lifetime. He knows what it feels like to experience the adrenaline-filled surges and heartbreaking setbacks that real life delivers. He has seen what works and what fails in the fraught, fragile, and, at times, ferocious circumstances in the Middle East, one of our world's most challenged and challenging regions. All of this has resulted in an unrelenting passion for results and eternal compassion for the well-being of people, families, communities, and cultures everywhere. Today, as Vice President of the NPS Foundation & Alumni Association, Todd bridges the divide between academia, industry, and the people and structures of military power. He understands how bureaucracy works and how to make it work for the better.

These deeply experienced authors recognize how challenging it can be to cross the chasm from ideas to implementation. They repeatedly hear how frustrating it is for leaders, especially young leaders, to wrestle with the bureaucratic resistance, procedural slow walking, and direct or disguised stonewalling that prevents the implementation of new practices and resists successful innovations.

Their students at NPS are among the brightest in the world, facing one the most challenging areas for innovation anywhere in the world. Have you heard the expression, "It takes a long time to turn a battleship?" NPS students are responsible for achieving something enormously harder. Once a decision is made and orders given, a battleship at full speed can turn 180 degrees in less than two minutes. But try installing 3D printers onboard that ship for the fabrication of urgently needed parts and equipment – and the time required to achieve success could be months, years, or never.

NPS students of innovation leadership must navigate inside the military's current systems, changing circumstances, existing practices, evolving technologies, competitive pressures, active conflicts, and layers upon layers of mandatory approval. And they must do this in a world where speed, adaptation, and effective use of new inventions are more vital for victory than ever before. Many leaders of innovation in business, government, and communities confront these challenges and navigate similarly confounding situations.

Denning and Lyons understand how crucial it is for leaders everywhere – in the military, in business, in society, and in life – to be enabled, encouraged, and empowered to succeed in one of the greatest challenges of our time, bringing new inventions to successful implementation. Why is this so difficult? What causes so many working inventions to fail at crossing this chasm?

One answer presented clearly in this book is that most leaders in business and government treat implementation as something they can "produce" with a well-managed process. This linear and step-by-step approach has a long history of delivering efficiency, productivity, speed, and cost reductions.

However, innovation in a community poses a completely different challenge. It requires winning agreement, gaining commitment, and guiding real people already familiar with their existing processes, policies, and practices, to participate in fundamentally adapting and adjusting the way they work and live. For the innovation leader, this means listening, appreciating, educating, explaining, guiding, and perhaps celebrating, too. All of this occurs and is achieved in conversations – and this demands a different set of skills from those required to streamline production or achieve a process improvement.

The lack of these skills creates an illusion the authors call the "valley of death" where inventions and their inventors die before they become successful innovations. Where can you learn these necessary and increasingly vital skills? Where can you discover the insights, learn the distinctions, practice the skills, and admire proven strategies for success? The answer to that question is in the forthcoming chapters of this book. Navigating a Restless Sea is filled with practical advice, surprising stories, abundant examples, and genuine pearls of wisdom. The authors make no promise that your crossing to a successful innovation will be easy or fast, but if you learn to lead with the skills you need, your efforts will not be doomed to fail.

A Personal Example of the Power in this Book

I define service as *taking action to create value for someone* and Uplifting Service as *taking the next action to create more value for someone you care about*. With these definitions, I have helped many leaders and organizations to *improve service performance* and *build uplifting service cultures*. These two outcomes are not the same.

The first can be individual or situational and only needs someone to put some idea into action. The second is more enduring. It's communal and relational and delivers more value and more well-being to more people over time. The first requires a service provider and a recipient (usually called the customer). The second requires a community of diverse service providers to embrace, adopt, improve, refine, implement, and sustain a series of new ideas and practices.

To lead people in attempting and sustaining this second effort requires a completely different level of focus, understanding, attention, and care for the service providers, customers, community, culture, past, present, and future. This level of listening and understanding, sensing and appreciating, communicating and coordinating, measuring, and mobilizing, and eventually trusting is precisely where this remarkable book will take you.

Be forewarned: do not underestimate the power of the authors to provoke the way you think and bring new insights to your attention. Educators of this caliber do not come along every day, and rarer still is when they make the investment to consolidate their teaching into a fascinating and accessible book.

Let me share this personal example. Peter and Todd took my definition of service, *"taking action to create value for someone,"* and changed it in Chapter 21 to read *"action that brings value to someone."* (They generously attribute this version to me.)

Notice this subtle yet powerful revision. Feel it. My version focuses on the service provider; taking action, creating value. Theirs focuses on the customer; bringing to, value for. Decades into my career, these two authors have pushed my thinking forward, and I am grateful.

Such positive and powerful teachings will challenge and delight you throughout this book, filled with stories and illustrations, examples, challenges, and practical tools you can use.

Immerse yourself in this voyage. Open your thinking, real thinking, to embrace what is being revealed. Invest yourself in the book's many experiments, practices, and techniques. Delight yourself and those around you as you embody new ways to serve and express your care – for those you lead, for those you love, and for life. Bring your curious mind, eager hands, and open heart to this adventure.

Read on.

~ ~ ~ ~ ~

Ron Kaufman
Author, *New York Times* bestseller *Uplifting Service*.

PREFACE

Innovation is the emergence of new practice in a community. What are the leadership practices that bring forth new practices?

• • •

Generative AI in the form of ChatGPT was offered for public access by OpenAI at the end of November 2022. It was a major leap forward for machine learning technology. It touched off enormous waves of interest. Within two weeks, 100 million users were trying out the new technology. Within two months, there were a dozen how-to-use-GPT books available from Amazon. Tech companies quickly announced plans to incorporate the technology into their browsers, office packages, online services, and other apps. Hundreds of proposals for start-ups appeared and venture capitalists backed them. The speed of adoption of Generative AI was astonishing. It all happened in conversations, which spread rapidly through word of mouth, the Internet, and the media. Many people started experimenting to see whether Generative AI would be a good advisor, artist, writer, or programmer. They shared their findings widely on social media and as preprints of research papers. Moods of awe, surprise and intense enthusiasm blossomed. They were later joined by moods of distrust and fear that the Generative AI technology might get out of control and cause great damage to humanity. The ideas and moods spread rapidly round the world.

The collective conversation took on a life of its own, stimulating innovation leaders all over, who initiated smaller conversations within the froth. These included first mover OpenAI, tech companies, experimenters, tinkerers, AI researchers, medical researchers, artists, writers, and programmers. Some AI experts started having doubts about the safety of the technology; they inspired an international conversation calling for government regulation to manage the dangers.

This is an example of emergence of innovation. It happened in a complex mixture of many conversations as users flocked to the technology. In their small social circles, they guided their local conversations to adoption. Their conversations and new practices built on each other. New practices emerged in the larger community from the collective work of leaders and users and workers at every level.

Innovation emergence is fostered by many leaders and many followers. This book explores how innovation leaders accomplish these feats. You can learn what they know and practice it yourself.

• • •

In *The Innovator's Way* (2010), Peter Denning and Bob Dunham introduced the idea that innovation is the adoption of a new practice in a community. Putting it this way, they thought, brought focus to the ultimate aspiration of innovators, that their community incorporates their ideas or inventions into everyday practice. They wanted to attend to the people who do the work. Denning and Dunham studied many successful innovations and formulated eight essential practices that innovators use to bring about adoption. They presented strong evidence that leaders of successful innovation engaged in those practices. The eight practices produced the successes – not heroic genius, charisma, brilliance, or pure luck.

The eight practices guide you in walking side by side with members of your community, mobilizing their commitment to a new practice that realizes a new possibility they are collectively seeking.

The focus on adoption reveals three severe limitations on traditional ways of thinking about innovation. First, the traditional way is founded in a factory production pipeline model that takes an invention into a market but brings no certainty that the market will adopt what the factory produces. Second, it takes one good inventor to get a production process going, but thousands of workers to get the results adopted. Adoption is about mobilizing workers, not inventors.

Third, a great many innovations are social – new community practices that resolve breakdowns and injustices. No inventors are involved. Adoption is a social process of mobilizing the many into agreement on new practices that get them what they did not have. Generating adoption requires mastery of conversations in the social spaces of communities.

Today, the need for innovation leaders who generate adoption is more urgent than ever. People who are trying to innovate are increasingly frustrated with bureaucratic impediments and the apparent waste of their efforts. Traditional leaders are doubling down on the familiar pipeline model, fruitlessly seeking modifications that produce better results. Innovation scholars are advocating expanding the reach of pipeline models – arguing that *every* project in an organization should be organized, managed, and controlled, which they say imposes discipline, optimizes efficiency, and minimizes the risk of failure. Even as the attempts to control become more pervasive, the results remain dismal. In desperation, some organizations resort to "innovation theater" in the hope that a dramatic public story will generate the momentum that eludes them. With much fanfare, they organize workshops, contests, and press releases to promote the claim that the technology they are developing is game-changing. Innovation theater has not worked.

In the meantime, we (the present authors) organized a course at the Naval Postgraduate School to teach the eight practices and see if our students were more successful at fostering adoption than those working with the traditional innovation models. Indeed, this has proved to be the case. Over half our students reported early adoption of their ideas in their communities by the end of the course, and many continued, driving the new practices to full adoption in the ensuing years. These students' successes are the direct result of their skill in the eight practices.

We are not here to claim that the traditional pipeline models are dead. We want to remove a blind spot, not poke out a good eye. The pipeline is an important model for organizing production. Many innovations depend on new technology produced at a scale sufficient to provide everyone in the community with the tools they need to carry out the new practice. Production, however, is not the same as adoption. All too often we produce widgets that no one desires or uses. Adoption is not an aspect of a production line. It is a social agreement in the community to embrace and embody a new practice – often (but not always) the practice of using a technology built on a production line. Forging community agreement to adopt new practice is where the skill of the innovation leader stands out.

Without an understanding of the workings of the social spaces of our communities, it is extremely difficult to nurture the processes of emergence. How do you lead a community conversation in the direction you want to go, especially when so much is unpredictable and moved by forces beyond anyone's control? Our answer is that, despite its unpredictability and uncontrollability, social space hosts amazing structures, beacons that enable a skilled navigator to find a path to adoption of new practice.

• • •

Most everyone who hears our definition of innovation embraces it. It surprises them that they can learn a set of leadership practices that will help them intentionally achieve innovation – and they are eager to learn. Give the practices a try and see if you find them useful. Be warned, however, that innovation leadership takes dedicated practice. Much of what we ask you to do will be unfamiliar and challenging.

Our goal in the upcoming chapters is to help you move from the beginner who cannot see what is happening to someone who is proficient in the eight practices. We will explain each practice and then provide you an opportunity to practice it on your own. We will encourage you to bring others together into your conversation so that you can practice with them. Even though the eight practices are presented in a particular sequence, please know that they are not severable or sequential. Each practice builds on the others. The more you practice, the more proficient you will become. A significant part of this book explores the linguistic concepts that underlie the practices. These concepts make up a language for the dynamics of social space. They will help you understand how to get moving when you feel stuck, how to get attention from when you feel unheard, and how to influence events when you feel disempowered. Anyone who practices these skills in a spirit of service and care will become a better leader.

Let's get in the boat and begin to navigate this restless sea.

• • •

We intend this book for a wide audience: anyone who seeks to bring about a change of practice in their community:

- Business leaders, who want to sustain and grow their companies
- Employees, who want to make meaningful contributions
- Entrepreneurs, who want their startups to succeed
- Venture capitalists, who seek better insight into which startup proposals might succeed
- Professionals, who want to develop offers that attract clients
- Political leaders, who want to connect effectively with constituents
- Citizens, who want changes in their local communities
- Activists, who want to start movements
- Family members, who want better practices for their family

The same eight practices work for all these cases. Our intention is to make the innovation practices accessible to everyone. Practice them until you become competent with all of them. You will be amazed at the results.

• • •

In closing we would like to comment on the style of this book. We sought to find a middle way between a heavily academic book with many citations and footnotes and a pragmatic book focused on tips and techniques for practitioners. Our approach to innovation is novel in its emphasis on the social aspects, which can seem quite complex. A heavily academic book would emphasize the important ideas and where they originated but would have little to say about putting them to use. A heavily pragmatic book would sound very procedural and would not address questions about how the techniques came to be or why they work. The middle way allows us to show the sources of important ideas and simultaneously guide the practice of putting them to use. Stay with it, try the practices we recommend, and we are confident that, by the end of the book, you will be a competent navigator of the social space of innovations.

Peter J. Denning, Salinas, CA
Todd W. Lyons, Pebble Beach, CA
June 2024

ACKNOWLEDGEMENTS

Over the years we have worked with master teachers, facilitators of our workshops and courses, and discussions about what innovation is. They are virtual co-authors of this work.

Peter is especially grateful to four teachers. Fernando Flores has guided and coached me for forty years and has shown me the richness and power of language for shaping the future. Chauncey Bell taught me a unique perspective on design and mobilization of people to engage new designs. Richard Strozzi Heckler taught me that I have a somatic body that silently but loudly declares me to everyone around me. Ron Kaufman taught me the power of service and care in all leadership.

Peter is also grateful to his co-author Bob Dunham, who has provided ongoing advice and insights into innovation over the years.

Todd is grateful to the mentors who have guided, empowered and supported him as he practiced the craft of innovation. These mentors were innovation leaders in their own right and led by example. Lieutenant General Vincent Stewart, Lieutenant General Michael Groen, and Lieutenant General Michael Dana are three Marines who showed me how to lead innovation at every rank and importantly not to wait to "get in the right position" to start. I am also grateful to my peer mentors like Colonel Randy Pugh, Colonel Adam Strickland and Colonel Bill Vivian for their support and encouragement as fellow travelers on the innovation journey. None of us are on this journey alone.

Over the years of teaching innovation leadership to our students, we have had the privilege of working with inspiring delivery teams and facilitators. We thank:

Tom Choinski　　　　Lindsey Horn　　　　Steve O'Grady
Mark Dalton　　　　　Garth Jensen　　　　Jim Roche
Dave Drazen　　　　　Alison Kerr　　　　　Yvonne Sanchez-Garcia
Patrick Foley　　　　　Renee King　　　　　Brandon Smart
Ann Gallenson　　　　Laura McKinney　　　Bridger Smith
Holly Gardner　　　　Martin Moebus　　　Warren Yu
Sue Higgins　　　　　Dave Newborn

Over the years of talking to people about innovation and leadership, numerous other people have contributed their insights, challenges, and provocations.

John Arquilla　　　　Andy Hernandez　　　Salim Premji
Frank Barrett　　　　　Sue Higgins　　　　　Randy Pugh
Brian Berg　　　　　　Wayne Hughes　　　　Saqib Rasool
Douglas Bissonette　　Erik Jansen　　　　　Ann Rondeau
Arthur Cebrowski　　　Adam Johnson　　　　B. Scot Rousse
Vint Cerf　　　　　　Jeff Johnson　　　　　Barry Scott
Aaron Darnton　　　　Ray Jones　　　　　　John Seely Brown
Rob Dell　　　　　　 Mathias Kölsch　　　　Bret Seidle
Nick Dew　　　　　　Joshua Kroll　　　　　Gurminder Singh
Gloria Flores　　　　　Bob Metcalfe　　　　　Kevin Smith
Pablo Flores　　　　　Bret Michael　　　　　Elizabeth Swayze
Josh Freel　　　　　　JanIrene Miller　　　　Emily Taber
Scott Gartner　　　　　Dave Nystrom　　　　Matti Tedre
Erol Gelenbe　　　　　Marko Orescanin　　　Howard Teibel
Bill Gladstone　　　　Kaitie Penry　　　　　Walter Tichy
Britta Hale　　　　　　Terry Pierce　　　　　Bill Warner
Lauren Hanyok　　　　Ned Powley　　　　　Chris Wiesinger
Karen Hargrove　　　　Lorien Pratt　　　　　Peter Yaholkovsky

PROLOG: THE ARENA

THE MAN IN THE ARENA. It is not the critic who counts; not the man who points out how the strong man stumbles, or where the doer of deeds could have done them better. The credit belongs to the man who is actually in the arena, whose face is marred by dust and sweat and blood; who strives valiantly; who errs, who comes short again and again, because there is no effort without error and shortcoming; but who does actually strive to do the deeds; who knows great enthusiasms, the great devotions; who spends himself in a worthy cause; who at the best knows in the end the triumph of high achievement, and who at the worst, if he fails, at least fails while daring greatly, so that his place shall never be with those cold and timid souls who neither know victory nor defeat.

--US President Theodore Roosevelt, April 23, 1910

With these words, Roosevelt celebrates those toiling and sweating in the arena, doing the actual work. There is no triumph without great striving. Many people will be quick to critique the "doer of deeds."

So it is with innovation. Many spectators stand outside, speaking with great authority to tell how to change the game even as their own track records with adoption are dismal. Those who immerse themselves into the game, those who sweat and toil alongside their comrades, those who take care of concerns in their community: they get innovations adopted.

This book is dedicated to those who play in the arenas of their communities. That means you. You can lead a change of practice to relieve suffering, frustration, and resignation in your community. You can help your community give voice to the muted concerns that matter to them. You can build a story of a future they want and give them a glimpse of how to get there. You can make offers to make things happen. You can work with them, tailoring the offer so that every subcommunity can join in the practice. You can defuse the resistance from those who are not sure they are ready for change. In the end, when your work is done, they and you will be immersed in the new practice and satisfied with how it has turned out. We will show you how to do all this even if you are a beginner with innovation leadership.

In so many communities, people complain that no one takes their innovation proposals seriously and that their community is losing ground to competitors. They speak, but no one listens. They want to be seen, but no one notices. They ask to be included but feel left out. Put an end to this cycle. With this book in hand, plunge into the game and change it.

Part I
The Basic Practices of Innovation

1
AWAKENING

> *It is only afterward that a new idea seems reasonable.*
> *To begin with, it usually seems unreasonable.*
> -- Issac Asimov

> *No problem can be solved from the same*
> *level of consciousness that created it.*
> -- Albert Einstein

> *The Defense Department does not have an*
> *innovation problem; it has an adoption problem.*
> -- Eric Schmidt (2018)

> *Managers feel overwhelmed. The new model of*
> *management, which favors social aptitude and coordination*
> *skills, is taking hold before the old one, which rewarded*
> *expertise and intellect, has loosened its grip.*
> -- The Economist

Imagine you are a long-standing member of your community. You value the work and the friendships it has brought you. You see dark clouds gathering ahead of a storm that may damage your community or make it irrelevant. You see a way your community could change its practice to ward off this threat. Your community has been successful and is governed by strong rules and regulations grounded in valued traditions. Citing these rules, someone always shoots down your latest proposal. You wind up feeling powerless and begin to harbor resignation or even resentment. You fear you will be disciplined by your managers or ostracized by your peers for trying too hard to push for change. You know what the Valley of Death feels like.

You are not alone. Many who seek change in their communities are in the same predicament. They want to generate a change of practice in their communities, but it feels like there is always something blocking the way. This feeling is so widespread, it is not a quirk of personalities; it is a phenomenon.

Part of the problem is that we are caught in a trap of history, which has bequeathed us an obsolete view of innovation. It traces back to the late 1800s, a time of explosive technological development, a time when innovation meant to drive inventions to market through factory production processes. Production processes became much more efficient with the work of Frederick Taylor on the scientific management of factories in the early 1900s. During World War II, scientific management enabled U.S. factories to outproduce others in the weapons of war, paving the way for Allied victory. After the war, the idea of managing innovation through production pipelines was deeply encoded into science policy and law.

> **We are caught in a trap of history tracing back to a time when innovation meant driving inventions to market through factory production processes.**

Today's environment has changed dramatically. There is much more attention to social innovation, which does not rest on technology and cannot be managed as a technological production line. Moreover, most traditional production processes are too inflexible and too slow to keep up with competitors. The emphasis has shifted from production to adoption. Adoption is a social process. It relies on a mutual agreement among community members to adopt a new practice. The leadership skills for production are not the same as for adoption. Our common sense of innovation does not inform us of

Awakening

what skills are needed to achieve adoption in a social community. The Valley of Death is the name we give to our ignorance.

One of the missing considerations is that it often takes thousands of workers and entrepreneurs to bring a single idea into adoption. To succeed with adoption, we need to mobilize workers, not inventors. Theodore Roosevelt put his finger on this long ago when he admonished arm-chair leaders for their blindness and celebrated the players in the arena for their courage to make things happen. Many of those who tell us how innovation should work have no idea there is a skill set for adoption and that the skills for adoption are not the same as for invention or production. The way out of the mess is to look precisely where the old discourse tells us not to look: the unruly social space we inhabit with our fellow human beings. *Innovations are not inventions; they are changes of practice.*

> **To succeed with adoption, we need to mobilize workers, not inventors.**

This book is an invitation to enter the innovation arena. It shines light into the blind spots of our thinking. Let it guide you as you find your way through your community's unpredictability, uncertainty, and resistance. Inventions are important, but are irrelevant if no one cares about them or wants to use them. Innovation leaders have mastered a skill set. When you master those skills too, the Valley of Death will be revealed as a thriving social space.

The Eureka Story

Much of how we understand innovation is captured in the Eureka Story, a story celebrating a clever new idea and the person who discovered it. The word Eureka in Greek means "I have found it!" It is associated with a story of how Archimedes suddenly realized, on climbing into his bath, that the volume of water displaced equals the volume of the submerged part of his body. He suddenly realized he had discovered a way to precisely measure the volume of an irregular object and thereby detect lead-laced gold bars by their increased volume. Archimedes, the story goes, was so excited about his discovery that he ran from his tub naked into the streets of Syracuse proclaiming what he had found.

This idea has become part of our story of Progress. Civilization has progressed through an endless series of innovations. The Eureka story attributes innovations to the insights of great inventors – for example Edison invented the light bulb, Ford the assembly line, the Wright Brothers the airplane. Many of us learned these stories in school, watched them in movies, and read them in books. These stories seldom mention the hundreds or thousands of others who experimented with the idea, found new applications, crafted reliable versions, and built businesses to bring them to society. There would be no progress without these hordes of implementers. Yet all our progress is attributed to a few inventors, rendering invisible the many who brought worthy inventions into adoption.

> **The Eureka story celebrates clever new ideas and their inventors.**

Today, our increased global connectivity and speed of technological change heightens the stakes of competition and generates a pervasive sense of urgency to increase the pace of innovation. This has led to an increased emphasis on stimulating more creativity and invention – a quest that has produced no noticeable improvement in the overall rate of innovation. By focusing our attention and energy on invention, the Eureka story has distracted us from the work of adoption. We do not understand how adoption works and how to get more of it.

Our students and other aspiring innovators are simultaneously inspired and discouraged by Eureka stories. They tell us often: "That's not me. I am no genius. My ideas are not brilliant. I haven't invented anything significant. I am an introvert. I have no money or

Awakening

connections. The deck is stacked against me." Discouragement and resignation seem to win out in the end. The hero stories inspire desire but not hope.

The Eureka story has four flaws.

- Many innovations do not start with inventions; they emerge spontaneously.
- The stories celebrate the relatively few inventions that changed the whole planet; the vast majority of innovations are tiny by comparison.
- The stories single out individuals who may have started the process and ignore the thousands of others who worked to improve the invention and get others to adopt it.
- The stories portray the inventors as heroes and geniuses; but a more careful look shows that most inventors did not have the heroic traits ascribed to them.

For these flaws, Eureka stories are largely irrelevant to most of the innovation we see.

The real lesson hiding out in the stories is that all the "heroes" share a common skill set. Those with the skills of the innovation leader are more likely to succeed, whatever their other qualities, traits, talents, and circumstances.

The Production Story

The Eureka story has a companion, the Production story, that also deflects us from seeing how innovation really works. It arises from the enormous progress of technological innovation in the 19th Century. That century gave us steam engines, railroads, electrification, photography, telephony, telegraphy, automobiles, audio recording, and motion pictures. A world fair in Chicago in 1892 celebrated the stunning possibilities of these technologies and looked forward to a fabulous future of new prosperity. The technological advances accelerated into the 20th Century with powered flight, electronics, radio, television, computers, and the Internet. The 21st Century has already given us gene editing and artificial intelligence, with more to come.

At the start of the 20th Century, innovation was seen as inventions pushed through large-scale production lines. Experts and laymen alike assumed that invention and innovation were virtually synonymous and that getting more innovation meant incentivizing inventors and hooking them up with production lines.

The production of 19th and 20th Century technologies occurred mostly in factories. For most of the 20th Century, managers and scholars sought to make the promises of new technology more widely and efficiently available by applying the scientific method to the processes of production. In the early 1900s, Frederick Taylor laid the foundation with his work on the scientific management of factories. Taylor argued that factory production could be optimized by defining best procedures for each individual worker's task from time-and-motion studies, and by putting managers in charge of building overall work plans. The goal was to control the workers to accomplish the repetitive tasks correctly and efficiently. Workers were seen as rote performers and managers were seen as the source of intelligence that ensured products were produced at the lowest cost.

The pipeline model interprets innovation as the product of a factory pipeline.

After World War II, the US government encoded the production-line idea into its policies for technology transfer. It has become known as the pipeline model. In this view, ideas are generated in basic research, refined in applied research, instantiated as prototypes, incorporated into systems, and handed off to a market. This staged, mechanistic view reflected a belief that we have found optimal ways to

inspire, plan, manage, control, and deliver innovation in government and business.

The Taylor view is the intellectual foundation of the pipeline model. It has come under increasing criticism. The idea that bosses have all the intelligence and transmit it to workers via work plans does not sit well now that it has become important to mobilize every ounce of intelligence from workers as well as bosses. Critics blame the sluggishness of innovation to the failure of the Taylor mindset to recognize the creative power of every worker. Business leaders in non-Western countries gloat that the West has become so entrenched in a Taylorized way of running businesses that it cannot keep up with them. Worse still, those competitors believe that the West won't wake up even when told explicitly how they are being beaten.

Workers in Western countries chafe under the constraints of Taylorism. By treating everyone as an "asset" filling a particular "position", organizations dehumanize not only workers but their customers. Professional specialists don't like being treated as rote workers who must comply with every policy cooked up by managers. They especially want to be involved in the conversations that determine what the work is.

> **Workers want to be involved in the conversations about what the work is.**

Modern advocates for the production story call for the pipeline model to be adapted for innovation projects large and small throughout an organization. Figure 1 is an example of a recommended pipeline model. In the Source stage, a team scans many sources to find problems worthy of investment. In the Curate stage, team members "walk the halls", talking to colleagues and customers about the good and bad of the problem statements, yielding a shorter list of opportunities. In the Discover stage, the team prioritizes the surviving opportunities and then analyzes and tests their assumptions carefully. In the Incubate stage, they build "minimum viable products" for their solutions. In the Transition stage one of the solutions is selected and passed on the entity that will put it into production and get it adopted. The numbers at the different stages suggest the culling rate, in this case a 4:1 reduction of possibilities at each stage. This is the environment in which many people must navigate. It conflicts with the much-admired lean and agile management principles. Ironically, it institutionalizes a high attrition rate, leaving many workers discouraged because they see small odds that their good ideas for change will survive the process.

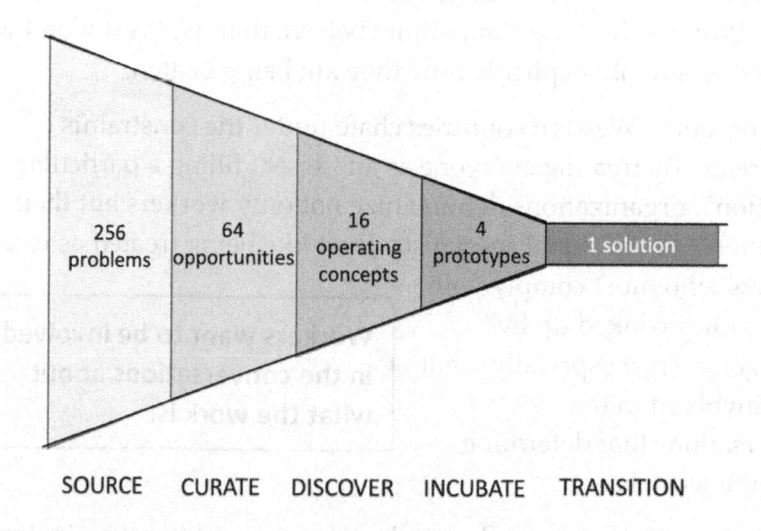

```
256          64          16           4
problems  opportunities  operating  prototypes   1 solution
                         concepts

SOURCE    CURATE    DISCOVER    INCUBATE    TRANSITION
```

Figure 1. Pipeline adapted for all innovation projects. (Adapted from an image in the BMNT book.[1])

---

[1] Sabra Horne. 2022. *Creating Innovation Navigators: Achieving Mission Through Innovation*. BMNT Publisher. The 4:1 attrition ratio is the author's best guess.

Awakening

The production story has four flaws.

- It assumes, as in the Eureka story, that innovation begins with inventions; but many innovations do not.
- It assumes that production is linear, following a sequence of well-defined steps; but it is nonlinear, often backtracking to a previous stage when a prototype does not work.
- It does not deal with contingencies – unexpected and unplanned events that interrupt production. Two recent examples of unexpected disruptions are the interruption of factory production in China because of COVID, and the geopolitical interference with supply chains that feed manufacturing around the world.
- It institutionalizes a high attrition rate, which means that the ideas filtered out by the stages are wasted effort and expense.

The root of the problem is that the Taylorized mindset behind the innovation pipeline believes that enough of the future can be controlled and managed by careful planning to make the process worthwhile. Unfortunately, this belief has a big blind spot: the dynamics of human social spaces.

An innovation happens only when a human community, through the churn of their conversations, and under the influence of innovation leaders and technologies, adopts a new practice. Our social space is neither predictable nor controllable. It is a turbulent, restless sea where waves constantly surprise you, sink you, or propel you somewhere you did not intend to go. It is better to learn to navigate the currents like a surfer or kayaker.

> **The Taylorized mindset has a big blind spot: the dynamics of human social spaces.**

Together, the Eureka and Production stories have dominated our thinking toward innovation. The systems we have set up to produce innovation come with a high cost. Business surveys and patent office statistics consistently show that the overall success of innovation projects and patents is around 5%. That means just 1 in 20 projects or patents meets their financial goal of getting an adequate return on the investment. No wonder we feel stuck. We live in a system that is stuck.

The Valley of Death

A third story has emerged to explain the failures of the other two. The innovation pipeline models typically label their final output as "transition", a term that means handing off to others for adoption. The Valley of Death story tells us that "transition" is a set of intransigent barriers obstructing hand-off and adoption (see Figure 2). Oft-cited examples include:

- Team or performers tired or overwhelmed
- Unexpected surprises and contingencies
- Supply chain disruptions
- Unexpected shifts in the environment or external markets
- Culture change needed but not achieved
- Adverse policies and authorities
- Poor investment choices
- Inertia of the status quo
- Unfavorable cost-benefit ratio
- Lack of supporting infrastructure
- Not scalable
- Key talent lost from the team

Awakening

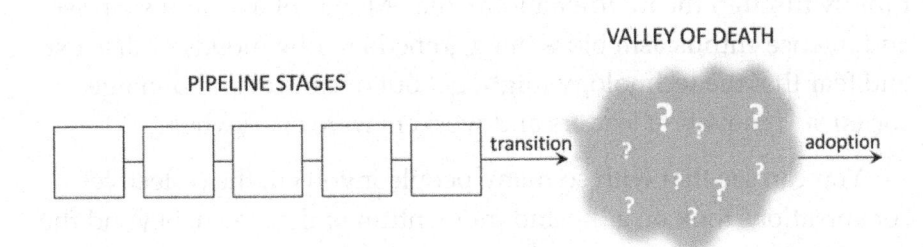

Figure 2. The Valley of Death is pictured as a new stage of the pipeline that thwarts the transition into adoption.

The problem with barriers is they focus our attention, energies, and resources, on obstacles. Passage through the Valley feels like a series of encounters with powerful opposing forces. Successful innovators see the spaces between obstacles and maneuver through them toward adoption. We once heard a conversation between mountain bikers illustrating this point. The newbie said, "It is so dangerous going downhill, I'm constantly dodging rocks. I have already had a few bad spills." The experienced biker said, "I steer into the empty spaces between the rocks; never had an accident."

Adoption Happens in Conversations

So, if pipeline thinking and its permutations are not reliable paths to adoption, what is? The answer is right under our nose: foster the conversations in which adoption happens.

Consider an example. Generative AI in the form of ChatGPT was offered for public access at the end of November 2022. Within weeks, 100 million users were trying the new technology, tech company executives were piling on with promises to put AI into their signature products, and entrepreneurs launched hundreds of companies with new capital from venture firms. The speed of adoption of Generative

AI was astonishing. All this happened in conversations, which spread rapidly through the internet and media. Moods of awe and surprise and intense enthusiasm blossomed, joined later by moods of distrust and fear that the technology might get out of control and damage societies. Innovation leaders and workers were everywhere.

You can see that with so many people involved, the collective conversations took on a life and momentum of their own, beyond the control of any one person. Adoption is unruly and chaotic. Local leaders guide their local conversations to local adoptions. Their conversations and new practices blend and accumulate. New practices emerge in the larger community from the collective work of leaders at every level.

A further lesson about emergence can be seen in the story of Steve Jobs and the iPhone. The familiar story is that Steve Jobs was a hard driving, difficult genius who had an idea for the iPhone and pushed it through despite resistance from the people working for him. A more careful look shows that Steve Jobs had been pursuing the idea of an intelligent assistant for almost twenty years. Early attempts like Newton failed because the technology was not able to support the offer he had in mind. By 2007, when he announced the iPhone, several technologies had converged, making his offer credible and enticing. Instead of offering a customizable intelligent assistant, Jobs offered a cool way to establish a customized, personal identity in a digital world. The Phone was not just an app platform, it was a social statement. The iPhone depended on several key components: a deal with the telecommunications companies to invent a "data plan" for customers sending data over voice links; the success of iPod, which became a component of iPhone; the success of the iTunes store, which became the model for an app store; the expansion of an existing community of Apple software developers into a community of app developers; and the availability of new technologies such as gorilla glass. Jobs combined all this into an offer that only Apple was positioned to make, and which appealed to a large number of people.

The Generative AI and the iPhone stories exemplify four core lessons about innovation:

1. Innovation emerges in the conversations of communities as they agree to adopt new practices that take care of their concerns.
2. The conversations of communities have their own momentum and cannot be controlled.
3. Innovation leaders appear all over, fostering conversations that generate local practices, which combine into larger community practices.
4. Innovations depend exquisitely on the moment of time. An innovation could not occur sooner because the components and concerns did not exist. It could not occur later because someone else took care of the concern already.

This interpretation of innovation has been around for a long time. It appears in the stories of leaders nurturing their communities to commit to new practices. Leaders do this by exercising a skill set consisting of eight conversational practices: sensing, envisioning, offering, adopting, sustaining, executing, embodying, and mobilizing.[2] We will discuss them shortly. All are essential because omitting any one of them is likely to block the innovation.

Unfortunately, the common stories of innovation leaders do not mention these practices. Instead, they emphasize personal qualities such as charisma, creativity, heroism, genius, brilliance, connections, extroversion, and sheer good luck. These qualities are helpful, but not needed for success – there are numerous successful innovation leaders who lacked these qualities.

Some innovations do not result from the purposeful intentions of leaders. They are wrought by necessity in response to unexpected

---

[2] P. Denning and R. Dunham. 2010. *The Innovator's Way.* MIT Press

contingencies. Examples are disasters such as hurricanes, earthquakes, or fires. Suddenly the everyday practices are no longer possible. Leaders appear as people start helping the injured, providing shelter, forming search-and-rescue parties, and transporting food and water, or setting up communications. All the individuals responding to the concerns suddenly brought forth by the disaster are leaders. They do not seek credit or fame for their help.

Prime Innovation Pattern

The actions of leaders in all innovations follow a common form, which we call the *prime innovation pattern*:

- Someone notices a concern around a breakdown or disharmony in their community and determines to do something about it.
- They see and describe a future where a new practice resolves the concern and they show a credible path to get there.
- They offer to make it happen and commit themselves to see it through.
- They form a team to assist in delivering the innovation and any technology needed to support it.
- With their team, they mobilize community members to join the new practice.

This pattern characterizes all innovations as social. Even though it may appear that technology drives the change, the actual innovation occurs when members of the community adopt the practice of using that technology. The change is always in human practices, enabled and supported by the technology.

The prime pattern as described in the list above appears to be linear, like a pipeline, one of the concepts we have been trying to avoid for understanding innovation. The linearity is a useful illusion for

Awakening

beginners because it neatly lays out the conversations they need to engage with to get to adoption. As they gain in experience, the illusion falls away and they see the practices as a tightly blended cluster. In the next section, we will show a nonlinear map of the practices (Figure 3).

The Innovation Leader Skill Set

In research for *The Innovator's Way*, we learned that leaders move through the prime pattern by marshalling a skill set consisting of five basic conversation practices and three advanced practices.[3] The five basics are:

1. *Sensing*: Listening for concerns of their community in what is said and unsaid, and what is revealed by their moods and practices.
2. *Envisioning*: Building a story about a future practice that could take care of their big concern and shows a credible path to get there.
3. *Offering*: Offering to bring the new practices into the community and takes responsibility to get it done.
4. *Adopting*: Getting commitments from early adopters for trials of the new practice.
5. *Sustaining*: Building trust in the capability, resources, and determination to continue the new practice for the long haul.

You can make substantial headway toward your innovation with these five practices, but they are not enough to attain the goal of adoption. Three advanced practices integrate the basic five with the social fabric of the community:

---

[3] In *Innovator's Way* the mobilizing practice was called "leading" and the practices were displayed around the circumference of a wheel.

6. *Embodying*: Exercising the skills above with sensibility and awareness of how people react in their bodies, which harbor moods and conditioned tendencies that can obstruct their best intentions.
7. *Executing*: Forming a delivery team to coordinate actions, deliver its promises to the community, and produce technologies needed to support the new practice.
8. *Mobilizing*: Energizing people into a movement to join the new practice and teach it to other members of the community.

Figure 3 shows the eight practices as a tightly interacting cluster, which is how we view them in the remainder of this book.

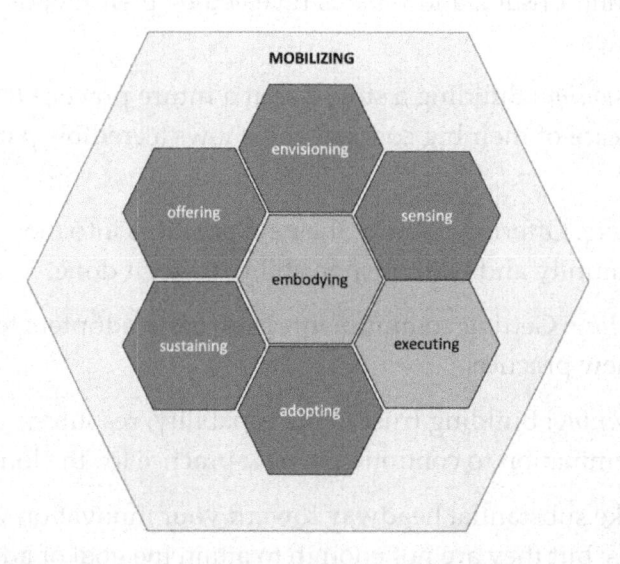

Figure 3. The eight leadership practices are not a linear sequence. They are a tightly blended cluster of interdependent practices. The basic practices (dark gray) do not require a high level of skill, whereas the advanced practices (medium gray) do. An "awakening" event starts the process with Sensing.

With these skills and knowledge of the structures of social space, we can navigate toward adoption, despite uncertainties, surprises, and contingencies. This is why we say that "innovation leaders are skilled at practices for bringing forth new practices."

Reflection on the Definition of Innovation

We have said that innovation takes place in the social space of a community, where it is adoption of new practice. Let's pause briefly to discuss what we mean by the key concepts of social space, community, adoption, and practice. These concepts permeate this book.

The *social space* is a space of communication and coordination of human beings, a space of relationships and power. It is always changing, always in motion. It has many dimensions – concerns, commitments, communication, coordination, action, speech acts, disclosures of worlds, moods, power, identities, values, norms, and histories. It is so familiar we hardly notice it. With all its fluidity along many dimensions, social space can confound you with massive uncertainty. You cannot know what people collectively will decide. You cannot predict contingencies or how people will respond to them. Nevertheless, there is enough structure in the dimensions of the space to enable you to move toward a future you have declared. We find the metaphor of a restless sea particularly apt. You can navigate toward your goal despite uncontrollable contingencies such as winds, waves, currents, land masses, storms, supply shortages, and repairs. Part II of this book looks deeply into the recurrent features of social space so that you can become a competent navigator. Every movement in every dimension originates in conversations. For this reason, we often say that *social space is a restless sea of conversations*.

The *community* is a set of people who share concerns, beliefs, and practices. It is sometimes called community of practice. It is the set of people whom we target to adopt a new practice. Communities are embedded in social space. Communities can be of any size – the world, your country, your region, your county, your city, your town, your team at work, your customers, or your family. The vast majority of innovations occur in small communities. The diversity of communities is good news because you do not need to aspire to change the whole world, at least not initially. You can start with your local team and, as you gain experience, you can expand your innovation into ever larger communities.

Adoption means that community members have taken on the new practice as an embodied skill. People progress with practice through developmental stages from beginner to master. They carry out the skillful practice without much thought because their bodies know what to do. It also means that mobilization is not only a process of bringing the community into agreement to adopt, it is a learning process that takes them from beginners to competent in the new practice. Innovation leaders are teachers and guides.

Practice means community ways of doing things: routines, habits, skills, and performances. This is the same sense as practices of law or practices of medicine. Practices are embodied: individuals learn them and perform them skillfully. Practices are embodied in communities as coordinated individual practices. Books and manuals can describe practices, but you learn and embody them only by repeatedly doing them. In fact, it is impossible to fully describe an embodied practice with sufficient detail that a reader can acquire the skill. There are many practices we "know" because we can see ourselves doing them well, yet we cannot describe how we do them. Everyday examples are riding a bike, tying shoelaces, typing on a keyboard, playing a musical instrument, playing on a soccer team, and driving on the right side of the road. Professional examples are mixed martial arts, computer chip design, systems programming, and warfighting. Practices are not applications of knowledge. Knowledge refers to descriptions, rules, and data can be stored as symbolic patterns in databases and books and organized as "bodies of knowledge". But no amount of reading about a practice can enable you to perform it. You cannot be a pianist without setting your hands on the keyboard and practicing, practicing until your teachers and audiences say you play well.

What Science Teaches About Innovation

Science is seen as a source of technology innovations as the community of scientists formulates and validates hypotheses about the natural world. Science specializes in defining standard observers of phenomena. That means many people can repeat the process for themselves and either confirm or deny a hypothesis. Science is not about discovering certainties. It is about navigating through uncertainties to find hypotheses that withstand the assaults of doubters.

There is a striking parallel between the community processes of science and of innovation. In his book *Science in Action*, the sociologist and philosopher Bruno Latour argues that science has two distinct aspects, which he explains with the metaphor of the Roman two-faced god, Janus. The wizened face looking backward sees all that has gone before and confidently summarizes with laws and rules of action. Latour calls that "ready-made-science" because it can be trusted and put to use. The youthful face looking forward toward the future cannot tell which rules might apply, if any. Latour calls that "science-in-the-making". The backward face sees certainty about what has happened, the forward sees only uncertainty about may happen. The uncertainty is like a fog that obscures the scientist's ability to see ahead. In the fog, backward looking explanations offer little guidance for forward looking navigation. Scientists need to understand this because the process of investigating the unknown is inherently uncertain and the past seldom resolves the uncertainty.

Innovators face the same dilemma. Models developed to explain past results look well-grounded because they are based on patterns and data that been observed from extensive experience. Innovators frequently face disorientation when, in the middle of the current situation, they discover that their retrospective model is not a trustworthy guide for next steps. With innovation, there is no logical reason that the past should forecast the future – after all, we are in the process of creating a different future. Ready-made-innovation in the form of models that produce innovation is a poor guide for innovation-in-the-making.

Science gives us one other lesson for innovation. The social spaces confronting innovators appear as enormous trees of possibilities, branching in many directions from the present. A step forward after choosing one of the possibilities may be a dead end and you must go back and try another possibility. And when you go back, the same set of possibilities may no longer hold. After you successfully navigate the labyrinth of possibilities, you can retroactively describe a path through this shifting tree that achieved the change you sought. Retrospectively, it looks like you knew what you were doing. But as you were navigating the path, you had no idea which branch was the way forward.

The popular pipeline model seems to characterize most retrospective paths. With hindsight, you can see ideation at the beginning, prototyping in the middle, and building out near the end. Yet, the moment you turn around and look toward the future, you cannot see the future path. All you see is a chaotic set of possibilities.

This kind of description invites the use of chaos theory, a branch of science that looks at complex adaptive systems by characterizing overall chaotic behavior and attempting to predict future unknown states of the system. Chaotic behavior is different from random behavior. The standard tools of statistical prediction for random processes fail for chaotic processes. We can statistically characterize the past chaotic behavior but cannot predict their future states with any certainty.

To many people, it is extremely disappointing that science tells us it cannot predict chaotic futures. This is exactly the situation innovators experience. The valley of death is a space of chaotic social events. Science and engineering alone cannot provide good answers about how to proceed.

Ready-made innovation *explains* the past but cannot *see or generate* the future.

Resolving an Apparent Clash

The pipeline and adoption views of innovation can appear as competitors; one wins and the other loses. Which one should a manager, executive, or scholar choose? In light of what Latour has shown us about science, this is a false choice. They co-exist. Bob Metcalfe captured the challenge of reconciling them with his famous saying, "Invention is a flower, innovation is a weed."

The pipeline models are descriptions of patterns we see when looking backwards after an innovation has occurred. They give us confidence that in the future, by following the same pattern, we can organize, manage, and control the costs and risks in producing new artifacts and handing them off to customers who might adopt them. The adoption view orients toward getting something new to emerge from the cloud of uncertainty surrounding the future. It gives us a skill to deal with whatever that cloud throws at us. As we will see in the rest of this book, this is a skill of navigating through contingencies that are constantly arising in the churn of conversations in a social space.

We need both views. Production comes into play when we need tools to support the new practices. Adoption comes into play when we seek our community's agreement to engage in new practices. Figure 4 visualizes how the two views can fit together.

The apparent clash of views has become more visible in recent years as the concern in business and government for more and faster adoption has increased. Pipeline advocates argue that the discipline and control of the pipeline should be extended deeper into organizations, touching every project. Adoption advocates argue that success is often compromised by trying to impose a linear order on the nonlinear process of emergence because it inhibits the very conversations necessary for adoption.

The logic of the pipeline is to organize the production of artifacts. The logic of adoption conversations is to generate community agreement on new practices. Pipelines do not generate adoption and adoption conversations do not manage pipelines. We need both.

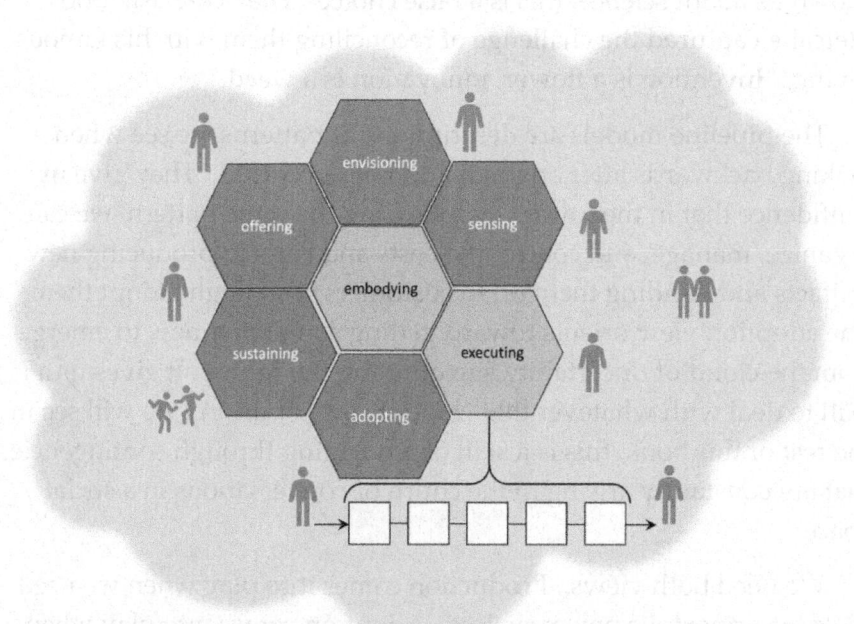

Figure 4. Adoption (of new practice) happens in social space under the guidance of leaders engaging in the essential conversations. When needed, production is managed in the executing conversation.

Awakening

Our difficulty in achieving adoption is not with production per se, but with our attempts to understand adoption as a form of production.

> **The problem is not with production per se, but with attempts to understand adoption as a form of production.**

Success at both adoption and production depends on personnel and managers being competent in the eight essential skills. Unfortunately, education in these skills is uncommon in technical fields, which favor "hard" over "soft" skills. Many find that the soft skills needed to get their work adopted are harder than the hard skills of their work. The good news is that learning the "soft" skills of leading adoption is not that hard once you know what they are. We will show you this in Part II of this book.

Layout of This book

Our narrative comes in three parts representing important stages in the learning of innovation leadership. The first part lays the personal foundation for generating adoption of new practice, the second navigates the social space in which the adopting community lives, the third focuses on the advanced skills for mobilizing the community into new practice.

Part I focuses on the personal foundation for generating adoption of new practice. We discuss what it means to be a beginner. Your community will be beginners in the new practice and you may be a beginner at the leadership practices. We introduce maps, which are pictorial diagrams of the conversations in the human social space that enable you to navigate to a future that cannot be precisely predicted or controlled. We introduce the eight essential leadership practices. We call attention to the problem of resistance, which is at the root of the Valley of Death. You will need to understand social space to become proficient at overcoming resistance and generating adoption.

Part II digs deeply into navigation of the social space in which the adopting community lives. Navigate means to find a path through a complex maze of obstacles and open spaces to reach your goal of a new future with your community. Understanding the workings of social space will turbocharge your ability to bring about adoption of your innovation proposal. There is much structure in social space – not enough to control or predict, but enough to navigate.

Part III examines the advanced, integrative practices that enable you to navigate tough situations and mobilize followers for your innovation. It examines how all eight leadership practices can show up in common situations of startups, new product lines in business, and bureaucracies. We will also examine how to measure progress in light of the interpretation of innovation in this book. We will examine Large Language Models, which are driving a revolution in Artificial Intelligence, to see why these machines cannot navigate in social space. We conclude with a section on mastery.

We recommend that you use this book as a guide for your innovation project. The three-part organization allows you to begin work immediately on your project. As you progress through the book, you will gain skill at the practices.

The innovator's work comprises a small number of elemental practices and social space comprises a small number of elemental structures. The complexities of innovation and maneuver in social space arise from the endless ways in which these basic elements can be combined. They are like the simple molecules of majestically complex DNA. Conversations are the atomic forces binding everything together.

To emphasize the simplicity of the basic elements, we have given single word names to all the chapters. Parts I and III concern elemental actions; all their chapter names are action word ending in -ing. Part II concerns structures in social space; all their chapter names are ordinary nouns. Throughout, we exhort you to practice with these elements in many conversations with people in your community. Practice is how you will bind the elements into a unity of your own making and style.

Conclusion

The eight leadership practices seem natural if you pay attention to the human level of innovation – the conversations that mobilize communities to new collective action. The Eureka and Production stories about innovation are blind to these practices. The eight innovation practices embrace the world of uncertainty, neither as a disaster to be wished away or bravely disregarded nor as a rash of risks to be reduced, but as a massive opportunity to create new community practices. The uncertainty is not an obstacle, but a constant unfolding of new possibilities to innovate. With this understanding, uncertainty becomes a positive force for you, the innovation leader.

2
BEGINNING

> *A beginning is a very delicate time.*
> *-- Princess Irulan, (DUNE)*

> *The first step towards getting somewhere is to decide you're not going to stay where you are.*
> *-- JP Morgan*

Every innovation begins with an awakening. It is the moment when someone senses a concern in their community and determines to do something about it. That person opens conversations with people in the community, initiating changes to their practices. In the beginning is the concern.

Innovation leaders likewise have their beginnings. When they decide to do something about a concern in their community, they find themselves beginners in the new game. Sometimes they also find themselves as beginners at leading innovations. As they improve their skills at listening and leading, they bring innovations into practice in a shorter time or into larger communities.

Community members are also beginners as they set out to adopt the new practice offered by the leader. They may have trouble learning the new practice. They may be suspicious of new ways to do things and of practices imported from other communities. They may resist any changes to the status quo, arguing there is no need to "rock the boat" or "cause troubles".

Even though there is demand for beginners, the supply is short. Many of us are not open to being beginners. We may be proud of our accomplishments and success in our fields and unwilling to expose our ineptitude at a new practice. We may have bad memories of when we previously tried new practices. We may believe children should be the beginners and adults should take care of grown-up things. We may believe we should be able to gain expertise in new areas much faster, given our prior experience in gaining expertise. After rising through ranks to become experts, we may see beginnerhood as a demotion.

We cannot be innovation leaders without being willing to be beginners again. We must have compassion and patience with ourselves, and likewise for the beginners in our community. We must become expert beginners.

The Smallest Thing Can Stymie

It can be easy to shy away from a large project because you perceive a breathtaking gap between where you are now and where you want to be. It looks like a long journey from beginner to expert.

In truth, project size is not what stymies beginners. Little things can get in the way in any size project. Consider an example from one of Peter's journeys as a beginner. He collaborated with Fernando Flores at Pluralistic Networks on a course to teach how to be effective on small teams. Most team breakdowns in business involve teams of five or fewer. Flores decided to use the World of Warcraft game as a laboratory for small teams. WOW offers a multitude of quests, each with a specific mission, and allows small teams of up to five players to pursue a quest. The game is so engrossing that people display the same conditioned tendencies, practices, and emotions as they do in real life. Flores dispatched observers to watch teams pursue quests and offer coaching in after-action briefings.

WOW is an enormous game with thousands of quests, huge territories, and over a million players signing in to play on any given day. It takes a long time to become an expert in the game. And yet people are willing to be beginners in the game because they like watching experts perform and want to be that way someday.

In WOW, the left hand is the most likely reason that a beginner drops out. Beginners in WOW need to master the skill of moving and rotating their avatar in three dimensions. This is done by using the left hand to tap 8 keys as needed for each movement – forward, backward, left turn, right turn, left sideway, right sideway, up, and down. The novice has no feel for this and is constantly forced to watch the keyboard to find the proper key – and in not watching the action on the screen their avatar is quickly killed in a skirmish. It takes around 50 hours of game play for most beginners to fully embody the left-hand movements. Then they move their avatars without thinking about it and pay attention to the surprises and challenges in the game itself. It is amazing how frustrated some novices are with their inability to master left-hand movement. Many just give up and quit the game.

Another example illustrates further how a seemingly small thing can confound a beginner. We ask our students prepare several 2-minute videos about their projects. We give them guidelines about setting up their webcam, proper lighting, and dress. Before they start, most are certain they can knock out their first video in under 15 minutes. But when they play their initial recordings, they are often horrified at the poor quality of their presentations. They wind up making half a dozen trials and spending two or three hours before feeling satisfied enough to submit a video – and even then they are dissatisfied because their recordings seem several notches below what they anticipated when they started. They discover there is a big gap between understanding what the guidelines say and actually performing to a standard.

Skillful Performance

Our emphasis on embracing beginnerhood is part of a larger emphasis on performance knowledge as distinct from book knowledge. We adopted the Dreyfus skill acquisition hierarchy as our guide to how we progress in expertise after starting as a beginner. It is helpful to see the community as a "game", a dynamic set of social interactions among players trying to achieve a purpose while subject to certain rules defining acceptable and unacceptable moves. People enter the game as novices and over time with lots of play advance to greater levels of skill and proficiency.

Beginners are newcomers who have just joined the community and are not familiar with their game. A teacher gives them rules, asks them to try them out, and commit them to memory. The teacher assists the novice in deciding when a rule applies to the current situation. This can be a time of great uncertainty and frustration at being such a poor player in the game. Beginners have no sense of how to move effectively. They can see others moving well in the game but cannot yet imitate them. After a while, the rules and facts become familiar and less confusing – the person has become an advanced beginner. After more play, the person becomes competent, able to carry out standard actions without much thought or serious mistakes. After still more play, the person can become proficient, where their play is so good that it inspires others to perform better and sets new standards of performance. After even more play and time, the person can become an expert, having accumulated so much experience that they can quickly solve problems that others find intractable.

This hierarchy defines levels of embodiment that people achieve over time while playing in the game. Beginners have no embodiment and can only act by figuring out which rules to apply. Experts have full embodiment and know from intuition and experience what the right moves and strategies are; they do not think about applying rules and cannot even say what rules if any characterize their play.

When Peter was Director of the Research Institute for Advanced Computer Science at NASA Ames Research Center in the 1980s, one of his missions was to form a world-class research group where computer scientists collaborated with NASA aerodynamics scientists to develop simulations of air flows around aircraft that would enable complete aircraft designs without wind tunnel testing. The computer scientists were experts with algorithms, parallel machines, and mathematical software. The NASA scientists were experts in fluid dynamics, the physics of smooth and turbulent air flow. But since the computer scientists were just beginners in fluid dynamics, there were unable earn the full trust of the NASA scientists, who would let them only do programming but not full-scale fluid dynamics research. The computer scientists felt sidelined and their expertise discounted. Only after they finally admitted they were beginners in fluid dynamics did they finally start making contributions that were respected by the NASA scientists. Specifically, they showed how to automatically map fluid dynamics simulators originally intended for supercomputers on to a new generation of much cheaper highly parallel computing architectures without rewriting any code.

The moral of this story is that expert status in one domain does not carry over as expert status in another. An expert in one domain may be a beginner in another. You are more likely to be treated as a full team member if you declare that you are still a novice in the game of the team's mission and you offer to contribute your expertise as needed to serve the mission.

The Beginner's Creed

Peter first gave voice to the insights above while working with a cohort of adult (age 30–35) graduate students in his operating systems class. Operating systems are a complex technology difficult to master and it is easy for students to fall into unproductive moods while studying them. The class was enjoying the subject until their first quiz. Many got worse grades they expected and fell into various bad moods including discouragement, anger, and even resentment. Hoping to return them into a mood of openness to learning more about operating systems, Peter decided to talk to them about their moods. He composed a poetic mediation that walked through all the moods a beginner is likely to experience. He called it "The Beginner's Creed". A copy appears at the end of this chapter.

Before handing back their quizzes, he asked his 30 students, "How many of you are an expert in some area?" Every hand went up. Then he asked, "How many of you feel like a beginner in operating systems?" Every hand went up. Then he asked, "How many of you *like* being a beginner?" Only two hands went up. He declared, "We need to have a conversation about that."

He handed out the Beginner's Creed and asked them to read it. When all were done, he read it aloud to them so that they could hear its moods. He asked them to read it to themselves every day for a week. For the rest of the course, the students were much more relaxed about their roles as beginners and were much more engaged in the work of the course. At the end of the course, when the project teams stood up to make their final presentations to the class, one team said proudly, "We are beginners! Look what we have accomplished!" In his concluding remarks at the end of the course, he declared, "Congratulations. You are no longer beginners. You are now advanced beginners. You are prepared to learn to be competent with operating systems." Some smiled with pride.

The Expert's Lament

The Beginner's Creed was a great success. We regularly use it in other classes to help students past their discomforts and resentments about being beginners. We use it in the innovation leader class because of the centrality of beginners at the start of innovations. After a while, students and colleagues began to ask, "What about those of us who are already experts? Do you have a creed for experts?" Peter thought about this for a while but could not come up with a creed. Instead, he came up with a meditation on the lament he had heard so frequently from experts who wished they did not have to be beginners. A copy of the Experts Lament appears at the end of this chapter.

Conclusions

When you are a beginner in a domain where you must now play, embrace being a beginner. When you welcome the process of being a beginner and accept the help of your teachers and fellow players, you will progress much faster. The same applies when you are proposing a new practice for your community. You may be a beginner at the new practice and you may not yet understand all its implications. Watch out for little practices – like the WOW left hand – that support everything else. Inability to master them quickly often discourages beginners and drives them away.

Take care of the members of your community. They are skilled at their current practice. The new practice must be sufficiently attractive that they are willing to sacrifice the old to get it. You will have to coach them through the discomfort that comes with being a beginner at the new practice. As an innovation leader, you will need to practice compassion for your fellow community members.

Finally, take care of yourself. As you learn the eight leadership practices, you may discover, to your surprise, that you are a beginner.

THE BEGINNER'S CREED

I am a beginner.
  I am entering a new game about which I know nothing.
  I do not yet know how to move in this game.
  I see many other people playing in this game now.
  This game has gone on for many years prior to my arrival.
  I am a new recruit arriving here for the first time.
  I see value to me in learning to navigate in this domain.

There is much for me to learn:
  The basic terminology
  The basic rules
  The basic moves of action
  The basic strategies

While I am learning these things I may feel various negative reactions:
  Overwhelmed at how much there is to learn
  Insecure that I do not know what to do
  Inadequate that I lack the capacity to do this
  Frustrated and discouraged that my progress is so slow
  Angry that I have been given insufficient guidance
  Anxious that I will never perform up to expectations
    on which my career depends
  Embarrassed that everyone can see my mistakes

But these moods are part of being a beginner. It does not serve my goal and ambition to dwell in them. Instead,

> *If I make a mistake, I will ask what lesson does this teach.*
> *If I make a discovery, I will celebrate my aha! moment.*
> *If I feel alone, I will remember my many friends ready to help.*
> *If I am stuck, I will ask for help from my teachers.*

Over time, I will make fewer mistakes.

> *I will gain confidence in my abilities.*
> *I will need less guidance from my teachers and friends.*
> *I will gain familiarity with the game.*
> *I will be able to have intelligent conversations with others in the game.*
> *I will not cause breakdowns for promises that I lack the competence to keep.*

I have an ambition to become competent, perhaps even proficient or expert in this game.

But for now,

I am a beginner.

THE EXPERT'S LAMENT

I am an expert.
    I spent many years building up to this
    I progressed from being a beginner to where I am now
    I have amassed and maintain much knowledge and experience

It has been rewarding.
    I have received recognitions for my accomplishments
    People ask me to find solutions that have escaped them
    They ask me to train them in advanced ways
    Younger people seek my mentorship
    All call me an expert
    They look up to me
    I like it.

But I don't want to hoard this expertise.
    I do not want to stagnate
    I want to bring it to others, make the world better
    I want to remove doubts that I can meet expectations about me
    So I have reached out to other groups.

Dealing with them has been a bear.
    They do not ask questions to tap my knowledge
    They do not invite me to their teams
    They do not appreciate what I have to offer
    They do not see how hard I work to maintain my expertise
    They do not respect me
    What is the matter?

So I asked them: why is it so difficult to be an expert with you?

And they answered:
>*You are not an expert to us*
>*You do not know our game*
>*Your proposals make no sense to us*
>*We see you trying to contribute*
>*But you cannot until you learn our ways*
>*To do so, you must be a beginner with us.*

And I replied:
>*But I was already a beginner once*
>*I do not want to go through that again*
>*It was so belittling and embarrassing to know nothing.*

And they replied:
>*We all know next to nothing, even in our own game*
>*The beginner is the gateway*
>*Go learn to be a beginner.*

And we will welcome you.

3
SKILLING

A finite game is played for the purpose of winning, an infinite game for the purpose of continuing the play.
-- James Carse

With talent and a great deal of involved experience, the beginner develops into an expert who intuitively sees what to do without recourse to rules.
-- Stuart Dreyfus

Think of your experience of trying out a new game. Perhaps you tried Pickleball in the real world, Beat Saber in the virtual, or Elden Ring on your computer and grew frustrated at not knowing what to do or how to move. Perhaps you stopped playing because you felt like you were not progressing as fast as others. You were a beginner who did not like being a beginner.

Every game has players whose skills at the game vary from new beginner to seasoned master. The players continually upgrade their skills, moving beyond beginner to competent and eventually to expert. A few even become masters, redefining the fundamental practices of their community. Even if being a beginner has no allure, being a master does. We are drawn to masters. We go to sports games, musical concerts, and Michelin star restaurants to see them in action. We seek out and admire masterful doctors, chefs, mechanics, carpenters, architects, writers, poets, teachers, pilots, artists, actors, movie directors, jazz musicians, and composers. These people not only solve complex problems with aplomb, they inspire us to reach for new heights. None of these masters was an "overnight success". They practiced consistently, diligently, and purposefully to attain their skill.

We all start as beginners. Welcome to the game.

The Game

In his famous treatise *Finite and Infinite Games,* James Carse lays out a framework for understanding the game as a universal description of how humans coordinate with each other in communities. A game has a playing field, a set of players, rules of acceptable and unacceptable play, and a purpose. A finite game has definite starting and ending times and the purpose is to "win" by achieving a specific goal. An infinite game has no definite starting or ending time and the purpose is to continue the game indefinitely across many generations of players.

The sports world gives concrete examples. Consider basketball. It was invented in 1891 to provide an indoor sport playable in the off-seasons of baseball and football. Over the years it grew into a major enterprise with a college network and a professional network. The college network, represented mainly by the National Collegiate Athletic Association (NCAA), consists of about 360 schools that sponsor student basketball teams. The professional network, represented by the National Basketball Association (NBA), consists of 32 teams based in various US cities. These organizations have major contracts with broadcasters to bring games to TV viewers and radio listeners. They operate a massive scouting network that finds the best talent from colleges and places them on professional teams. They operate museums, fan clubs, halls of fame, and all-star games. This enterprise is built on an extensive schedule of finite games, each playing two teams with one the winner. The enterprise itself is an

Skilling 41

infinite game, seeking to keep basketball healthy for an indefinite future.

The Philharmonia Baroque Orchestra of San Francisco was founded in 1981 to present masterful performances of music from great composers and singers using instruments and musical conventions from the Baroque, Classical, and Romantic early music periods. They have evolved into one of the world's most famous and accomplished early-music orchestras. They have formal relations with major music schools to find new talent. They play numerous concerts every year to rave reviews from audiences and critics. They continue to be a brand name over many generations of musicians playing in their orchestra – none of the players in today's orchestra was a member of the original orchestra. They are an excellent example of an infinite game that is unbeholden to any finite game.

A feature of all games is thirst for talent. They seek skilled and proficient players. Some cultivate "farm systems" of young people who gradually grow in skill and eventually qualify to be full-fledged players. Developing young talent to acquire the skills needed for professional play is a never-ending quest.

Human Ecosystems as Games

Every human community of practice can be interpreted as a game with finite and infinite elements. It has players (usually a great many), social norms, rules of play, and a purpose. This way of looking at a community leads to several immediate conclusions relevant to innovation:

- There are many people in the game, all coordinating actions toward the purpose.
- Innovation means that the play of the game changes – perhaps from new rules, norms, strategies, or responses to

contingencies. Our innovation definition – adoption of new practice in a community – fits this aspect of a game.

- The game existed before most of the current players arrived and will continue to exist (with other players) after they are gone.
- Players have different skill sets appropriate for their roles and positions.
- Players have different skill levels, from beginners to seasoned experts. The game accommodates players gaining in skill over time.
- Adoption of new practice necessarily means players move from beginner to competent in the new practice.

Players who look for ways to win the game regardless of the cost operate as finite players. Players who look for ways to nurture relationships and talent so that the game can continue indefinitely operate as infinite players. Successful innovation leaders are infinite players in their community's game.

Acquiring the Skill to Play in the Game

In the early 1970s, Hubert Dreyfus started to question claims being made for Artificial Intelligence, especially the claim that software "expert systems" could become expert performers. The heart of expert system software was an "inference engine" that applied rules to situational data to deduce conclusions. In Dreyfus's interpretation, expert performers do not apply rules to determine moves, but instead call on embodied experience (intuition) to know what the right moves are. He argued that computers are rule followers and are therefore not powerful enough to be experts. Needless to say, this did not endear him with the AI leaders of the day. Over the years, he was vindicated: the best expert systems were deemed "competent", but none "expert".

During the 1970s, Hubert and his brother Stuart studied how players of games acquired the skills needed for competent and expert play. In addition to software expert systems, they studied foreign language acquisition, chess, and flight instruction. In 1980, the US Air Force contracted with them to propose better methods of training pilots to fly aircraft. They developed a model with six stages of skill development: beginner, advanced beginner, competent, proficient, expert, and master. Their model attracted wide interest among educators and instructors and has become known as the Dreyfus hierarchy.[1]

The Dreyfuses took issue with the common notion that performance comes from "applying knowledge". In standard usage, "knowledge" is useful information that can be recorded and retrieved, and "understanding" is being able to explain something using available knowledge. Skill defies such explanation. Much of what we "know" is in the form of embodied practices rather than descriptions and rules – knowing-how rather than knowing-that. Even if we can describe a practice, reading the description does not impart any skill at performing the practice. Michael Polanyi, a philosopher, called this "tacit knowledge". He captured the paradox in his famous saying, "We know more than we can tell." Typing on a keyboard and riding a bike are examples of tacit knowledge, where knowing and doing are two vastly different things. The Dreyfus framework gives a rigorous way to interpret skills without having to invoke "knowledge". Skills can only be gained from practice, often under the watchful eye of a coach or teacher.

The table at the end of this chapter summarizes the Dreyfus hierarchy and its performance standards. The hierarchy is a continuum from beginner to master. The performance of beginners is

---

[1] S. Dreyfus and B. Scot Rousse brought the philosophical framework up to date: "Revisiting the six stages of skill acquisition." 2021. In *Teaching and Learning for Adult Skill Acquisition* (E. Mangiante and K Peno, eds), Information Age Publishing.

all rule-based with no embodiment and no sensitivity to context. The performance of masters is intuitive, fully embodied, and exquisitely sensitive to context.

The power of the framework becomes strikingly apparent when we compare how masters differ from beginners. The master fully embodies the skill whereas the beginner has no embodiment at all. The beginner learns by following the rules. The master learns by embracing new possibilities with joyous gusto while constantly experiencing "flow", and in the process defines new rules that future beginners will learn.

To learn more about being a master, watch the 2010 film *Being in the World*, produced and directed by Tao Ruspoli.[2] In 80 minutes it celebrates eight masters including a juggler, jazz cellist, jazz horn player, jazz drummer, speedboat racer, chef, carpenter, and flamenco singer. Its numerous scenes of these people in action inspire awe and amazement. In between are comments by prominent philosophers and teachers about what these people are doing that makes them masters. These commentators all celebrate Hubert Dreyfus, the nineth master in the film. You wind up wanting to be more like these masters. You gain insights on how you might achieve that.[3]

Welcome to the Game of Innovation

We titled this chapter with the word "skilling" for the work of acquiring skill. The uncommonness of the word reflects the uncommonness of paying attention to performance rather than application of knowledge. Embodied skill is sometimes referred to as "ready-to-hand" practice because your hands feel ready for action without conscious decision by your brain. Your muscles "know" what

---

[2] https://www.youtube.com/watch?v=fcCRmf_tHW8 (October 15, 2023)
[3] See https://www.youtube.com/watch?v=dIFsZ9uTrpE

Skilling

to do. Sam Snead, a famous golf pro and master teacher once said, "Practice puts brains into your muscles."

The Dreyfus hierarchy is about skilling. It makes practices visible and provides a language to talk about them. It distinguishes knowledge and rules from practice and performance. If we rely only on knowledge and rules as guides to action, we wind up stuck at advanced beginner no clue about how to get better. Our success at bringing about adoption of new practice depends on working with everyone involved, members and their leaders, to advance their skills in the game.

Dreyfus Skills Hierarchy

Stage	Summary	Performance Standards
Beginner	Basic rules	Person knows of the domain and desires to learn. Commits to learning the domain. Capable only of following rules given by a trusted teacher. Can be very slow and tentative while g and trying out the basic rules. Easily confused and frustrated. Little or no sensitivity to context.
Advanced Beginner	Rule oriented with domain familiarity	Person is familiar with common situations. Learns and uses maxims -- tips and rules of thumb to be used when certain symptoms appear. Likely to cause breakdowns when not supervised. Faster about figuring out and making the moves.
Competent	Performs standard practices well, customers satisfied	Person has learned the norms of the domain. Common situations all look familiar, and the person knows what to do right away. Does not require supervision. Avoids common mistakes. Satisfies customers. Asks for help when facing with an unfamiliar situation.
Proficient	Exceptional performance, sets standards others imitate	Person has a high level of skill that others admire. Sets new standards of performance. Inspires excellent performance. Handles complex situations smoothly.
Expert	Superior problem solving ability honed by long experience	Person has extensive experience. Quickly sees solutions to problems that baffle others. Sought out as a teacher, manager, and problem-solver. Community recognizes as
Master	Full embodiment, continual flow, joyful gusto, reshapes field	Person has developed a long view of the domain. Sees nuances that are invisible to others. Sets new contexts that change the game everyone else is playing.

4

LEADING

Leadership is about setting a direction. It's about creating a vision, empowering and inspiring people to want to achieve the vision, and enabling them to do so with energy and speed through an effective strategy. In its most basic sense, leadership is about mobilizing a group of people to jump into a better future.
– John P. Kotter

Good ideas are not adopted automatically. They must be driven into practice with courageous patience.
– Hyman Rickover

Admiral Hyman Rickover retired from the US Navy in 1982 after 63 years of active duty service. He was the driving force behind the Navy Nuclear Submarine fleet from its conception. He became known as the "Father of the Nuclear Navy". He was a safety fanatic who felt responsible for every stage of a ship: "I am responsible for the ship throughout its life – from the very beginning to the very end." The nuclear submarine fleet under his command had the remarkable achievement of never having a nuclear accident in 30 years. The Soviets suffered 14 accidents in their nuclear submarine fleet during the same time. Rickover's demanding leadership style in a highly bureaucratic and change-resistant Navy made him many enemies. Several times other Navy leaders tried to force his retirement, only to be blocked by his powerful political allies in the White House and Congress. You do not need to be easy to get along with to bring forth new practices.

At his retirement, Rickover attributed his success to his cultivation of the virtues of responsibility, perseverance, excellence, creativity, and courage. In our view, these virtues supported his success but did not generate it. If you examine his record and his public statements, you can clearly see him practicing the prime pattern of innovation leadership. He articulated a deep concern in the Navy – that the Soviets would develop a more powerful submarine fleet than the US. He envisioned that nuclear powered submarines would be virtually undetectable and capable of long missions undersea for months at a time – the perfect platform for launching nuclear missiles. He enthusiastically promoted this vision and offered to make it happen, and he was selected to do it because of the reputation he had built for "getting things done". He set strong standards of responsibility and expertise in operating nuclear reactors undersea, which paid off with the almost mythical record of zero accidents.[1] He personally interviewed everyone who was going to serve on a nuclear submarine and selected only those who convinced him they would meet his standard. He mastered the art of working with military and political power to mobilize allies in Congress and the White House to protect his agenda from Navy naysayers. At the end of his career, he articulated his view of service and care:

> I do not believe that nuclear power is worth it if it creates radiation. Then you might ask me why do I have nuclear powered ships. That is a necessary evil. I would sink them all. I am not proud of the part I played in it. I did it because it was necessary for the safety of this country. That's why I am such a great exponent of stopping this whole nonsense of war. Unfortunately limits—attempts to limit war have always failed. The lesson of history is when a war starts every nation will ultimately use whatever weapon it has available.
> (Hearing, Joint Economic Committee of the US Congress, 1982)

Rickover's actions exemplified the eight essential leadership practices we are studying here. You can learn and master them

---

[1] His seven rules: https://www.taproot.com/admiral-rickovers-7-rules/

yourself – in your own style and with your own personality. We begin with an overview of the practices.

The Basic Conversations of Innovation Leadership

Figure 1 visualizes the eight practices of innovation leadership. The eight practices are conversations in social space, interacting in a tight pattern to generate adoption of new practice. Each conversation has its unique purpose, which is achieved by commitments elicited during it.

We call attention to some important relationships among the conversations. First is the *awakening*, the moment when someone realizes that something that matters needs to be taken care of and determines to do something about it. The awakening opens the sensing conversation. It is not explicitly depicted. Second, embodying is shown at center because it supports all the surrounding practices – all take place in our bodies. Our bodies generate and react to what is said (by ourselves or others) and influence the outcomes. Third, mobilizing is shown at the outside because all the other practices combine to support it. Although the inner practices seen to form a ring around a hub, they take place simultaneously – they have no linear order.

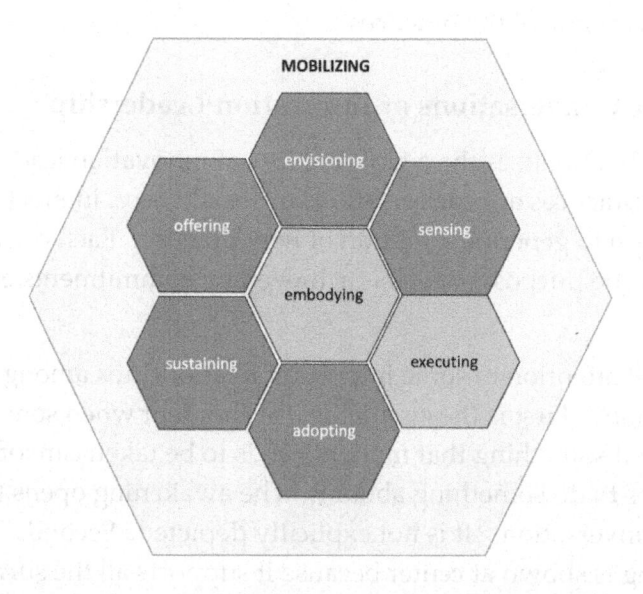

Figure 1. Mini-map of the conversational practices in social space that generate adoption of new practice in a community. The dark gray shapes are the basic practices and the lighter gray shapes are advanced practices. Embodying appears at center because it supports all the others. Mobilization appears at the outside because all the other conversations support it.

Here is a summary of the eight practices.

SENSING. This is a practice of deep listening. You give voice to a deep concern in your community. Concern means an issue that people care about and draws their attention, time, and resources. Common sources of concerns are breakdowns, disharmonies, threats, and opportunities. Two warnings: First, the concern may be felt but is not articulated. It is your job to bring it forth and give it a voice.

Leading

Second, it is all too easy for your imagination to smother your listening. You unwittingly substitute your own conception of what they need – you focus on "your concern for them" instead of "their concern". The danger in this is that they don't share your concern and thus anything you offer will not seem relevant. Having given voice to their concern, you declare you want to do something about it and you set out to make it happen. The listening practice behind sensing is essential for you to maintain connection with the concerns of your community.

ENVISIONING. This is a practice of story-telling. You build a story of a future in which the concern has been addressed. Your story is plausible in the possibility of resolution. Your story shows how the future is reachable via credible paths from the current situation. You summarize the big idea behind your story as a punchy, crisp, conversation-starting declaration. Many of us are acclimated to the "research paper", a form common in academic papers, government reports, and company progress reports. Research papers make the path to the results look simple and linear – "we started with the problem statement, formulated an approach, implemented it, tested and validated it, and arrived at a solution." The object of a research paper is to present and explain a result, not to get it adopted. Many of us were brought up on a diet of research papers – term papers, theses, and technical reports – and don't know how to tell a real-life story that shows how someone can overcome obstacles while aiming to take care of a concern. Research papers seldom discuss the many dead-ends encountered, what was learned from them, and all the contingencies that had to be navigated. Innovation is complex and nonlinear. Achieving it requires a compelling story that attracts people to the new future where the community's concern is resolved.

OFFERING. This is a practice of making attractive offers to your community. An offer is a conditional promise to provide something – in this case a resolution of the concern – if they accept the offer. The offer will be attractive when it addresses the concern and the plausible ways it can be resolved. Because we seldom accomplish anything all by ourselves, we are almost always assisted by a team, an organization, supply chains, and more. Implicit in the offer is a promise to coordinate team members and necessary external entities in fulfilling the offer. In addition, an offer of a technology will be more compelling if you can show a prototype that demonstrates that the core idea of your innovation is feasible and worth developing.

ADOPTING. This is a practice of bringing on board the early adopters in your community – eliciting commitments to join the new practice on a trial basis.[2] Early adopters are generally eager to try out new things and, when they like the new things, they become voices that exhorting the more risk-averse majority to join. The offers that attract early adopters usually involve more risk and shorter time frames than offers that attract the majority.

SUSTAINING. This is a practice of bringing on board the majority adopters in your community. Majority adopters tend to be more conservative and risk averse. When the innovation involves a technology, they want assurances that the technology is reliable, stable, well-tested, and available from multiple sources. They want help and technical support while they learn the technology and when it breaks. They listen attentively to early adopters' experiences. When the innovation involves a social movement, they want assurances that the movement has already produced useful results and is being taken seriously.

These five are the basic practices. The next three are more advanced practices require greater skill and experience.

---

[2] In his classic book, *Diffusion of Innovations*, Everett Rogers demonstrated that every community consists of inventors, early adopters, majority adopters, and laggards. These groups are a progression. Each group on average takes longer to adopt than its predecessor groups. These groups also represent mindsets, dispositions about risk and adoption that must be addressed in the offers presented to them.

EMBODYING. This is a practice of recognizing and working with the somatic aspects of conversations. Somatic refers to the integration of mind and body in fulfillment of commitments. Skill acquisition is somatic because it is the embodiment of new practice. Community adoption of new practice implies embodiment of the new practice among community members. All skill acquisition follows the development path of beginner, advanced beginner, competent, proficient, expert, and master. Part of achieving embodiment is dealing with moods, emotional reactivity, and conditioned tendencies, of ourselves and our communities, for they can pull us strongly in directions contrary to our aims and intentions. For the innovation leader, embodying takes place on multiple levels simultaneously. The innovation leader embodies the new practice as a demonstration for their community. The innovation leader deepens their embodiment of the innovation leadership practices. And the community comes to embody the new practice shown by the leader.

EXECUTING. This is a management practice of forming a delivery team, aligning them to a shared mission, dividing the labor among them according to their skills and talents, gathering resources to do the jobs, and coordinating all team conversations to reach their conclusions in fulfillment of the mission. The manager is responsible for keeping all team members focused on the team's promise – lone-wolf performances can obstruct coordination, break cohesion, and impede deadlines. Team members who interact with others – internal and external customers – do so with the aim of leaving them satisfied with the interaction. Similarly, the manager is a customer of the next level of leadership, responsible for keeping them informed on progress and asking for their assistance when contingencies threaten to block the team.

MOBILIZING. This is the practice of bringing people into a social movement for adopting the new community practice. It orchestrates the other conversations to support mobilization. It empowers those who join the movement to become leaders who bring others into the movement. Thus, the leadership of the movement is not vested in a single person but is distributed in the community. All the leaders are committed to the same goal. We encourage you develop others as leaders as part of your mobilization work. When the work is done, mobilization complete, they are satisfied with a job well done and welcome the reaction prized by Lao Tzu, "We the community did it all by ourselves!"

We recommend that you master the basic practices first. When you are competent at them, turn to the advanced practices to support the continued growth of your innovation project.

For both early and majority adoption, you are likely to encounter resistance, typically from people whose power or status in the community is threatened by the new practice. They can resist passively by ignoring you, or actively by using their social power and resources to block you. You will need to master the skill of coping with resistance.

The map in Figure 1 is a navigational guide. The eight practices are not a linear procedure leading to adoption. Innovation leaders are always sensing, envisioning, offering, adopting, and sustaining. The evolution of these conversations will depend on the circumstances that generated the awakening. For example, if the awakening is generated by a sharp external event like an earthquake or hurricane, most everyone immediately senses the need for new practices and the leaders can begin immediately offering new practices for recovery. The urgency for action makes sensing and envisioning less relevant at the start. Sensing and envisioning will become important later as the situation stabilizes and new contingencies arise. If the awakening was more gradual, articulating the concern becomes the most important practice, for it generates energy for all the other practices. In a more orderly environment where the innovation is brought about over time,

Leading

leaders constantly return to sensing, envisioning, and offering when they meet resistance or learn that an experiment has failed.

The map alerts us to the need to start conversations when something is missing and stick with them until the results are produced. For example, if no one is adopting your offer, perhaps, you are addressing the wrong concern or your envisioning story is not compelling. Even when a surprise event occurs, the map can show you what conversations need to be started. If you are aiming to generate adoption of new practice in your community and you are not engaged in frequent conversations with them, you will not realize your aim.

> **Train yourself so that your first reaction to a breakdown is "what conversation is missing?" rather than "how do I fix this problem?"**

Listening

We are used to thinking about communication and conversations as means of exchanging information via messages conveyed back and forth. This view of conversations is too limiting for understanding innovation. It is far better to think of conversations as a way of sharing a space of possibilities and relationships. We shape the space through the commitments we make to each other.

Listening is an essential practice for successful conversations. Listening means to attune to the way the other person sees the world and the concerns they have while moving in the world. Listening does not mean to verify to the other person that their message has been received correctly. The technique of active listening – repeating back what the other has said to see if you got it right – is not a method of attunement. It cannot reveal concerns that are unsaid. People often have concerns they are not fully aware of and therefore cannot speak of them directly. Or they are aware but choose not to share directly. A different kind of listening is needed to achieve attunement with the other.

We are particularly interested in listening for the "orienting concerns" of the people in our community.[3] Concerns are issues that people care about, to which they devote their time and resources. Orienting concerns are the deep values that guide them in life and give meaning to their actions. We cannot sense, envision, offer, generate adoption, execute, or mobilize well without becoming aware of the orienting concerns people we interact with.

Asking people directly what they are concerned about is not a reliable way to get them to disclose their concerns because they can be poor about expressing what they really seek. Consider a notorious example. Software engineers begin their projects by asking their customers to tell them the functional requirements. And yet, no matter how hard they try to get requirements right, the customer response they fear the most during final testing is, "Yes, that is what I asked for, but not what I want." Once customers have said what they want, the engineers must go back to the drawing board and create a better next version.

How might we listen for orienting concerns? This takes some practice. Here is what to practice.

- Get them to tell stories about themselves, their histories, and their communities. Their stories will disclose their deeper concerns.
- Listen for what they see as breakdowns (events or condition that block progress toward their goals).
- Listen for their moods. You can do this by listening for the assessments they make in their stories. Listen for grounding and ask questions to clarify grounding. Inquire about the standards they are upholding in their assessments.

---

[3] We thank our colleagues at Pluralistic Networks, B Rouse and Gloria Flores, for bringing this term to our attention.

- Listen for things that make them anxious, bother them, or trouble them. Anxiety is a sign they care about something because they fear it will be taken away.
- Listen for differences between how you see things and how they see things. Do not confuse what you are concerned about with what they are concerned about.

Put yourself into a mood of curiosity for these conversations. Your conversations are a way to explore their world. What does their world look like?

An Example of Deep Listening

A common difficulty for beginners is listening for breakdowns that exist in the background where they are experienced but not seen. Beginners take statements of breakdowns at face value and miss the deeper concerns behind them. They have an impulse to fix the breakdown rather than to have more conversations to understand why the person sees things that way. Here is an extended example.

Our students often express dissatisfaction with the "climate" of their organizations. They say they distrust their leaders and managers, who seem so wrapped up in an obsession to fulfill mission that they do not take care of their people. The resulting toxic moods are often described euphemistically as low morale.

Government leaders have long been concerned with fostering positive climates throughout their organizations. One of the important tools they use for this purpose in the military is the climate survey. The survey anonymously polls members of a command for their attitudes on a range of issues. The commander is required to publish the results to their people and describe what actions they will take to resolve negative findings. The commander's superiors may figure the results into promotion decisions.

Despite these policies, there are numerous complaints that commanders do not effectively correct problems. Many unit members perceive that nothing changes from one year to the next. They blame the lack of action on problems with the survey itself, for example:

- The survey is a collateral additional duty on top of all other responsibilities of commanders.
- The free-form comments offer no suggestions for improvement.
- Because of poor morale, few unit members take the survey seriously.

In short, the survey is the perceived breakdown. Corrective action focuses on fixing the survey and on stronger inducements for commanders to fix the problems.

But fixing the survey is the wrong place to look for a solution. If you were to interview unit members and listen as described above, you would begin to see what is really bothering them:

- They want connection, but see their commanders as aloof, disconnected, and detached.
- They feel alone, not sure whether others see it the same way, and are afraid to ask.

In other words, the unspoken concern is: "My commander does not care about me or anyone else as an individual." Nobody actually says this. Most likely they are unaware that *lack of care is the real issue*. If they are aware, they are afraid to bring it up. If you, as a deep listener, bring it up, they are likely to respond, "Aha! Yes! That's it!" The breakdown of care is not a problem with the survey or its governing policies. It is a problem in the practices of the commander and the unit members. New practices are needed. Here examples of practices by which commanders have successfully produced positive climates:

- Find ways to give credit, rather than take credit. Remember Harry Truman: "There is no limit to how far you can go if you don't mind who gets the credit."

Leading

- Cultivate practices of gratitude and appreciation. Not as fleeting emotions that come and go, but everyday practices. Look for the gifts that people bring and be thankful. Find something to appreciate what another does and let them know; there is always something. Gratitude and appreciation are a foundation of trust.
- Organize processes for major decisions that emphasize conversations with people before final decisions are made. It is important to let people know their opinions and recommendation will be heard. Robert Gates, a former Secretary of Defense who was a master at fostering positive climates in his organizations, said "Involve the people who will be doing the work in the decisions about what the work is."
- Look for opportunities to show and take care. They are all around. It might be something simple like delaying the start of a meeting so that a missing team member can be found and take part in the meeting.
- Show respect in all interactions.

In other words, climate changes come from leadership actions of commanders, starting with the declaration *Commanders care about their people*. Sometimes "taking care" is like "tough love". General James Mattis, former Commander of US Central Command and a Secretary of Defense, exemplified a commander who took care and was revered by those who served under him. He insisted that unit commanders live the precept "commanders care about their people" and train them so well that they are unlikely to make mistakes in battle. Their intensive training instills the attitude of "having the backs" of other team members and having full trust that other team members will have their back. Thus, the training was rigorous and hard. But when these units were in the field, they performed well and were grateful to Mattis for insisting on the conditions that not only made them more successful but brought more of them home safely.

Conclusion

When our goal is to produce products in quantity, the production pipeline is the better model. When our goal is adoption of new practices that integrate use of products into the habits and routines of the community, the conversation space is the better model. We sometimes need to satisfy both goals, when an innovation based on a product needs to be scaled up for a large and growing community.

Conversations are the medium that brings people together in spaces of shared possibilities and relations. They generate commitments to coordinated action. Deep listening for orienting concerns is essential for successful conversations.

These basic conversations compliment the view of community as a game (see Chapter 3). They are conversations that shift the play of the game by changing rules, strategies, practices, and sometimes even the purpose of the game.

These basics are not sufficient to generate the outcome of adoption of new practice. We must master three more advanced practices – embodying, executing, and mobilizing. These are integrative, holistic leadership practices and that incorporate the innovation into the community as a whole. To do this, we need to educate ourselves on the dynamics and structures of the social space of communities. We will examine them in the next several chapters (Part II) and return to the three advanced leadership practices after that (Part III).

5
NAVIGATING

A map does not just chart, it unlocks and formulates meaning; it forms bridges between here and there, between disparate ideas that we did not know were previously connected.
– Reif Larsen

You can't use an old map to explore a new world.
– Albert Einstein

"Why are you looking for your keys under this lamppost when you know the keys are elsewhere?" asks the policeman. "Because this is where the light is," replies the searcher.
– Folk Legend

The tales of ancient mariners who crossed the open seas are stories of navigation. Somewhere over the horizon, unseen, is the destination. How does the ship reach its destination when the direction is not completely known? What should the crew do when winds and storms blow them far off course? Where do they get supplies to keep the crew going and make needed repairs? How does the captain maintain discipline on a journey whose end cannot be predicted?

Innovation leaders face the same dilemmas. How do I achieve my innovation goal, which is over the horizon of my sight in a direction I do not completely know? What should I do when surprises and contingencies drag me away from the course I have planned? Where do I find the resources needed to keep going? How do I keep my team and my community on board with the changes before they are fully implemented? Like the ancient mariner, the innovation leader is a navigator.

Navigation is about the journey, finding your way even though the path is obscured by a fog of uncertainty. Just as mariners sought maps to guide them across the seas, innovation leaders ask for maps to guide them through the social spaces of their communities. In this chapter we discuss what we mean by maps of the social space. Many of the chapters coming up provide maps for navigating particular aspects of the social space.

Map making is an ancient tradition. The earliest maps marked territory held by a king or warlord. Explorers striking through a territory or sailors crossing a sea developed maps to help them, and those following them, find their way. Many of these maps recorded only what the explorers could see. They had large areas labeled "terra incognita", tagged with sketches of dragons that might devour new explorers. Over the years, land and sea maps became ever more complete and accurate, resolving border disputes and enabling reliable trade routes. In the 20th century, technologies such as triangulation, satellite imagery, and GPS enabled maps accurate to within a meter anywhere on the planet. Today, these worldwide maps download to personal devices that give directions to the desired destination.

Our experience with modern maps has given us a common sense that maps are *complete* and *accurate* – no more "incognita". That in turn has led to an understanding that the purpose of a map is to give directions to a destination. This understanding does not work for innovation leaders because, almost by definition, the new territory

Navigating

being navigated is "incognita". The best we can do is map recurrent features of our social spaces like signposts we can use for navigation.

Throughout the ages, explorers of old had to find their way despite numerous uncertainties. A telling example of human ingenuity for navigating uncertainty is the Micronesian stick map, used by the Polynesian peoples to find their way in canoes among the Marshall Islands across large expanses of open sea (Figure 1). The sticks represented swells and wave patterns generated by unseen islands. The mariners developed skills of reading swells, bioluminescence, and flights of birds to locate themselves with these maps. Our maps of social spaces are rather more like stick maps than a GPS receiver. They will help you get to where you want, but you will need the skills of the eight practices to use them well.

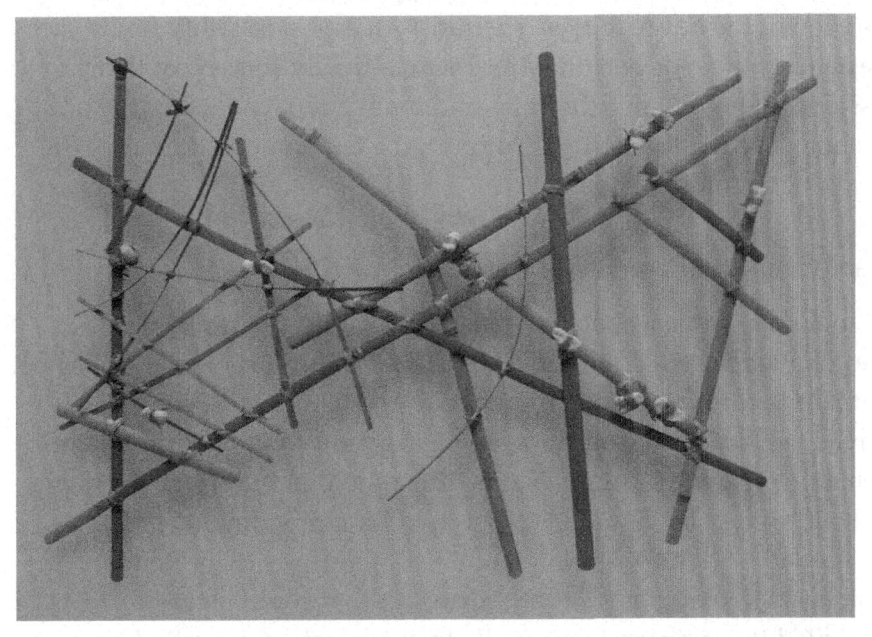

Figure 1. A Micronesian Stick Map. Sticks represent wave swells, beads represent islands. (Source: Wikipedia Creative Commons)

Consider an example of navigation. One of our students was a young naval officer who wondered why ships consistently leave shipyard maintenance behind schedule and over budget. He knew that every day the ship spends in shipyard maintenance is a day lost to performing its mission. He identified the maintenance scheduling process as the bottleneck. It was done daily by a daylong manual process on a whiteboard. The biggest fear of the planners was not loss of ship readiness, but erasure of the whiteboard. He offered to create a software program to automate the maintenance tracking process. His prototype did the old job in one tenth of the time. In the process of showing off his prototype, he discovered a group that had been charged with doing the same thing he was trying to do. They were frustrated because they had not been making good progress. Because he had a prototype, he quickly gained their confidence and worked with them to muster the resources to support a full design and adoption of the new process. He transformed a possibility for resistance into an opportunity for them to finally succeed at their mission. They became advocates and innovation leaders for the new tracking practices. With their support, the new practice became "the way things should be done."

Lost Without a Proper Map

In his *Seven Habits* book, Stephen Covey tells the story of a salesman who traveled to Chicago to close an important deal. His host sent him a snippet of a downtown map and a business card. When he arrived, he located the address on the map and found his way there. To his surprise the business had no offices in that building. He called his host, who said, "C'mon, it's not that difficult to find our address. Try harder." So the salesman redoubled his efforts to locate the business by looking at alternate addresses that could be lost to typos. He visited those places to no avail. In exasperation, he called his host again. Now his host, obviously annoyed at the delay, berated him and asked him to adopt a better attitude or it would not be worth visiting.

The salesman tried again with a more upbeat attitude about the goodness of the pending deal, but he still could not locate the office. By this time, the intended start time of the meeting was long past. In anger and frustration, he returned to the airport and went home. After he calmed down, he called his host again to try to reschedule. His host said, "I'm so glad you called. I inadvertently sent you a Detroit map instead of a Chicago map. No wonder you could not find us." The moral of the story: no amount of trying harder or attitude adjustment will get you to your destination if you are using the wrong map.

Many who seek innovation feel stuck, like that hapless salesman. Their maps are books that tell them how to form startups, get new product lines going in their organizations, defeat change-resistant bureaucracies, or cultivate the right leaders. Executives, managers, and working professionals try to follow the guidelines advocated by the experts. When they face challenges, they follow the steps, try harder, and adjust their attitudes. Yet, their overall performance at adoption is poor. Business surveys confirm that 95% of innovation projects end in failure. That is unchanged from the failure rate we found when writing *The Innovator's Way*.

There are widespread efforts to increase the rate of successful innovations, including leadership development courses, management training, creativity workshops, crowdsourcing, hackathons, and design thinking events. Hackathons and design thinking are particularly popular today. They make people feel that they are exploring a new space and generate lots of new ideas. While these approaches can significantly reduce the cost of ideation to identify solutions to problems, they do not seem to make a measurable impact on the overall rate of adoption.

What if the common mental maps about how innovation works are like Covey's Detroit maps – descriptions of the wrong territory?

The Pipeline

The pipeline is an abstraction of factory assembly line inherited from the industrial age. It assumes that we can linearize the production process into a sequential series of stages. It tells us that ideas for problem solutions are the input to a pipeline, whose successive stages refine the ideas into products ready for "transition". Transition (short for "technology transition") is usually defined as a hand-off to another organization (such as a military program of record) or an offer made to a target group of potential customers. Transition seldom equates to the adoption of new practice. Many programs of record within the government fail to achieve adoption of their technologies.

Figure 2 is the Research & Development ("technology transfer") pipeline used by the US Defense Department. It assumes that ideas for new technology are discovered in basic research, turned toward specific problems in applied research, developed into working prototypes, tested, validated, and incorporated into large systems. After the last R&D stage (6.9), the technology is ready for transition into programs of record. Each stage has its own separate budget and funding authority, its own personnel, and its own supply chains. The stages are often done in different locations. The communication channels between stages are most commonly reports, data sets, artifacts such as software, and occasional personnel transfers.

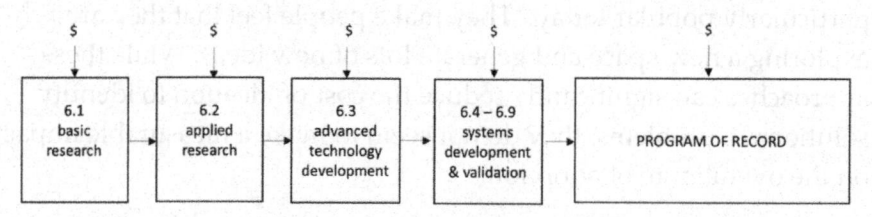

Figure 2. DOD R&D pipeline. Each stage has its own budget (the $). Projects often take ten or more years to flow through.

Companies operate with a similar map for generating ideas in research and pushing them through a corporate pipeline toward the expected market for a new product. The companies often fence off their research labs from their profit and loss flows. They reason that by insulating the researchers from customers, researchers will have maximum freedom to be innovative. The researchers get to explore new technologies and practices unfettered to a specific customer or use case. Unfortunately, this does not always work as expected: research that is unconnected to customer concerns often leads to products of little interest to customers. Even when the research connects with customers, it often yields prototypes that cannot be scaled up. There are many stories of companies creating industry-leading research arms whose technology were ultimately are taken into adoption by a competitor instead of the company that invented it. Famous examples include digital photography, which was pioneered by Kodak, and the modern office network with graphical user interfaces, which was pioneered by the Xerox Palo Alto Research Center. These companies were supremely successful at fostering invention – and spectacularly unsuccessful at innovation.

Mapping innovation as a progression through a pipeline with delineated stages has not proved fruitful for adoption. The basic problem is that pipelines don't show how new practices are adopted by communities. An even bigger problem is that these diagrams are not treated as maps at all. They are treated as flowcharts for control of a production line, with each stage carefully governed by a plan set by managers, as envisioned by Frederick Taylor in his pioneering work with scientific management of factories. Managers are responsible for setting the overall plan, defining measures of performance for each stage, and controlling the stages to stay within their time and money budgets. Advocates of this model for innovation extol its ability to

Frederick Winslow Taylor (1856-1915) was a mechanical engineer who worked his way up through the ranks at Midvale Steel Works, eventually becoming chief engineer of the works and shop foreman. From his first hand experience he concluded that his workers were not as efficient as they could be and through time-and-motion studies aimed to find out what the most efficient workers could do. He came up with a new way of managing the workers in which he determined the best practice for each position, trained the workers in that practice, and showed managers how to plan and administer the overall work. His methods were very successful at improving worker productivity and significantly lowering labor costs of products. His book *Principles of Scientific Management* (1911) became a classic success worldwide. He was considered the father of scientific management, which gave birth to the modern field of industrial engineering. He made his fortune from patents for tungsten alloy steel.

Source: Wikipedia Creative Commons

define the skills and responsibilities of managers and workers, provide the means for managing budgets, maintain discipline when contingencies arise, and minimize risks of failures. They even propose it as a model for managing all projects, not just technology transfer pipelines. The pipeline has ceased to be a navigational map and has become a tool of control.

With pipeline models, "getting more innovation faster" means pushing more stuff through the pipeline – by generating more ideas for input, prototypes will come faster and validation tests sooner. The pipeline also encourages leaders and managers to optimize each to reduce its transit time.

The Pipeline Model Institutionalized

At the end of WWII, the western powers were effusive in their admiration of university researchers who had helped the war effort – for example, the invention of radar and the electronic code-breaking computer. In the post-war US, Vannevar Bush, the science advisor to President Roosevelt, advocated that the government should support university research as an enterprise to assure a constant state of readiness in case of another war. He introduced the ideas of basic and applied research. Basic research is investigations that lead to fundamental understanding with little regard for utility. Applied research is investigations to solve specific problems. Bush argued that the government should support basic research because the time until use exceeded the horizons of most companies. Leave applied research to industry, he argued. The National Science Foundation was chartered in 1950 to implement Bush's ideas as science and technology policy. The US Defense Department refined the Bush ideas by expanding the spectrum into six stages of technology transfer (refer to Figure 2). Government planners determine the overall timeline of the stages of major projects, the facilities, the personnel, and the funds to be allocated. The goal is to eliminate as much uncertainty as possible because uncertainty is perceived as an enemy of progress and an escalator of cost. The pipeline is also seen as a management plan to control the process and keep it focused on its ultimate goals. Managers are seen as "drivers" who force projects along and keep them on schedule and budget. In other words, the pipeline is seen as a well managed, risk-reducing process of technology generation and transfer.

Three generations have grown up with these ideas and believe that innovations begin with ideas invented in research that flow along pipelines that transform them into useful products at the end.

Unfortunately, pipeline models are a much poorer guide than they seem. One flaw is that they do not explain the large class of social, spontaneous, or dark innovations that "emerge" rather than "get produced". Mothers Against Drunk Driving, for instance, is a social innovation, which started in the 1980s as movement to change the laws and attitudes toward drunk drivers, who at the time got light sentences when they caused accidents and deaths. MADD was successful in changing practices and attitudes about drunk driving. Black Lives Matter is another social innovation, founded in 2020 after the death of George Floyd with the declaration to heal the past, reimagine the present, and invest in the future of Black lives. Many policing and police oversight practices changed as a result. MADD and BLM are recent examples of spontaneous social innovations. Patent trolls and black markets are examples of dark social innovations, which are new, parasitic practices that bring no benefit to the majority of a community.

Another pipeline flaw: the models provide no guidance for how to respond to unexpected surprises and contingencies. Another: they do not reveal who is responsible when things go off track. Still another: the sheer complexity of pipeline management over the years. Figure 3 is a diagram of the pipelines of the acquisition process in the US Defense Department. There are pipelines within pipelines within pipelines. Detailed management processes have been worked out for all these pipelines. Complying with them all makes the process opaque, dreadfully slow, and unresponsive to contingencies. This situation is rather like that of the ancient astronomer Ptolemy in the second century, who believed that planets and stars moved in perfect circles around the earth. But the observations of planets did not bear this out. Astronomers invented epicycles – circles within circles within circles – to explain the observed motions. Although more accurate, these models were too complex to be generally useful. Fifteen hundred years later, the Copernican revolution reframed the whole picture by putting the sun at the center and allowing elliptical orbits. Today, pipeline scholars have been trying to modify the pipeline model so that it works better. In terms of the ultimate goal – adoption of new technologies – none of the modifications has been particularly successful.

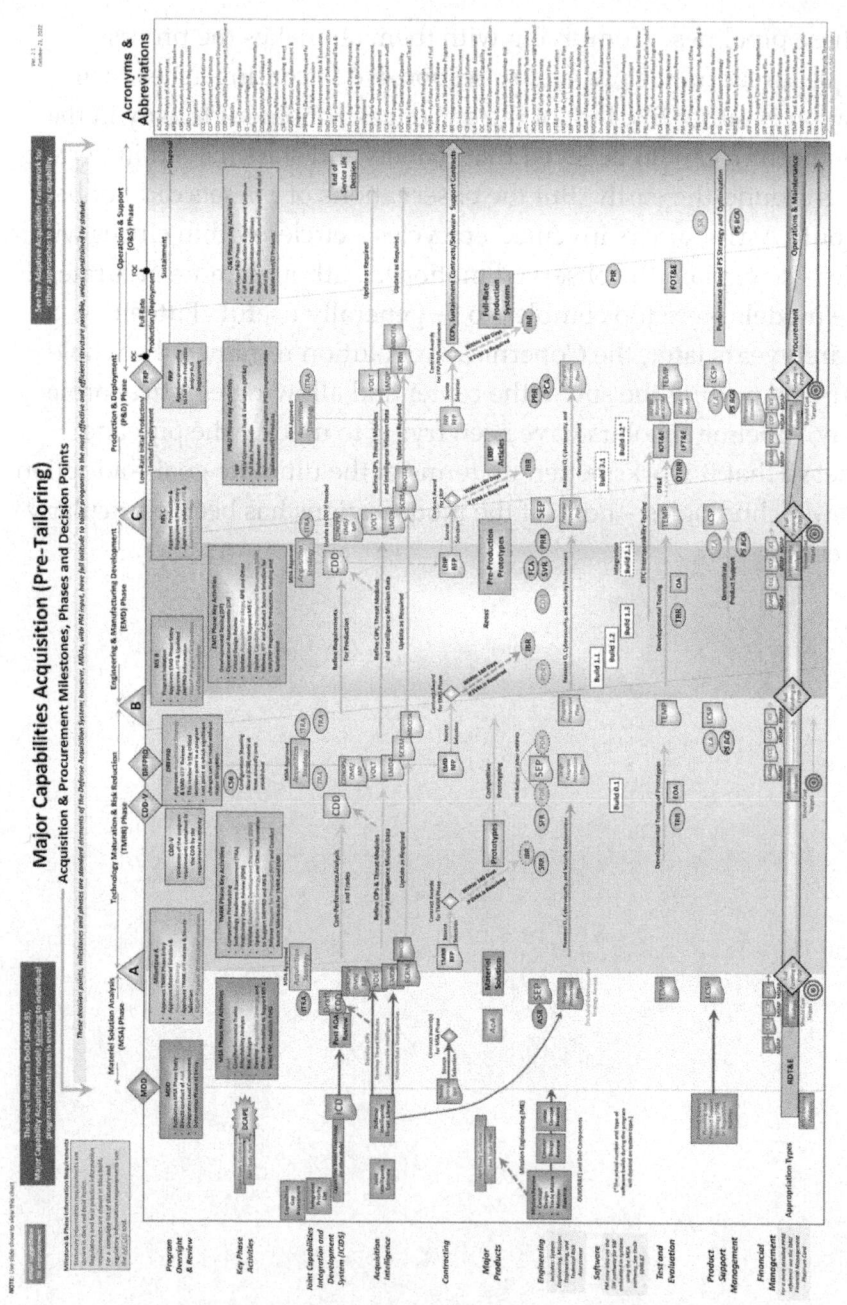

Figure 3. Pipeline chart of the DOD acquisition process.

Responses to Pipeline Flaws

Businesses and governments have responded to these disappointments in two ways. One is to blame a "valley of death", a metaphorical haven of mysterious forces bent on killing innovators who try to venture through the later stages of the pipeline. Some have even added a "valley of death" stage into the government pipeline in the transition from large systems to program of record. No one seems to know how to get through the valley of death successfully.

The other response to the failure of the pipeline model is adding patches (modifications to theories) that aim to address the weaknesses of the pipeline. An important example is the *innovation funnel*: a set of many ideas is progressively winnowed at each stage of the pipeline by reviews, iterations, and market tests, until the few with greatest merit make it to the transition. Figure 4 is a typical example. This patch assumes that a high failure rate is inevitable and tries to beat the odds by "taking many shots on goal" and "failing fast." This is not a realistic option for the many small groups with limited resources. It is wasteful because many projects are scrapped, and their effort lost.

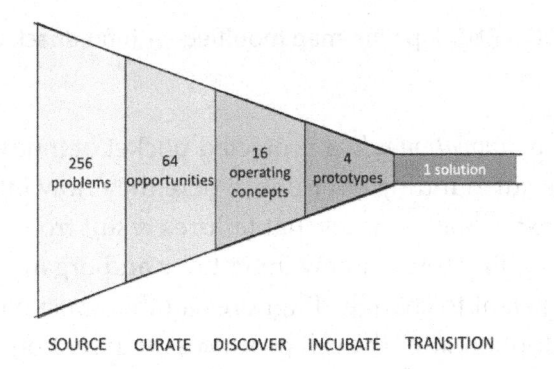

Figure 4. Innovation funnel pipeline applied to project management. (Adapted from a figure in the BMNT book.[1])

---

[1] Sabra Horne. 2022. *Creating Innovation Navigators: Achieving Mission Through Innovation.* BMNT Publisher.

Five more modifications of pipeline theory are popular.

The first is *feedback*. Feedback loops are added to the pipeline so that information about problems can be sent back to earlier stages for adjustments and adaptions (Figure 5). For example, a limitation discovered in applied research is conveyed back to basic research for more investigation. A bug in a prototype sends the prototype back to applied research for further improvement. Adding feedback increases the visual complexity of the diagram without changing the basic idea of staged flow.

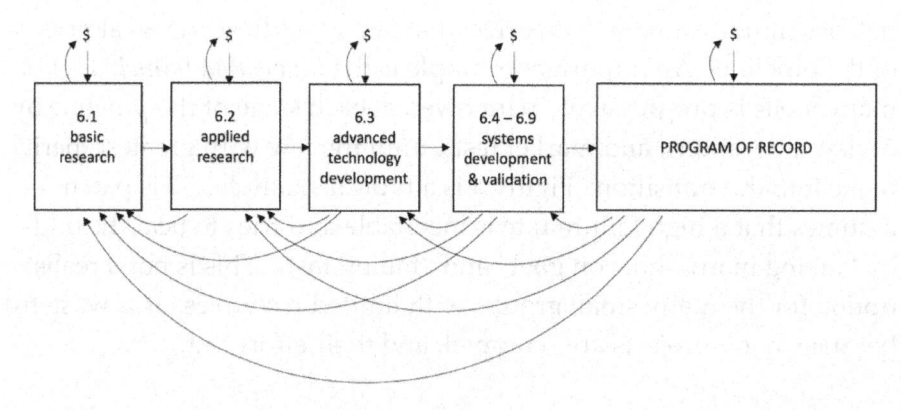

Figure 5. DOD R&D Pipeline map modified with feedback paths.

Second is the *innovation cell*: a protected pocket of innovators spins off ideas into the surrounding environs, where they flow into local pipelines. This extension assumes that failures result from organizational hostility toward new inventions and organizational inertia that is resistant to change. It ignores all that must happen to move toward adoption after the cell produces an invention.

Third is *intellectual property*: patents serve as proxies for innovation. This extension assumes that those with the most patents are in a position of power because their inventions are protected from competitors, who can legally use their patent claims only by purchasing licenses. However, the correlation between invention and eventual adoption is very weak: according to the Patent Office, only about 5% of patents return the inventor's investment.

Fourth is *diffusion*: an innovator injects an idea into a social network, where it spreads out across the communication channels of the network until everyone has a chance to adopt it. Unlike the pipeline, this model makes human agency of adoption explicit. Members of the community explicitly decide to join the innovation. Segments of the community (inventors, early adopters, majority, and laggards) use different criteria and take different amounts of time to reach their decisions. Like the pipeline, diffusion models the innovation process as flows through a network originating with a single source. While diffusion is a significant departure from the pipeline, it still does not deal with spontaneous innovations, dark innovations, competing innovation proposals, or unpredictability of the environment.

Fifth are *agile* management and *lean* management. Agile management means, first, to include customers on project teams so that their perspectives are immediately available to influence the design and, second, to do a lot of rapid prototyping so that customers are well informed in their feedback. Lean management means to identify and eliminate waste in the process, notably steps that do not add value to the final product. Principles of agile and lean management have been added to the management of teams within the stages of the pipeline. And yet the pipelines are not significantly more successful at leading to adoption.

There is one other theory, Clayton Christensen's *disruption*: established businesses are nibbled to death by small challengers with a different business model that offers a low-grade version of their product to customers the established business does not want; eventually the alternative matures and disrupts their main business because they cannot compete with it. This model treats businesses as organisms in an ecosystem in a constant churn of survival of the fit and destruction of the unfit. It has been a useful guide to business leaders who struggle with the question of how to defeat a competitor who offers cheaper versions of their product using a more efficient business model. Disruption theory is about business survival, but not attaining adoptions of innovation.

Each of these "pipeline patches" is based on a large kernel of truth. But each one breaks down for many common examples of innovation. None of the patches has materially improved the productivity of the pipelines involved. These models *explain the past*, but they are insufficient to *generate the future*.

Maps of Human Ecosystems

Innovation happens in human ecosystems, not factories. We human beings live in a social space of conversations. Conversations can be as small as two persons talking or as large as a world community (thanks, Internet). The whole of humanity is connected in a tight, yet unseen network, each person and group engrossed in their own affairs and realities. Innovation in their communities arises in their collective conversations as they respond to collective concerns.

Resistance is a common example of a breakdown confronting innovation leaders. They have sensed a concern, proposed a better future, and offered to make it happen. But one or more subgroups of their community feels threatened and mounts a campaign to sideline their innovation proposal. Those who view innovation as pipelines see resistance as a new stage, "valley of death", which comes with no guidance on how to get through. Those who view innovation as adoption see resistance as a signal that the concerns of important groups are not being addressed. The response is to seek conversation with the resisters to find a way to include them – sensing their concerns, reframing the envisioning story, and modifying the offer. This is what navigation in the face of resistance looks like.

Navigating

Innovation leaders are more like mariners who navigate a restless sea than managers who manufacture products according to a plan.

Conclusion

Our definition – innovation is adoption of new practice in a community – makes no distinction between technological and social innovations. All innovations are social, and some are enabled by technology. The technology is not the innovation; the practices it enables are the innovation.

Throughout this book, we will give you maps of social space to aid you to visualize the phenomena we are describing. Although these phenomena are pervasive, they are mostly invisible. We are not used to seeing them. Visualizing them makes it possible to talk about them and navigate with them. Navigation means you can intentionally shape the world and not just be shaped by it. We intend to reframe the picture of innovation with new maps so that we can consistently achieve the adoptions we seek. You do not have to be in the situation where you are trying to find your destination in Chicago and all you have is a Detroit map, but you don't realize it's the wrong map.

• • •

We turn now to Part II of this book. Its nine chapters map out nine critical dimensions of social space. Even though the space itself is constantly shifting and changing, these dimensions are recurrent and can become visible to you. They are like buoys guiding you in the fog. You can generate movement through the acts of commitment you make in language, through your conversations. We will turn to the three remaining innovation practices in Part III. Your knowledge of social space will enable you to be proficient at these practices.

Part II
Navigating Social Space

6
CONVERSATIONS

> *We make things happen in the commitments*
> *we make to each other, and we make these*
> *commitments in conversations.*
> – Fernando Flores

> *Commitment is an act, not a word.*
> – Jean-Paul Sartre

> *The revolution begins when computers can engage in conversations.*
> – James Burke

The moment we say that innovation is the adoption of new practice in a community, we acknowledge that innovation is a social process. The idea that innovations are phenomena in social space takes some time for many of us to adsorb. We are used to looking at the world as a place of objects, data, information, control, scientific explanations, and problems that can be solved with rational thinking. In social space, we see conversations, relationships, care, identities, commitments, emotions, moods, skills, and power. The structures of the rational world feel familiar and natural. Those of the social world are much less familiar and we often feel uncomfortable with them.

With this chapter and the remainder of Part II, we explore social space to deepen your understanding of the leadership practices. Our students frequently tell us that the distinctions we make are so sharp and clear, they are life transforming. They often ask, Why isn't this taught in school?

To answer this, we need to look at some history. Four hundred years ago Europe was embroiled in the Thirty Years War (1618-1648), a conflict which seemed destined never to end. René Descartes, mathematician and philosopher, thought that the problem was that people get overwhelmed by their emotions and cannot have a rational discussion to work out their differences. He developed the philosophy of *mind-body dualism*, which holds that the mind is the noble master seeking to make rational decisions and the body is a debased hulk pulling in all sorts of irrational directions. By separating them, he advocated rising above the body by working with rational thought. This resonated with many who were weary of war and wanted a better way. His philosophy became extremely popular and remains so today as Cartesianism or rationalism. Over the past 400 years much thought has been devoted to understanding rationalism, striving for a well-ordered society that can work out differences rationally.

In recent years there has been a rising interest in the emotional body. Examples of "nonrational decision making" appear in linguistic philosophy, cognitive science, medicine, and economics. People almost never make decisions by using logic to reach their conclusions. Rather, they do what they feel is right, and create a rational explanation after the fact. Much has been learned about how this works but little of it has reached the school curriculum. Innovation takes place in a social space that does not use logic to motivate action. Our account of social space is built from language-action philosophy, somatic philosophy, and our own research on the practices of serial innovators. We need to be skillful masters at navigating in this space. The eight practices are our navigation tools.

Conversations

Our goal in Part II of this book is to help you understand your community's social space and learn how to navigate it as you seek to bring forth a new practice – that is, move toward the goal when the path is unclear. Although social spaces are complex, adaptive, and unpredictable, they have discernible structures that allow us to navigate. It is a real joy to see how much structure there is in social spaces and how useful it can be for getting to your innovation goal.

We mentioned that a way to understand social space is as a game with players, rules, and purpose (Chapter 2). This view is not sufficient for navigation. A deeper look reveals that the dynamics of social space are defined by our conversations and other interactions among ourselves. Without conversations, there can be no coordination of action, no means for practices to change, and, indeed, no game. Fernando Flores, an international business and political leader, identified the primacy of conversations with his philosophical axiom: *the world is constituted from conversations and practices*. This is our starting point for learning about our social space.

What do we mean by "conversations"? Our usual understanding is that a conversation is the exchange of messages. While this view of communication is a powerful engineering paradigm, it is not powerful enough for navigating a social space.

We turn to another powerful Flores insight: *actions follow from commitments made in conversations*. We will see that there are only five kinds of commitments, which we make in our conversations by "speech acts". From there, we will characterize the "conversation for action", in which two parties coordinate their commitments to generate an outcome. The conversation for action is a molecule for growing the complex networks of commitments in our organizations and communities.

We will then highlight three additional kinds of conversations that provide the background of obviousness in which the conversation for action takes place: the "conversation for possibility" generates possibilities for action, the "conversation for context" reveals meaning and purpose for possibilities, commitments, and actions, and the "conversation for relationship" builds a foundation of care and trust.

What are Conversations?

Conversations are the essence of human interaction. Our relationships grow and are nurtured in our conversations. Everything we do in social space is a form of conversation. Some interactions, such as talking or exchanging emails, are in words; others are non-verbal gestures, movements, nods, winks, facial expressions, and postures.

Our everyday understanding of conversation tends to be much narrower. The common understanding is that a conversation is an exchange of messages between parties. They transmit their messages over some sort of channel, such as brain-to-mouth-to air-to-ear-to-brain. As the parties receive messages, they update their mental models of the situation. Over repeated exchanges, they overcome misunderstandings caused by noise or distortions in the channel. Once their mental models agree, the parties can coordinate their actions successfully.

The message-exchange idea was encoded into communication engineering in the late 1940s by Claude Shannon's remarkable "information theory". Shannon demonstrated that it was always possible to find encodings for messages that would allow the receiver to reconstruct the message over a noisy channel. The more redundancy in the code, the more noise could be overcome. This theory was the basis for engineers to build communication systems with 100% reception accuracy.

Navigating in social space demands much more than an understanding of channels, noise, and codes. Navigation is about coordination and, more importantly, relationships. It begins with our awareness of how our every action, verbal or non-verbal, affects others and ourselves. We communicate in language, which we learned as children. In our many interactions as we grew up, we accumulated various understandings – *interpretations* – of what others mean and intend when they speak certain words and make certain movements. Our entire history, including our ancestors going back hundreds of years, shapes our present interpretations. We use the term *listen* for the particular way a person interprets conversations. Day and night our brains are constantly listening and updating our interpretations. It is little surprise that two people in a conversation can have different interpretations of the expressions in language they exchange. The ambiguities of human conversation are too complex to explain as mere machines exchanging unambiguous signals.

Consider a very simple example. Alice and Bob are cleaning up after dinner. Alice says, "please take out the garbage." Bob says "OK" and takes out the garbage. Alice is satisfied. This interaction seems to be explainable within the engineering model of communication.

Now consider a variation. Alice says, "tomorrow is garbage collection day." Bob knows from past experience with Alice that this means to take out the garbage. He says "OK" and takes it out. Again, Alice is satisfied. Bob's awareness of his past history with Alice enables him to see her true intent, which was not obvious simply from the words she said.

But that is not the only possible outcome. Alice's sentence is not formulated as a request. In the context of their experience together, Bob interpreted it as a request. What if Bob had interpreted Alice's words as information about the town's garbage collectors? In that case, Bob might say "Thanks for letting me know." If Alice intended it as a request, this would have created a breakdown because Bob does not take out the garbage. We cannot explain either scenario with the message model, because the encoder has no way to know Alice's true intention when encoding the sentence for transmission.

We therefore need an interpretation of conversation that looks at how we listen. When I say words, what will the other person listen? Will they listen what I intended? Or something else? The communication will not succeed if the other's listening does not match my intention. For me to be a successful communicator, therefore, I need to skillful at *listening to the other's listening*.

When Alice and Bob are poor at listening to their listenings, their attempted coordination can spiral into

> **A successful communicator is skillful at listening to the other's listening.**

an emotional unhappy ending. Here is a possible scenario. When Bob does not take out the garbage, Alice gets mad and says, "Didn't you hear me say to take out the garbage?" Bob says, "No I didn't, I just heard you giving me information." Alice is now more dissatisfied. She says, "You are trying to get out of your chores with word play. Dang it, take out the garbage!" Unhappy and perhaps resentful, Bob takes it out. Alice remains dissatisfied because she has lost trust that Bob will carry out his responsibilities. Both Alice and Bob take some blame here. Bob is not listening for Alice's intention, and Alice is not listening for whether Bob is interpreting her words as a request. Had either been listening, the conversation might take a different direction. Bob might ask, "Would you like me to take out the garbage?" Or Alice might ask, "Did you hear my request to take out the garbage?" Either way, they avoid the breakdown, Bob takes out the garbage, and both are satisfied. Their mutual trust is intact.

Ask yourself this question. Do I habitually listen for the other person's listening? When I intend a request, how do I know they listened my intention? If I am not listening or validating their listening, I should not be surprised if my conversations lead to breakdowns accompanied by negative emotions and the erosion of trust.

We are sometimes given the advice of "active listening", which means we repeat back what the other person says and ask whether this is what they said. This is a good practice. Unfortunately, it may be unreliable because the other person can say you got the words right even though you do not understand their actual intentions. Active listening is not true listening; it is more like an engineered communication channel that asks for a resend in the hope of overcoming noise.

In other words, the workings of our everyday conversations do not resemble the engineering model except perhaps in very superficial ways. Communication breakdowns will plague you as long as you interpret communication as exchange of messages.

What happens in conversations when we say we are communicating? We make commitments that produce actions, we coordinate actions, and we listen for the intentions of others. We build trust. We take care of our relationships. We reveal our concerns and what we care about. We articulate possibilities. We tell stories that help others see what we see. We express joy, sadness, anger, and a host of other emotions and moods. If Alice and Bob saw their interaction space in this way, they would be able to listen to each other's listening and avoid many breakdowns in their communications.

Speech Acts

John L. Austin, a British philosopher, was one of the first to call attention to how our language is laced with verbs that "do the action they say."[1] This idea also fascinated John Searle, an American philosopher, who studied it in depth and wrote a book on speech acts.[2] An example is the minister who proclaims, "I hereby declare you husband and wife." From that moment the two are joined into a union

---

[1] Austin, J.L., How to do things with Words, Harvard University Press (1962)
[2] Searle, J. *Speech Acts*. Cambridge University Press (1969)

recognized by law. Another is the judge who says, "The jury's verdict is not guilty." At that moment, the defendant can once again move freely in the world.

These works were initially seen as a theory of language and did not attract much attention. In 1979, Fernando Flores, a student of Searle, saw that this theory was of immense practical importance for business and management because speech acts are the commitments that drive action. Chauncey Bell, a student of Flores, summed up what Flores had grasped:[3]

> We invent all our ventures and enterprises with declarations. We make offers which, when accepted, become our promises to customers, investors, employees, and friends, family, and others. Everything that is new begins with assessments we make about insufficiencies, messes, opportunities and obsolescences. Our enterprises are created as networks of requests, offers, and promises. Everything else that happens starts with requests and offers. We make sense of ourselves and our worlds through assessments and assertions. Money lives in the middle of all this as a collection of commitments, often in hidden and secret ways.

For Flores, the job of a leader is not to make decisions, but to *manage the network of commitments making up an organization*. This is not such a daunting task because there are only five kinds of commitments:

> Request
> Promise (and Offer, which is a conditional promise)
> Declaration
> Assertion
> Assessment

Let us consider what each of these speech acts do.

---

[3] Bell, C., *Mobilize!*, Victoria Ruelas Publisher (2020), p 28

REQUEST. The purpose of a request is to ask another person to provide something you do not have. When the other person supplies what is missing, it is now a part of your world. A common communication breakdown occurs when you believe you made a request, but the other does not listen a request. If you are unaware that the other party has not interpreted what you said as a request, you wind up clueless about why they did not act. *There is no request unless the listener listens a request.*

PROMISE (AND OFFER). The purpose of a promise is to deliver to another person something they do not have. A promise is usually made in response to someone's request. If no one has made a request, you can still make an offer, which will become a promise when another person accepts it. An offer is a conditional promise. A common communication breakdown occurs when you do not keep your promise. This might be because you do not have the competence or resources to keep it, or you do not care enough to keep it. Whatever the reason, if you repeatedly break your promises, others will stop trusting you. It is better to decline a request up front than to break the promise later; the upfront decline gives the other person the opportunity to find another performer.

DECLARATION. The purpose of a declaration is to bring a new state of affairs into existence. The state of affairs can be a new way of existing (such as "we are now married"), a new possibility (such as "I have a solution to your problem"), or a specification of a game (such as "Here is our org chart showing who has what authorities to declare policies and fill positions."). Anyone can declare a new possibility. Declarations often depend on having appropriate authority; for example, a minister has the authority to declare marriages, a boss the authority to hire. Declarations do not have be the logical next step after what has gone before.

ASSERTION. The purpose of an assertion is to represent that something is true in the world. Widely accepted assertions are often called facts. Assertions can be verified by anyone who wants to check them out or who has witnessed what is asserted. Assertions are used as evidence to support arguments. Scientists claim a hypothesis is true where there are enough scientific facts to support the hypothesis and none to oppose it. Similarly, lawyers seek to prove allegations by offering sufficient facts that the jury will no longer have a reasonable doubt.

ASSESSMENT. The purpose of an assessment is to express an evaluation, a judgment, or an opinion. Unlike assertions, assessments cannot be true or false. Instead, they can be grounded or ungrounded. Grounded means that the speaker provides sufficient relevant assertions to support the assessment. Assessments are often made to give purpose to proposed actions. Listeners are more likely to accept and act on grounded assessments. People are more likely to act as you recommend if you have given a well-grounded assessment of why the action is worthwhile. Many assessments are made to characterize or classify people or situations. Your reputation is a story based on many people's assessments of you and your actions. If you want to change someone's assessment of you, you need to take new actions that provoke new assessments. Arguing with them will not change their assessments.

Commitments *produce action* now or in the future. They also *generate an expectation,* beginning immediately, that the action will happen. Thus commitments change the state of the world from the moment they are said. The table below is a compact summary of the descriptions above. The abbreviation "COS" means "conditions of satisfaction", a specification of an intended outcome. Alice, Bob, and Charlie are speakers.

Speech Act	Effect	Commitment	Expectation
Request	Alice asks Bob to provide a COS that Alice does not have	Alice commits to receive the COS when it is delivered	Alice will be satisfied if the COS is delivered
Promise (and offer)	Bob will provide a COS to Alice who has requested it. An offer is a conditional promise – if Alice accepts, Bob will perform	Bob commits to provide the COS to Alice	Bob will provide the COS
Declaration	Charlie declares a new state of affairs in the world	Charlie commits to being part of the new state of affairs	Charlie and others will act in accord with the declaration
Assertion	Charlie claims that something is a fact	Charlie commits to provide witnesses and other evidence attesting the claim	The claim is true and relevant to what Charlie says
Assessment	Charlie makes an evaluation or judgment; if Charlie provides sufficient relevant evidence to support evaluation, the assessment is "grounded"	Charlie commits to the assessment and orients future actions around it	Charlie can provide a rationale for the course of action

Many military commands, government agencies, and businesses are hierarchical. We interpret their organizational charts as trees of declarative authorities. At each level the incumbents can declare certain policies, start certain conversations, and resolve conflicts below them. A common error is to view organizational charts as the allowable paths for communication. Military officers, for example, are told to "follow the chain of command" in making requests, offers, or reports. That means they ought to pass the request up toward the root and down toward the desired performer. This is inefficient and often results in garbled messages reaching the intended performer. It is easy to generate misunderstandings when your conditions of satisfaction are re-interpreted by each level of the tree through which they pass. It is often better to make a request directly of a performer even if they are in a different branch of the hierarchy. In that case, it is important to keep the chain of command informed of relevant requests and that you structure the conditions of satisfaction to include their concurrence.

Speech acts change the state of the world through action and expectation of action. Something is present after the act that was not present before. Speech acts are tools we can use to open new paths of action in social space.

Kinds of Conversations

For navigation, we work with four kinds of conversations. They are Conversation for Action (CFA), Conversation for Possibility (CFP), Conversation for Context (CFC), and Conversation for Relationship (CFR). Worlds are the realities generated by these conversations. Figure 1 is a map of the relationships among these ideas. We will discuss the Conversation for Action in detail in Chapter 8 (Coordination), Worlds in Chapter 7, and the others here.

Conversations

CONVERSATIONS
- reveal concerns
- set context
- care for relationships
- generate worlds
- generate possibilities
- make commitments for actions
- coordinate actions
- generate trust

NOT JUST
- convey information
- exchange messages
- overcome noise

WORLDS
CFC
CFR
CFP
CFA

CF (conversations for)
- C - context
- R - relationship
- P - possibility
- A - action

The realities we perceive
1. Generated by conversations
2. Generate new conversations

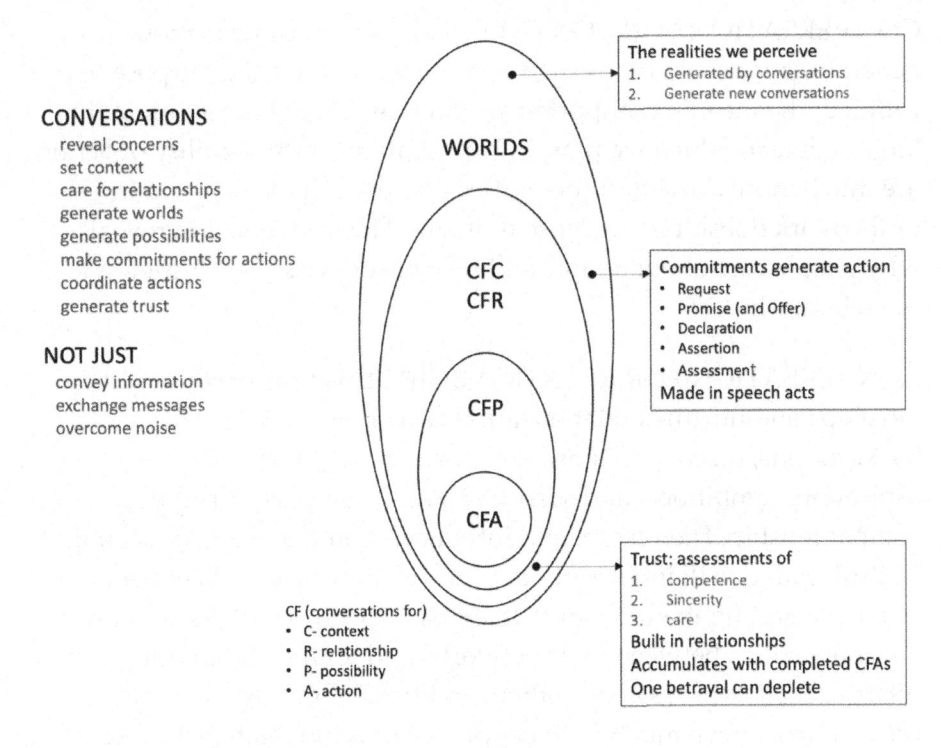

Commitments generate action
- Request
- Promise (and Offer)
- Declaration
- Assertion
- Assessment

Made in speech acts

Trust: assessments of
1. competence
2. Sincerity
3. care

Built in relationships
Accumulates with completed CFAs
One betrayal can deplete

Figure 1. Map of conversation types.

CONVERSATION FOR POSSIBILITY. This conversation creates possibilities for action but does not commit to any one of them. This conversation is needed if a previous commitment failed to materialize or a contingency came up. It is conducted in a mood of speculation – an openness to possibilities. By contrast, the Conversation for Action is often conducted in a different mood – resolution – the determination to bring something into action. Since it is not easy to switch between those two moods, it is better to keep the conversations separate in space and time. For example, speculate with someone while walking or ideating on a white board, then sit down at a conference table later to map out actions. Breakdowns are likely if you try to switch from generating possibilities to generating actions in the same meeting.

CONVERSATION FOR CONTEXT. This type of conversation generates awareness of the big picture and explores the purpose to be fulfilled, the meaning, importance, and relevance of our work in the larger game in which we play. Conversations for possibility or action are much more difficult if the parties do not understand the purpose or the work doesn't make sense to them. This conversation reveals why people care about a topic and the concerns they are bringing to the relationship.

CONVERSATION FOR RELATIONSHIP. This type of conversation develops and nurtures relationships with others. We learn backgrounds, discover histories, connect, bond, share concerns, aspirations, ambitions, and sorrows. We develop trust, respect, companionship, friendship, and intimacy. You may have noticed that skillful leaders will inquire about your relationships and connections as part of getting to know you. It is easier to work with them if there are connections between their networks and yours. From our relationships, we care about others and the community. It is very difficult to achieve much with people we have no relationship with.

You must practice all these conversations and mix them artfully as you lead your teams. Many teams get so focused on "action" they cannot generate new possibilities when a breakdown occurs, they lose their senses of purpose and meaning, and they become detached and distant from each other.

Somatics of Conversations

We cannot talk without the speaking and listening apparatus in our bodies. Our bodies have physical reactions as we move in conversations. The physical reactions can reinforce our progress (for example, when we are elated about a positive development) or they can interfere (for example, when we are fearful that your audience will reject us). We call the space of physical reactions the *somatic side of*

Conversations

conversations. Somatic means "pertaining to the felt body". Somatic practices are integrative: they aim to bring harmony to mind-body interaction. As you practice the innovation leader skills of this book, you will develop a sensibility about the somatic side of conversations. This will not only help you navigate, but it will also eliminate your tendency to believe that communication is some sort of brain-to-brain information transfer.

> **Our bodies' physical reactions affect our progress toward goals. Somatic practices train our bodily reactions to support our goals.**

All conversations have a linguistic aspect (the structure, the intent, the speech acts, the disclosures) and a somatic aspect (bodily reactions during the conversation). We have discussed the linguistic aspects of the first five practices (sensing, envisioning, offering, adopting, sustaining). As you are doing these things, you experience reactions in your body. You might get sweaty palms when it is time for you to speak your envisioning story or offer to a group. You might feel overwhelming anxiety and water down your offers. You might pepper your declarations with hedge words to relieve responsibility.

These somatic aspects can either derail or support you. If you radiate interest and concern, your listeners will be more receptive to your offer. If you clam up and do not speak your offer, you will generate no action. Because of the somatic aspects, there is a profound difference between the performance of an offer and the abstract idea of making an offer.

Somatic responses in conversations can be proactive or reactive. *Proactive* responses are cultivated by somatic practices such as centering and learning to sense other people's energy, moods, emotions, and anxieties. Sustained somatic practices

> **There is a profound difference between the successful performance of an offer and the abstract idea of making an offer.**

can bring you to *emotional fortitude*, meaning that your emotional reactions do not throw you off center. (We will discuss emotional fortitude in the later chapter on embodying.)

Reactive responses appear as emotional reactivity and conditioned tendencies. Emotional reactivity is often expressed as frequent strong emotional reactions to seemingly minor issues. For example, your hot-headed angry reaction when someone disagrees with you derails you from the conversation you want to have. Your fear that your offer might be rejected derails you from making your offer. Your tendency toward road rage when someone cuts you off can turn you into a reckless, vengeful driver.

Conditioned tendencies are practices we learned at some previous time to cope with somatic reactions. Even though the original reason for a conditioned tendency may be long gone, the practice is latent in our nervous system and can be triggered by something in the present. You might have been brought up to "respect elders" by never saying no to their requests. To stay out of trouble, you learned to say yes to everything. Now that you are older, the conditions that generated this conditioned tendency are no longer valid. Nonetheless, you continue to say yes to all requests, even though your plate is full and you do not have the capacity to satisfy them all. You wind up in a mood of constant overwhelm about all my unfilled promises. You earn a reputation for being flaky and undependable and cannot explain why this happens.

There is good news. Once you recognize the conditioned tendency, you have the opportunity (with the help of a coach) to train a new practice to replace it. You can learn to decline requests that you have no desire or capacity to fulfill. You can eliminate the mood of overwhelm by relieving the "overflowing plate" and earn the trust of your coworkers. In the later chapter on embodiment, we will discuss what is involved in recognizing conditioned tendencies and retraining the unwanted ones.

Conversations and Machines

How ought we think of "conversations" in a world increasingly populated by the large language models of generative AI? These are the first of a new generation of machines that can converse with us. What can our philosophy of action in language teach us about their power and peril? The most important insight is that generative AI, in all its current forms, cannot care. Generative AI cannot "listen for listening" with purpose or intent. Large language models do not have a body that has physical reactions, conditioned tendencies, or empathy. For some people, disembodied AI systems are less prone to bias and capable of more objective decisions. For others, inability to care is the fatal flaw that makes AI so alien and possibly dangerous. We will discuss machines and language in depth later (Chapter 20).

Care is essential for success at innovation leadership. The leader who cares about their community is more likely to mobilize people around offers that address their concerns. The leader who does not care about the concerns of the community, the breakdowns they face, and how they react to proposals for change, is likely to fail. That leader will engender resentment, resignation and a host of other unproductive moods that may make the situation worse.

Conclusion

Practice being fully present so that you can recognize when each kind of conversation is appropriate. When you first meet someone, a Conversation for Relationship is a good start, looking for common elements of background on which to form connections. A Conversation for Context is important before launching or reviewing a project because it refreshes everyone's awareness of the meaning and purpose of the requested action; otherwise performers may not see the point of their work. If one of your Conversations for Action gets bogged down, step back for a Conversation for Possibility before returning to action.

This chapter has been a "conversation about conversations" to enable you to develop sensibilities you will need to navigate in social space. The maps of conversations give us ways to reveal:

- What each person has committed to do.
- How work is completed when we do it well.
- Which clients are dissatisfied and why.
- How to restructure our networks for greater satisfaction.
- When we have lost trust and how to rebuild it.
- Who is responsible for particular actions.
- How to diagnose what is going wrong.
- Somatic body reactions that interfere with our intentions.

Many breakdowns in our communities result from long-standing habits of speaking and listening. With the help of the new maps, we can diagnose what is happening and build bridges to better futures.

As we diagnose the situation of our community, we can bring to light the conversational practices that led to this situation. We can discover why our community has been unable to escape from its current traps despite the efforts of many capable and responsible people.

Chauncey Bell sums it up nicely: "Until the moment in which this new language and practice of mapping coordination appeared, this dimension of human experience – the coordination of action in language – had not received formal attention from the right mapmakers. Over the years we have learned that working with the loop reveals miraculous things about how we human beings invent our futures in language. This is how we make the future happen: speaking and listening in conversations with each other."[4]

---

[4] Chauncey Bell, Mobilize!, 2020, p 37.

7
WORLDS

> *The world is constituted not of objects*
> *but of conversations and practices.*
> – Fernando Flores

> *Reality is merely an illusion,*
> *albeit a very persistent one.*
> – Albert Einstein

We are driving and the phone rings. We answer in hands-free mode and get into a lively discussion with our friend about a project we are working on. Ten minutes later, when the call is over, we suddenly realize we missed our intended freeway exit, because we were so deeply engrossed in the call that we were hardly paying attention to the road. We feel lucky that we didn't get into an accident and embarrassed that we must figure out how to backtrack to the proper exit. We start to wonder if hands-free phoning really prevents driver distraction.

What happened here? We found ourselves in the world of conversation with our friend, and the world in which we were driving nearly disappeared. The conversation generated a new world. The power of a conversation to take us into a different world – the world of the conversation – is astonishing. It's not simply that we got engrossed or distracted. The world we were in disappeared. We entered a new reality, the reality generated by the conversation itself.

> **Conversations generate realities, which we call worlds.**

Sometimes people wonder why when driving they can have a lively conversation with their passenger and yet not be distracted from the road and traffic. The answer is simple: you are in the same conversation with the passenger; both of you are part of the same world. Your conversation does not transport you into another reality.

Why are we interested in worlds? First, adopting a new practice changes the world of a community. Knowing something about how worlds work will help us achieve adoption. Second, many innovations are rooted in the cross appropriation of practices from another world. We need the power of seeing other relevant worlds and then entering into them far enough to appropriate their practices. For example, the Ukraine military entered Elon Musk's world of Starlink Internet and found that fast, cheap communication conferred a military advantage. Now other militaries are seeking to establish a Starlink practice for themselves. Third, when we first encounter a new world, we are beginners there. Our practices for being effective beginners (Chapter 2) accelerate our entry into a new world where we can appropriate their practices for our world.

In this chapter, we will help you come to see why conversations generate new realities. This will become the basis for your ability to navigate in whatever worlds you enter or create.

What is a World?

World means a perceived reality generated in a social space. Common examples are the fashion world, the academic world, and the military world. The people in a world have their own language, mutual understandings, and shared concerns. And when they are fully engaged in their world, other worlds do not exist for them.

The most striking aspect of a world is that it seems fully real. Our biology cannot distinguish a world generated by conversations from "the real world": the world we experience in conversations and practices *is the real world*. The experienced world is seamless. You can sharply focus your attention on part of it, but the rest is still there, dimmed out.

> **Our biology cannot distinguish a world generated by conversations from "the real world".**

A world is not the same as a community. Community refers to a set of people who have common interests and concerns and who take care of each other through their interactions. The world is the reality in which a community finds itself. Worlds generate a common background of obviousness that everyone there shares implicitly. We live in multiple worlds – for example, work and family. Our relationships provide bridges that enable us to move between worlds.

In the 1970s, Fernando Flores designed dramatic demonstrations of how conversations create realities. One he called the World Game, which lasted about three hours. The other he called Business 2000, which lasted five days. Both involved groups of about 60 participants. Here is an account of the World Game; Business 2000 was similar but went much deeper into the reality generated by the game. Flores divided the group into 10 teams of around 6 persons. Each team represented a company operating in the world economy. To start, he asked each team to get organized: declare its mission and select its officers and roles. When this was done, he asked each CEO to introduce the company mission and team to everyone and make its initial offer. Then he asked them to start interacting from their mission statements, offers, and roles. Occasionally a Big Voice would speak up on the PA system announcing some event in the world to which the companies could respond, for example, "An earthquake has just shaken Tokyo and 500 have been injured." Within about 30 minutes this cacophonous assembly no longer seemed like a game. People were having the same emotions they would in real businesses. People with valuable skill sets emerged as leaders. People were elated when deals closed and dejected when deals died. They experienced gratitude when someone met their part of a deal, and anger when someone betrayed their deal. Some CEOs were already experienced and did well at the CEO job and others, lacking the skill, generated resentment in their teams. When finally Flores ended the game (through an announcement of the Big Voice) he asked for reports what people experienced. Group members immediately told stories that sounded like the stories of real companies. Some of the stories included deepfelt complaints about the behavior of their CEO or their head of marketing. Others praised the heroic skills of their CEOs. Several times Flores reminded us that it was all a game and the game was over: let the game be over. After listening to the reports, he told us many had not grasped the point. The game was not about the companies. It was a demonstration of how a set of imaginary companies became real in the conversations we generated in that room. That came as a shock to many of us. We realized we had indeed taken it as real and had not seen that we jointly invented a reality in our conversations. Flores closed by noting that our biology cannot distinguish between the "reality" of external world and the "reality" of the world generated in conversations.

People from different countries live in different worlds and often cannot make sense of how people in another country see things. For example, in the Russia-Ukraine war, Russians believed that the Western allies of Ukraine provoked the war, while the West believed Russia started the war unprovoked. Finding a resolution to the conflict is difficult as long each set of players cannot see how things look from the eyes of those in the other world.

People of different political persuasions also form their own worlds. They believe the realities of their world are the truth and stoutly defend their truth against any critic in another world that holds different beliefs. The common genre of "wicked problems" appears when deeply conflicting worlds try to cooperate.

The term "bubble" commonly refers to a world whose participants believe they have special knowledge that will enable them to achieve a lofty goal such as becoming wealthy. These groups are sometimes called echo chambers because each person reinforces the ideas and sentiments of others. Many bubbles, such as those in finance, housing, and cyptocurrency, come to an untimely end when they burst, an outer world rushes in, and many participants are ruined.

Social media have come under fire because they are fertile environments for generating intolerant, conflicting worlds. The term "filter bubble" indicates how algorithms induce bubbles by feeding people only the information the algorithm deems to be of interest to them. These algorithms track data that people generate in conversations, searches, browsing activity, purchases, visits, and more. The filter bubble has become a disparaging term because it suggests that people are lured in by advocates who manipulate them by feeding them only information they want to hear.

The common feature of all bubbles is that they are generated by and held in place by the conversations and practices of their members. It is astonishing what we come to perceive as real from the conversations in which we engage.

The social space in which innovations emerge is chaotic and messy. We cannot eliminate the conflicts, but we can navigate through them to generate innovation in our communities.

Realities Objective and Subjective

It is useful to distinguish objective and subjective aspects of realities in a world. Objective reality refers to the aspects of the world that can be represented, measured, and verified by third parties. Subjective reality refers to an individual (or group) interpretation of the world. These two are deeply intertwined. Consider an example. My car is traveling at 70 mph in a 60 mph zone (objective). My front passenger says I should slow down (subjective). My rear passenger says we'll be late, go faster (subjective). The arresting police offer says I exceeded the speed limit by too much (subjective). This gets interesting when we challenge whether an objective fact is really a fact. In court, I tell the judge that the police officer's radar might be miscalibrated (subjective). The police officer lays out the details of how the radar was calibrated (objective). The judge says that the officer's testimony is more credible (subjective) and declares I'm guilty. What about that last statement? Was it objective or subjective? It seems to be both. It could be objective because it was a fact the judge said it, or it could be an opinion because the judge is authorized to hand down verdicts.

Thus, it looks like we cannot make a final determination of which parts of our stories of our worlds are objective and which are subjective. The reason is that both exist in language. Language gives us both the *ability to represent* and the *ability to shape*. We can and do shift between these abilities as the situation evolves and our interpretations change.

The funny thing is that we think good communication is about exchanging representations and we are mostly oblivious to how we shape others and they shape us in our interactions. Kari Granger, CEO of Granger Network, an executive consultancy, comments on how AI is shaping our reality without our awareness:

> Fewer and fewer people are familiar with the basics of semantics, grammar, and syntax. It's even rarer to find individuals with whom I can delve into the deeper philosophical aspects of language. It's unnerving to think that AI, on the other hand, is rapidly surpassing our own understanding of language's nuances and uses. And that means it is almost certainly shaping subjective reality in a way we

don't understand—because we don't even understand our own ability to do that.[1]

Granger goes further. She notes that when she asked executives what is an offer, their responses varied quite a bit while centering on sales. When she asked ChatGPT-4 the same question, it replied "An offer is a speech act." She concluded that the machine has a better understanding of the shaping aspect than the executives.

In this book, we are particularly concerned with our underdeveloped ability to shape. We aim to awaken our understanding of this side of language so that we can move people to change their practice. And while we're at it, we can learn how to coexist with machines whose conversations appear human.

The Background

Our language depends upon and conveys the ripples of previous conversations, passed down through years and centuries from prior generations. Our beliefs, customs, mannerisms, practices, and values are inherited from the conversations of our forebears, combining with the conversations we live in. We think, speak, and act in the context this historical background of presuppositions and prejudices without being aware of it. This background is boundless, with no definite beginning or end, extending beyond every horizon.

The conversations making up a world include many assumptions and understandings that are never mentioned explicitly and are taken for granted by those involved. For example, the request to bring a glass of water presupposes that we understand what a glass is, the glass is clean, what water is, the water is free of contaminants, what thirst is, how much water should be in the glass, the proper temperature, and much more. We don't need to talk about these

---

[1] Kari Granger. 2023. Introducing leaders to our new human peer (blog). Available: https://grangernetwork.com/introducing-leaders-to-our-new-non-human-peer/

things because they are "obvious" to everyone. What we call "common sense" is all that goes without saying in this tacit "background of obviousness" that nevertheless makes sense when revealed and brought into conversation. Indeed, if you reveal something from the background, people will respond "That's obvious!" because it fits the background even though it was not obvious the moment before it was revealed.

It appears that this ability to sense context from the background is integral to our ability to be in a world. This ability is a product of our human biology. We do not know if it can be transferred to machines, or even whether machines could read context for us.

In the 1980s, the field of Artificial Intelligence focused on expert systems – software systems that could perform like human experts. The software was programmed with logic languages that could make deductions from the given information. For instance, a medical expert system would diagnose illness and prescribe treatment given the patient's symptoms and data from the patient's test results. Despite extensive interviews with physicians to capture their rules and knowledge into a database, expert systems never rose to the level of human experts. The failures were attributed to missing "common sense facts" that were unspoken but obvious to human experts and their clients, but were not obvious to the machine. Expert system designers sought compendia of common-sense facts that the machine could use. Perhaps the most famous of these efforts was the Cyc project of Douglas Lenat, which after 40 years had accumulated 30 million common sense facts. Yet even that treasury was not enough to add up to a background of common sense and make expert systems smart enough to be experts.

In 2020 a new genre of machines called Generative AI emerged into the public spotlight, powered by neural networks trained from billions of documents found in the Internet. They operated in a conversational mode, responding to text "prompts" with text strings

Worlds

that were statistically probable in the training texts. They generated surprisingly good responses to their prompts. These machines were called Large Language Models (LLMs) because of the large amounts of human generated documents that trained them. The documents are written by people who, like the rest of us, are mostly unaware of the tacit knowledge they readily draw upon in their context. Tacit knowledge goes unrecorded. Like expert systems, these machines do not have access to the hidden background and cannot use it to generate outputs that make sense. As a result, LLMs are prone to fabrications and misguided musings called hallucinations.

The experience with LLMs shows it is doubtful that the background of obviousness can be revealed from statistical inference by machine. We continue to rely on our sensing skills to uncover what is hidden.

Imagination is another human ability that flows from our tacit background. It is a capacity to conceive possibilities that do not exist but can become incorporated into our shared background once articulated. Although LLMs have generated some surprisingly imaginative poetry, their outputs may be statistical inferences that surprise us rather than genuine creations relative to the background. This question on the limits of machines and machine methods deserves more exploration.

Exercise: Walking in the Neighborhood

Chauncey Bell designed an exercise to get you in touch with how our worlds are constituted from conversations. The exercise is in the appendix at the end of this chapter. Please pause your reading here and do the exercise. When you resume, and the rest of what we say here will make sense.

(Pause)

When we ask our students what they learn from this exercise, we get two main answers. One is that this is an excellent exercise in mindfulness, becoming fully aware of what is around you. The other is that it opens connections to other people and nature. Both are useful and valid lessons. These answers reveal how common it is for us to move around in a bubble of in-our-own-head-conversations and not see the possibilities of interactions with others. That can be lonely. The exercise wakes us up.

Yet these two answers miss Bell's point. The point is that the world you perceive as real is generated from conversations. The world is constantly unfolding and shifting as its conversations unfold and shift. Bell sees three main lessons from the exercise:

1. Everything you perceive has a name and a story.
2. Everything you perceive emerged from or was decided in past conversations, often a long time ago.
3. The identities of the persons in those conversations have not survived, but the effects they generated are still present today.

Names allow us to coordinate action around the named thing. Things that have no names are often invisible or very hard to discern. It is usually impossible to discover when or where the name of something emerged. We use term "emerged" rather than invented, created, or discovered because the phenomenon did not exist until a name for it appeared and the appearance was a community phenomenon. If Archimedes had run into the street to proclaim his Eureka discovery, and then immediately collapsed from a heart attack, his discovery would be lost. It would not exist for anyone because it did not become part of anyone's conversation.

Why is this important? The world is shaped by prior conversations and the current conversations will shape the future world. We have seen how the actions generated from conversations are the results of commitments made in them. A small number of conversational moves, the speech acts, can generate an infinite number of futures. Realizing this and mastering the moves will give you enormous power to lead changes (innovations) in the conversation space of your community. Mastering the eight-practices skill set enables you to put them together in the right way for innovation leadership. This new sensibility opens increased mobility of movement in the world.

Why is it so easy for us to miss this point? Bell answers this way:

> Once we grant to ourselves a richer, greatly expanded understanding of what is going on as we are speaking and listening, the notion that we invent our worlds and futures in language appears simple, all but obvious.
>
> Over the years, however, I have discovered that it is actually quite obscure. As I have endeavored to train younger consultants, I would ask where they thought things came from, and the answers were almost always more or less like the naive Lean syllogism "if you ask why 5 times, you will get to the root cause." This is absolute nonsense. Not that there's anything wrong with asking why repeatedly. That's a good practice. The nonsense is there is no such thing in human experience as a root cause. In physics and chemistry, sometimes, yes. If you mix hydrogen, oxygen, and a spark, you will get an explosion and water. In human interactions, never. Complicated biological, neurological, historical and other factors underlie the intrinsic conversational and intellectual laziness we all embody. We settle very fast for answers about why things are happening, where they come from, and what keeps them in place in our worlds. (Bell, *Mobilize!*, p38)

What is your first impulse when confronted with a breakdown? For most people it is to see the breakdown as a problem and look for a solution. For those who accept that the world is generated in conversations and practices, it is to ask what conversation is missing. When you can make this your impulse, you have access to the considerable power of language to turn your visions into reality.

Conclusion

Our realities are generated by our conversations, practices, and histories. Adopting a new practice brings the community into a new reality. Leading them in making the transition from their current reality to a new one that serves better is a challenge made easier when you understand the dynamics of social spaces as worlds created by ever-unfolding conversations.

Appendix: Bell's Walking in the Neighborhood Exercise

The exercise that follows is designed to awaken our raw sensibility to where our worlds come from. The exercise is best done with a partner, but you can do it alone. It is extremely simple. Print out the following prompts – questions you will ask yourself during the exercise – and then take a walk in your neighborhood. As you walk, follow the prompts that appear below, asking each question in your conversation with a friend, or talking to yourself as you walk and observe what you find in your neighborhood.

1. Yourself

- What is your name, and where did it come from? Who named you, and in what traditions did they name you?
- What are you wearing, and where did the clothing come from? Who defined the articles of clothing you are wearing, who branded them, and who taught you to wear those clothes?
- In what way do you think about the kind of person you are, and from what traditions and what speakers do you take the discourse about the kind of person you are?

Worlds

2. Town or city

- What is the name of the jurisdiction in which you are walking, and who gave it that name, when, and in what tradition?
- What are the boundaries of the jurisdiction? Who defined those boundaries, and when?
- In what style or political tradition is the jurisdiction governed, and what recent changes are appearing in the rules and habits of behavior in the jurisdiction?

3. Roads and paths

- How did these get here? Who asked for them, who paid for them, who designed them, who installed and who maintains them?
- What are the traditions of driving and walking in the jurisdiction? Right or left side of the road? What about the signage? What kinds of rules prevail? Traffic lights? Stop signs? What are the consequences of following or not following the traffic instructions embodied in the signs?
- Do people in this jurisdiction follow instructions or not?

4. Conventions

- Do strangers greet each other when they pass? Do they smile at each other?
- How close to each other do people stand when they are talking?
- How are others dressed?
- Who picks up the litter? Do you stop and pick up litter?

5. Homes

- Are the homes in the neighborhood well- or ill-kept?
- How are the boundaries of properties marked? Are numbers visible on homes?
- What rooms are located on the public sides of the homes? Kitchens? Living rooms? Why? Who put those rooms there?

6. Woodlands

- What are the names of the trees and plants you see there? Do you know some of those names? Who gave them those names? Where would you go to find out what their names are and what is the history of naming and thinking about those names?
- Who put those trees and plants there? In what kind of conversation did they define what would be there, and how they would be arranged?
- Who cares for the trees and plants? Why?

7. Enterprises

- Are the names of companies displayed on buildings? Why? Why not?
- Why are there people in those buildings?
- How did they get there, really – not that they walked or drove – what language-actions led to their being there?

8. The Sky

- Glance at the sky.
- How many features of the sky can you name? Where did those features get their names?
- Why are those features important? Why do their names 'stick'?

9. The Earth

- Feel the earth under your feet.
- What sensation does it give you? What do you call that sensation?
- Where did you learn to name the sensation as you called it?

10. Divinities

- As you have walked and observed, have you experienced the emotions we call 'gratitude' or 'awe'?
- How did you express those emotions – to yourself privately or out loud?
- Do you refer directly to the divinities ("the gods" or God) or do you avoid speaking in that way?

Now walk back home and explore what shows up as you read and reflect on the few sentences below.

1. The terrain you are exploring is local and familiar; we are not asking you to figure out stuff that does not belong to your own neighborhood. There is enough 'data' in the background of our normal everyday common senses so that you can bring pretty rich conversations about how a particular fireplug happened to arrive at a particular spot without having to undertake a major research project.

2. The exercise opens the opportunity to reflect on the connection between the way that the world of artifacts – things in our worlds – intersects with our customs, laws, and historical conversations.

3. The exercise enriches an already existing narrative that we share with others about what is already in our everyday world in a way that allows a rich conversation and the possibility of glimpsing something transcendent.

Like it or not, paying attention or not, each day we participate in shaping our worlds. Most of the time we participate in ways that are innocuous, harmless, and to which we are asleep, ignorant, or blind. We go along with what is happening. Sometimes we are thrilled by something: a sunset, the smile of a child, wonderful weather, magnificent music, a well-prepared meal. Displeasure is more common, and it is far easier to make a negative assessment than to acknowledge something that contributes to us. We complain to ourselves or to those around us, or to the gods. "It should not be this way!" "Why doesn't someone do something about this!"

Some of us will set out to deliberately and passionately take responsibility for (and brave the risks) that are involved in generating new futures. We can learn to pay attention to the moments in which we glimpse and then confront phenomena and situations that are unhealthy for us, or that suggest new possibilities and openings for us. In those moments, sometimes we can encounter ourselves as people who are being offered the gift of participating in the creation of important features of our worlds. And sometimes in the moment that some of us are granted those opportunities we are actually aware of what is happening – that new worlds are being disclosed in our conversations!

In our experience, this exercise can dramatically increase our capacity to observe the world being invented and reinvented around us every day, and to appreciate the capacity we have as human beings to participate in the creation of our worlds.

8
COORDINATION

> *In order to win, we should operate at a faster tempo or rhythm than our adversaries — better yet, get inside their observation-orientation-decision-action loop, confusing and disordering them.*
> – Colonel John Boyd

US Air Force Colonel John Boyd formulated the OODA loop based on his experiences as a fighter pilot in the 1950s and 1960s. He noted that pilots are constantly cycling through practices to observe, orient, decide, and act. Observe means to be aware of everything around you. Orient means to make sense of what you see. Decide means to choose an appropriate response or course of action. Act means to carry out the response. Boyd insisted that getting to the "act" was the most important part of effectiveness. It's all too easy to get caught up in analysis and hesitate. Hesitation, even momentary, makes all the difference between winning and losing. Boyd trained pilots on this loop until they could execute the loop very fast. He was a role model for his teaching. He was known as "40 Second Boyd" for his boast that he could take down all comers in air-to-air combat within forty seconds or he would pay them $40. Col Boyd was reputed to never have paid the $40. His paradigm of the OODA loop found its way into the operations of government and business. Many saw practicing the OODA loop well as a key to success, whether in the office or the skies.

Boyd saw how a linguistic structure could define a practical skill for producing action. Around the same time, linguistic philosophers were beginning to see that certain structures of language, which they called speech acts, were not simply descriptions of action, they *were* action. The modern concept of speech acts was first developed by J L Austin ("How to do things with words", 1962) and elaborated at book length by John Searle (*Speech Acts*, 1969).

In 1979 Fernando Flores (*Management and communication in the office of the future*, his PhD thesis at UC Berkeley) took these ideas into the pragmatic world of business and deep into everyday life. He argued that the world does not simply contain language, it is constituted from language, specifically conversations and practices. Everything we perceive comes to us through language. Everything that is part of our current environment originated in conversations often years, centuries, and even millennia in the past. Everything we say and do leaves an imprint in the world that becomes part of everyone else's world. Learning how language works gives us the powers of navigation and mobilization. Applying Flores's conception to the OODA loop, we see that the observe part is a conversation for context, the orient part a conversation for possibility, the decide part the making of a commitment, and the action part the fulfillment of a commitment.

> **The world does not simply contain language, it is constituted from language.**

In this chapter we focus on how we use the language elements to coordinate action. We define action as events that change the state of the world, leaving an imprint that is part of other peoples' future action. This is a broader view of action than the basic idea of things in motion that produce effects. In our view, conversations produce commitments, commitments produce action. If something is missing, we ask what conversation is missing and initiate it.

Coordination

The speech act theory says there are only five kinds of commitments: requests, promises, declarations, assessments, and assertions. These are the molecular elements of language that can combine together in countless ways to produce the mystery, complexity, and unpredictability of the world around us.

Conversation for Action

Requests and promises are the two commitments most directly connected to action. The strong interplay between them can be represented as a loop called Conversation for Action (CFA). In the CFA, one person (the "customer") cooperates with another (the "performer") to bring a *condition of satisfaction* (COS) into their world. Figure 1 depicts.

In the diagram, Alice (A) is the customer and Bob (B) is the performer. Their loop is composed of four speech acts: request, promise, delivery declaration, and acceptance declaration. Alice initiates by making a request that specifies the desired Condition of Satisfaction, or COS. Bob responds in one of four ways: *accept* the request, *decline* the request, *defer* giving an answer, or *counteroffer* with a modified COS. Bob's acceptance is his promise to deliver the COS. When Bob finishes the work, he declares delivery to Alice. Alice reviews the work and on concluding that it meets the COS, declares her satisfaction. That ends the loop with the parties satisfied and the COS present in the world.

If Alice and Bob participate in multiple successful loops together, they will build mutual trust and satisfaction. On the other hand, if Bob

> **Completing your loops consistently builds good relationships, satisfaction, and trust.**

repeatedly does not deliver on time, or delivers shoddy work, Alice will not only be dissatisfied, but she will also come to distrust any promise Bob makes. The common business slogan – "close your loops" – reflects this wisdom. Completing your loops consistently builds good relationships, satisfaction, and trust.

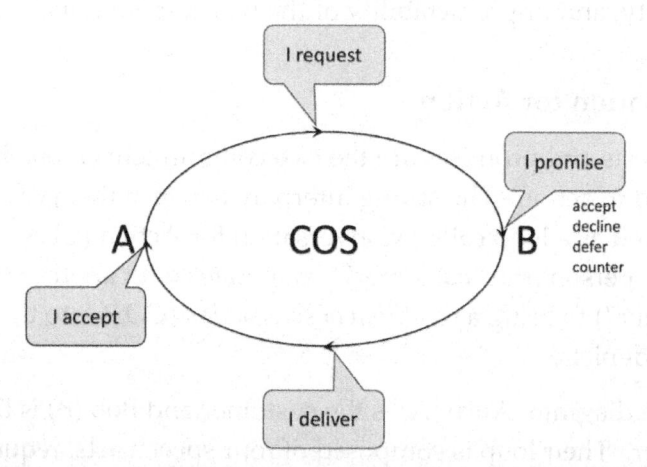

Figure 1. Conversation for Action. Alice (A) is the customer and Bob (B) the performer. They coordinate through four phases to create a condition of satisfaction (COS). Request preparation culminates with the speech act "I request". Negotiation culminates with "I promise". The work culminates with "I deliver". Acceptance culminates with "I accept". This diagram is not a flowchart; it is a map to aid in listening to the flow of commitments.

Let us return to our example with Alice and Bob in a previous chapter. When Alice makes a clear request "take out the garbage" (the COS), Bob responds with "OK" (meaning "I accept"). After completing the task, Bob declares to Alice, "I have done it." Alice completes the loop by saying "Thanks" (informal equivalent to "I am satisfied").

Coordination

The CFA is a super simple way to describe cooperative action that brings something new into the world. Even though we can see ourselves engaging in these loops all the time, many of us find we are not skilled at completing them and thus a lot of intended actions are never completed. One of the pitfalls is that people often use imprecise or vague words, believing that the meaning is obvious. The meaning is often not obvious. In our scenario, imagine that Alice said "tomorrow is garbage day." It is perfectly obvious to her that she meant for Bob to take out the garbage now, in preparation for tomorrow. She implicitly assumed, from their mutual experience together over time, that they share this meaning in their mutual background of obviousness. In one possible next step of the scenario, this is exactly what happened; Bob recognizes and responds to Alice's request. In another possible scenario Bob interprets Alice's statement as information but not as a request and the loop is never completed. If they both realized they were in a CFA, they could have taken corrective action. On seeing that Bob was not responding, Alice could have asked "Did you hear my request?" or on seeing that Alice seemed to be expecting something more, Bob could have asked "Do you want me to take out the garbage?" In this case, neither asked and both wound up dissatisfied.

When you look at examples in this way, you soon discover numerous ways loops can fail. The parties might pose the four speech acts in ways that the others do not listen that speech acts have been made. The condition of satisfaction may be ambiguous. The customer might be missing, such as when a performer undertakes a task that no one has requested. The performer might be missing, such as in an office where no one watches the inbox for new requests. These seven possible failures are just the beginning. Our students have no trouble coming up with dozens of ways to break a loop.

That raises the question: If it is so easily broken, what is the value of the loop?

The answer is that the loop is not a flowchart of actions but is *a map of commitments made and listened by the parties*. Each speech act takes the loop closer to completion. The CFA map enables you to notice when something threatens to break the loop and allows you to take corrective action. Even when you are only a third party observing a loop, you might intervene to guide the parties back into coordination. The ideal is that everyone embodies the map and knows how to guide their loops toward completion without having to stop and consult the diagram or be warned by an outside observer.

> **A loop is not a flowchart of actions; it is a map for coordination of the listenings of the parties. Use it to guide wobbly coordinations back on track.**

The CFA loop differs from OODA loop in a fundamental way. The OODA loop is a map of a personal skill. The CFA is a map of a cooperative skill. It takes at least two people to make a new condition of satisfaction appear. One person acting alone cannot do that. John Boyd realized this truth. His personal OODA loop was interacting with the adversary's. By "getting inside their loop", he meant to make unexpected maneuvers such as apparent retreats, that would confuse them and force them to take longer to orient and decide.

Workflows

CFA loops are almost never performed in isolation. In any of the four loop segments, the customer or performer can request someone else to assist in completing that segment. That request initiates a subloop necessary for the main loop to complete. It is easy to draw a map of all a team's loops linked in this way. Figure 2 shows an example of a workflow consisting of eight recurrent loops that fulfill an order for a customer. The main loop, "purchase product" is an interaction between a customer C and a sales agent SA. During the request phase, C accesses a web service WS to see the catalog and

Coordination

obtain an order form; the request is made when C submits the form. Then the sales agent checks credit (queries the credit bureau CB) and product availability (queries the warehouse WH) before accepting the request. The agent then asks the warehouse to pull the item and give it to the shipper. When this is done, the agent can declare order completion to the customer. Because customers commonly want to track their orders, the customer service agent CSA responds to tracking requests. If there are other service issues, such as billing mistakes, the CSA fixes the mistake.

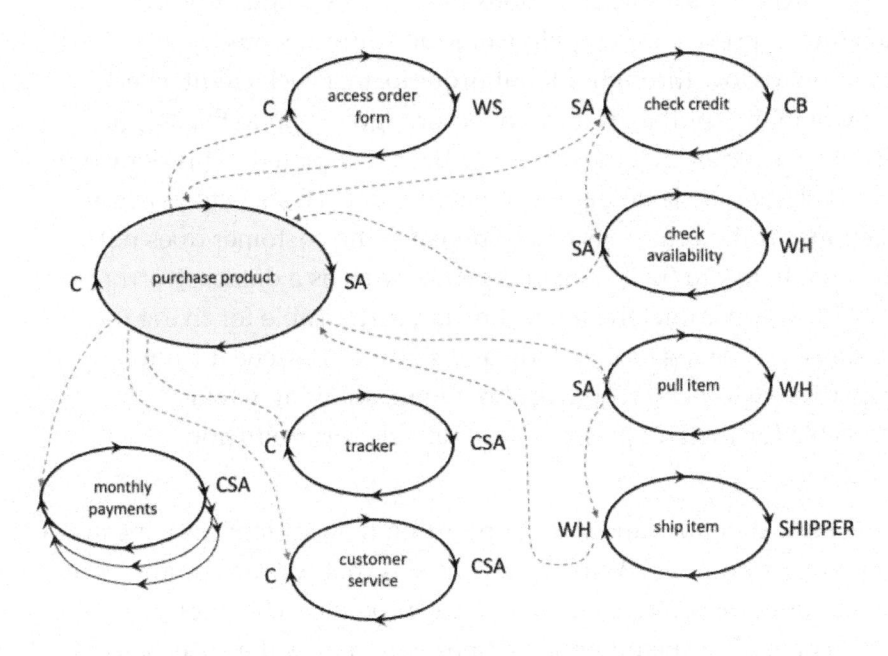

Figure 2. A workflow map. The main loop (purchase product) triggers a network of other loops that complete actions needed for the main loop. The stack of loops at lower left represents the processing of monthly payments for the purchase.

An important role of a manager is to *manage the network of commitments* make sure that all the team's loops are moving toward completion. The manager is responsible for keeping wobbly loops from going off track. If a result is missing, the manager identifies what conversation is missing and initiates it. The manager is not a decision-maker acting on information collected from the network. A manager is rated by the quality of the team's work, not by the decisions made.

> **A manager manages a network of commitments.**

Take a moment to reflect on how the absence of a good map can lead you astray. Most organizations have a procurement process, which they represent as a pipeline of input-output steps for a requisition to flow through: fill out order form, check credit, check item availability, pull item from inventory, give item to the shipper, notify the customer that the order has been completed. This depiction does not show who is taking responsibility at each stage to perform the actions. If the process is not responsive, the customer does not know who to ask to fix it. A contingency, such as a database error, can stall a pipeline completely: the technician responsible for fixing the error does not see the broken loop and so cannot rescue it from dissatisfied customers. The workflow map, showing who is responsible for each loop, is far more reliable for producing satisfaction.

We need pipelines and their supporting data systems as a means of organizing production. What is new here is that we can combine the understanding of conversations with the pipeline. The workflow map sets the context for the pipeline, defines who makes the speech acts that drive action in the pipeline, and shows who is responsible at each stage. As a manager, don't let your team look like a disembodied pipeline to your customers; design your interactions so that every loop produces satisfaction not only for its local customer but also for the end customer of the main loop.

Coordination

To what extent are the ideas of Conversations for Action and Workflow maps universal? The speech acts are universal: every culture has its ways of making requests, promises, declaration, assessments, and assertions. Likewise, the workflow patterns are universal. But different cultures can have large differences in the ways they move in workflows. For example, businesspeople in Oman prefer to delay requests until the end of a meeting whereas Americans prefer to make them at the start. The Oman people prefer to build up to a request by establishing a relationship, whereas Americans prefer to state "the bottom line up front" and work on the relationship later. In some cultures, making a direct request is considered intrusive and impolite; they prefer to drop hints and let the performer make an offer.

Although the CFA appears in every culture, social customs around speech acts and their timing can vary widely. Savvy business people educate themselves on foreign cultures before visiting them to make deals. When you visit any community, it pays to learn their customs for conversations for action, possibility, context, and relationships.

Conversations as a Fractal Universe

The description of a Conversation for Action, or CFA, as a loop with four speech acts easily hides the context in which the two parties coordinate. Reflect on this for a moment. When Alice says "I request" she implicitly assumes that her words make sense to Bob. Similarly for Bob when he says "I accept". Both Alice and Bob assume implicitly that they agree on the meanings of the words in the Condition of Satisfaction. Where do these assumptions come from?

They came from previous conversations. In the garbage example, the ideas of "garbage", "taking it out", and "collectors come tomorrow" refer to long-standing practices that have been worked out over the years by previous people engaging in their own

> **Every CFA contains images of prior CFAs that created the meanings of its assumptions.**

CFAs. Many people were involved in those conversations. Our ability to engage a CFA today rests on the completion of those prior conversations. Moreover, what we say today will become part of the assumptions that enable future conversations. Thus, we can say that every CFA contains images of prior CFAs that created the meanings of its assumptions.

In this sense, the conversation space in which CFAs take place has a fractal structure. The term fractal was coined to name geometric forms that, when studied at close range, are composed of the same forms at smaller scales. Benoit Mandelbrot, a pioneer in fractal geometry, told that his interest arose from the question "How long is a shoreline?" The ragged edges and undulations render a linear measurement impossible. When you try to zoom in on a ragged region, you see more ragged edges and undulations. This keeps happening at all scales as you keep zooming. Mandelbrot discovered a geometric form, now called Mandelbrot set, which when you zoom in on its edges is composed of identical copies of the set. Keep on zooming and you keep on seeing more sets, all the way to infinity. So it is with conversations. Zoom in on a conversation, and you discover the meaning depends on previous conversations, all the way to infinity.

Even though the outcomes of previous conversations can reverberate over immense periods of time, the names of those in the conversations are rapidly lost. What they took care of lasts, but their names do not last.

Remarkably, if you ask Alice or Bob where their assumptions came from, they will respond, "They are obvious, aren't they?" All those prior conversations are invisible. Their residual echoes show up in our present context as the "background of obviousness". What we see in our world today makes sense because it is obvious. We take the background of obviousness as a feature of life without seeing the great fractal mystery behind it.

9
DECLARATIONS

> *And for the support of this Declaration, with a firm Reliance on the Protection of divine Providence, we mutually pledge to each other our Lives, our Fortunes, and our sacred Honor.*
> – US Declaration of Independence (July 4, 1776)

> *We invent all our ventures and enterprises with declarations.*
> – Chauncey Bell

The story of coordination through Conversations for Action is incomplete without looking at the context. The Conditions of Satisfaction are intended to bring something new into the world. What is going on in the world that makes it worthwhile to bring in new conditions? How does one create a compelling context for action? We create context by telling stories and by making declarations and assessments. Here we focus on declarations and assessments. Declarations initiate a new state of affairs. Assessments evaluate or judge a state of affairs.

The Declaration of Independence

One of the most famous declarations is the US Declaration of Independence, signed on July 4, 1776. By this declaration, the thirteen British colonies in America severed their relationship with the King of

England and precipitated the Revolutionary War to expel the British from their midst.

Our colleague Chauncey Bell once analyzed the Declaration to see how the framers used language to ground their assessment of illegitimate government and declare a new future for themselves. He found that the Declaration could be seen as three parts, as in Table 1.

Table 1. Bell's Speech-act Analysis of Declaration of Independence

Section	Words	Percent
Opening declaration: a preamble declaring our interpretation of the world, who we consider ourselves to be, the standards to which we will hold ourselves, and the authority by which we speak.	230	17%
Middle complaint: We make a serious complaint against those who have governed us for (1) many actions they have taken without concern for our well-being, (2) the damage and suffering produced by those actions, and (3) not listening to and acting upon our proper requests. We ground our complaint.	940	71%
Closing declaration: We declare a new order, and in support of that we promise "our lives, our fortunes, and our sacred honor."	160	12%

This beautifully crafted document declared standards for assessment of good government, provided a grounded assessment that the King's colonial government had callously violated these standards, and declared a new order. Notice that the actual declaration is just 12% of the document; the rest sets the context. The framers knew that their declaration would spark a war. Skirmishes between British and colonial troops had already begun in 1775 and turned into a full-scale war soon after the Declaration. The Declaration created the context for a war for independence. France entered the conflict in 1781 and helped the colonial forces defeat the British. Fighting formally ended in 1783.

All this set the stage for the US Constitution, which was another big declaration written in 1789. The Constitution defined the United States and the rules of the "US game." It has stood the test of time through its ability to evolve and adapt to new contexts.

The Declaration is a dramatic demonstration of the power of declarations and assessments. These two speech acts are not limited to formal declarations – they appear everywhere in our daily conversations. We can learn to recognize them and practice them effectively. In the innovation leadership practices, for example, we declare what we have sensed, we declare a better future, we declare our offers, and we declare our calls to mobilize people to join us in the new practice.

An important lesson from this story is that the most effective declarations are combined with supporting assessments. Our assessments evaluate our situation. We ground our assessments by assertions to make it easy for others to accept our assessments as a basis for their own actions. Our declaration opens the new future and creates a space to initiate actions to get there.

Declarations

A declaration creates a new state of affairs. A minister pronounces a couple to be husband-and-wife. A judge pronounces a defendant guilty or not guilty. The boss declares someone is promoted. Bob declares he is responsible for taking out the garbage every Sunday night.

Many declarations can only be made by persons who have the authorities to make them. The minister must be licensed by the state, the judge appointed by a state process, the boss officially appointed as a supervisor. Authorities are previous declarations from those who have authority to make them, and so on. Authorities are often spelled out in special documents such as constitutions, bylaws, or company policy statements. These documents also specify who can delegate what authorities, how people are selected to fill positions of authority, and how to change the document itself.

Of course, anyone can make a declaration, speaking on their own authority. The framers of the Declaration of Independence had no authority from the King of England. So they declared their source of authority in their preamble and then defended their authority by mobilizing themselves to war with the King's army. Many innovation leaders are in this situation: they must mobilize followers while speaking on their own authority. Without followers, their new "state of affairs" will not survive.

The declaration changes the game and therefore the dynamics of the evolving play. In general, a game can be changed by amending its purpose, playing field, equipment, rules, or strategies. The game can also be changed by inventions of new subgames. It is popular to say that an innovation proposal is a "game-changing" declaration.

Exercise: Walking in the Room

Making a declaration is not easy for everyone. Some tense up before a crowd and cannot get themselves to say the declaration. Some start to speak it, but only water down its fire by tacking on explanations to make it seem logical. Many have not experienced the feeling of successfully opening a space for a group. These reactions are not merely in our heads, they are ingrained in our bodies through years of practice. We use the term "somatic" to focus on what is happening in the body.

Declarations

The walking-in-the-room exercise develops a somatic sensibility about how to open space in a moving crowd and get their attention with a declaration. The newly opened space represents the invitation of the declaration to step in and be part of it.

To set up the exercise, we push all the furniture to the sides of the room and ask the group to stand in a circle. The teacher says, "This walking-in-the-room exercise explores how we coordinate with others and make declarations when it might seem we have nothing to do with each other. You already know how to walk – so start walking!" At this point the people start walking but are obviously uncomfortable. They quickly fall into a mood of confusion because they don't know what is happening and they don't like it. We do this purposely because walking in the room together generates a new world for them in which the rules are not known. We want them to experience how easy it is to find themselves as beginners end begin to explore their conditioned tendencies around being beginners.

While everyone is walking, the teacher maintains constant patter about what is happening. "The other people are going about their business and you are moving among them. You don't know their business and they don't know yours. They are engrossed in their own affairs and with their own experiences of reality." At one-minute intervals, the teacher issues an instruction to change the flow as follows.

1. Notice that we have fallen into a pattern and are walking slowly. Speed it up to be more like real life.

2. Notice that we are paying more attention to our feet than to the other people. Eyes in the room.

3. Notice that our rhythm has improved but we are still slow. Faster!

4. You hear a beep from your smartphone. Take it out and deal with the text message that just arrived.

5. Notice how we lost our rhythm and slowed or even stopped. Put those phones away and get back into the room. Now you are reminded why working your phone is seen as such a distraction when driving.

6. Notice how we have fallen back into the old pattern again. Mix it up. Go to a new position. Go in reverse. Be a little unconventional.

7. Now we become aware that when walking in a crowd, collisions are possible and could be harmful. Let's become safer. Consciously avoid collisions.

8. Notice that slowed us all down again as we became cautious. Let's stop paying attention to possible collisions. Walk into the empty spaces.

9. Ah, good, that restored our rhythm and pace. Open spaces represent new possibilities for movement. We coordinate better when we are blending our possibilities. Pick a partner and stop for a conversation. Ask them, "Will you have a conversation with me about what is going on in this world?"

10. (Partners talk for a minute.)

11. Now come back to the walking. Notice the difference when you learn these are real people with real concerns and interpretations that may differ from yours.

12. After allowing the flow to resume, the teacher suddenly moves to the center in a wide two-step turn with arms extended; he stops and makes a declaration; he holds his pose for a noticeable pause. He then says, "I just opened a space in the crowd, which parted and made room for me, and they stopped walking to pay attention. When we resume, the space I created with my declaration remains open and you can walk into it." He resumes the walking.

13. Now the teacher calls each person by name and asks them to come and take the space in the center and say the declaration of their project; then return to walking. This is a somatic interpretation of making a declaration. When everyone has done this, the walking part of the exercise is over.

At this point, everyone stands in a circle for a group discussion about what took place. Almost everyone experiences initial confusion because they were not told what was happening. Many say they feel silly, dislike not seeing the point, or even like they were wasting their time. Most are annoyed that the teacher did not explain the purpose and relevance of the exercise before we started. As it evolves, they become more comfortable and see they were being prepared to make a public declaration of their project. Many say it made quite a difference when they walked into empty spaces compared to avoiding collisions. At the end, they see they *created* open spaces that invite others to walk into them.

We ask them to notice how pausing to have a conversation changed the mood in the room. The other people seemed less like strangers than before. We ask them to notice how easily they felt uncomfortable. Discomfort arises when you enter unfamiliar practices. Discomfort is very common when leading others into adoption of new practice while maneuvering in a fog of uncertainty. Might you learn to interpret discomfort as a sign that a change of practice is occurring, which is what you want? Might you learn to comfortable with the way change feels?

In life, you can have similar experiences and reach similar epiphanies because you are always "walking in a room". Some of you have participated in military or civilian parades where synchronized walking was the point. How was the synchronization taught and learned? How did it feel to get lost in a group rhythm of synchronized walking?

Another example is walking in the streets of a city. Most people have observed that walking in New York City is different from San Francisco, and even more different from Rome or Ho Chi Minh City. Each city has its own style and hidden assumptions. New Yorkers who want to move faster than the sidewalk crowd have learned tricks like pointing their fingers where they are intending to walk and watching the crowd part to make room for them. This trick does not work in San Francisco. Travelers to Rome notice that residents appear to be about to collide when suddenly and smoothly they turn their shoulders sideways and pass narrowly. Travelers to Ho Chi Minh City realize that they must look forward and move at a steady pace in crossing a street for otherwise a moment of hesitation is likely to cause a massive pileup of cars. Next time you are in a crowd, pay attention to how others are moving, how you fit into the flow, and whether you felt a rhythm to the flow or felt resistance. Reflect on how you feel and what you learn.

Envisioning Stories and Big Ideas

Your envisioning story, developed in the envisioning practice, is a declaration of a new future that resolves the breakdown or disharmony articulated in the sensing practice. Envisioning stories start the process of mobilizing people into a new practice. They are developed over time in conversation with people in the community, evolving into a story that resonates with the community.

It very useful to articulate the *big idea* of your story: a single declarative sentence that captures the breakdown and its resolution. This short declaration is often a good way to open your story. Thus, your declaration takes on two forms: the big idea and the narrative of the new future. These declarations open the space for your offer, which is what you will do to move toward the new future.

Let us illustrate this with the story of "Marco", a Philippine communications expert who was hoping to move home to work at the

Declarations   133

operations center of an Asian export-import company. He told their executives that they were not planning well for possible conflict in the region and they ought to upgrade to 5G technology. His envisioning story laid out the merits of 5G technology. It gathered no interest.

Marco decided to bolster his claim with logic. He argued they ought to be planning for the probable GPS blackout due to jamming of satellite signals during a possible conflict. He cautioned against adopting a "zero trust" authentication protocol that checked credentials with a secure remote server whenever a user started a new app; a regional conflict would sever Internet connections, leaving their local network inoperative. He argued that it would be logical to bring 5G technologies into their operations to resolve these problems.

His revised story was more interesting but still fell flat. His listeners did not see why the lack of 5G technology was a problem or how it would solve the jamming and authentication problems. Marco responded by adding to the story an offer to host a conversation with the company executives to help them see the wisdom of an upgrade. It still fell flat because the executives did not see why talking about it would change anything.

We coached Marco to start with a punchy declaration, tell a story of the breakdowns in the current situation, and conclude with an offer the executives would find attractive. He came up with this:

> The Philippines export-import company is not prepared to operate in case of a regional conflict. Their communication technology and practices will fail under those conditions. The company's plan for heightened security rests on a Zero Trust architecture, which requires validation of credentials on entry to each app. Validation requires interaction with a remote authentication server over the Internet. This puts us at risk of total failure if communications are severed. We could implement a trusted architecture that is locally based and puts the responsibility and authority in our hands instead of some external entity accessed by an uncertain

Internet. I offer to drive the adoption of that communication system that meets our unique challenges.

He got the job.

Marco's story illustrates how a big idea declaration can turbocharge an envisioning story by taking a clear stand on where everyone is going and stirring up emotion energy to get there. Declarations can be even more powerful than envisioning stories. The Declaration of Independence was like this. A dramatic modern example is the Volvo car company, whose declaration and motto are: *No one will die in our cars*. With this declaration, everyone in the company understands that their work is essential. Even the smallest cotter pin out of alignment can undermine safety. Volvo cars are rated among the safest in the world.

Manifesto

Sometimes the breakdown in the community is deeply embedded and the mood of resignation is pervasive. In these situations, we encourage our students to consider developing a manifesto. A manifesto is a big declaration about an innovation you are offering for adoption in your community. It identifies a big breakdown that causes great concern in your community, for which no one sees a resolution. The manifesto shows that the concern cannot be resolved within the current ways of thinking and calls for a new way. It is a call to action.

You do not show up as a personality in "your" manifesto. Instead, you will show up as a committed player in the new game you are declaring. Lincoln's Gettysburg Address is an historical example of a manifesto in which he acknowledged the great breakdown of the Civil War and offered a new interpretation of the nation – one from many (*e pluribus unum*). Fernando Flores's story of Louis Pasteur and the Dying Cows, recounted in the prolog of *The Innovator's Way*, shows how to choose an innovation that will be valued by your community:

every community has its share of metaphorical dying cows and longs for a way to heal.

Many manifestos come in the form of policy documents or white papers issued by the governments or politicians running for office. A few are incendiary confrontations between an existing and new order, as with Karl Marx's *Communist Manifesto*.

The manifesto we have in mind is neither a policy document nor a confrontation. It leads the reader from the present conundrum around a persistent breakdown to a new way of thinking and being that resolves the breakdown. It follows the progression of the prime innovation pattern (see box), which as we have seen is the universal pattern of conversations leading to adoption of new practice. Organizing the declaration around the pattern offers a natural progression from a breakdown to change in community practice.

Prime Innovation Pattern

- Someone notices a concern around a breakdown or disharmony in their community and determines to do something about it.
- They describe a future where a new practice has resolved the concern and they show a credible path to get there.
- They offer to make it happen.
- They form a team to assist in delivering the innovation and any technology needed to support it.
- They mobilize community members to join the new practice.

The table below lists seven key elements of a manifesto. We suggest that you start by treating them as questions and sketching out how you would answer them. Discuss and refine your answers with friends and colleagues in your community. At first, you may discover that some of your answers do not resonate with members of your community. Have conversations around these points of friction. It is likely that you will find places of convergence. Then it is time to convert your answers into a coherent document.

Manifesto Elements

1. Declare and articulate a breakdown in the current situation in your community that is causing suffering and other costs.

2. Articulate the limitations of the "current common sense" and its inability to deal with the issue. This is why the "obvious solutions" do not and cannot work.

3. Declare a new world (interpretation) that opens possibilities for resolving the situation and dissolving the breakdown. This is where you state your "big idea" – the start of a "new common sense".

4. Introduce the key operational distinctions that you will employ and will be the basis of a plan.

5. Outline a plan for bridging from the current world to the new world.

6. Build trust in your commitment to carry out the plan and achieve the new world.

7. Make a specific proposal for action with the current audience – the next steps – addressing concerns, risks, and benefits.

How long must a manifesto be? There is no one answer to that. We've seen one-page manifestos, essay-length manifestos, and even book-length manifestos. The best answer is "as long as it needs to be but no longer". This is why it is important to have conversations with friends and colleagues. They can help you tell when you have not said enough, and when saying more would add nothing.

Declarations

An Example: Innovation Manifesto

Chapter 1 of this book is a manifesto about achieving innovation. Here is a sketch of how the manifesto elements appear in that story.

(1) *The Breakdown.* Many people are frustrated with their inability to achieve innovation. This breakdown is widespread. Organizations report about a 5% success rate with their innovation projects. Few organizations have the resources for so many failures.

(2) *The Current Common Sense.* When asked to define innovation, most people respond that innovation is the creation of a novel idea or artifact that brings value to someone. They are frustrated when their valuable ideas go nowhere. Their common sense does not tell them that the work of ideation is different from the work of adoption. It blinds them to the actions they need to achieve adoption.

(3) *A New Common Sense.* What if we define innovation as adoption of new practice in a community? That seems to be what people really want. People who accept that definition organize their projects to bring about adoption. Invention and creativity would start that process, but other actions would be needed to drive adoption.

(4) *Key Operational Distinctions.* The terms adoption, practice, and community need clear definitions for this context. The needed actions can be formulated as a skill set of eight essential practices that can be taught and learned. If any one of the eight fails in its goal, the whole innovation is likely to fail.

(5) *A Plan.* We developed a basic course, "innovation leadership", that teaches and coaches the eight practices. We cultivated contacts at other naval institutions and helped them implement local versions of the course. During the coronavirus-induced lockdown we learned how to teach the course effectively online. We developed plans for an intermediate and masters class in innovation leadership. We developed a network of facilitators to teach the practices widely.

(6) *Trust.* Our team accumulated considerable experience in teaching the course and coaching students. We receive strong positive assessments from students and participating faculty. We compiled a list of nearly one hundred prior students who have taken their innovation projects into their Navy and Marine Corps work and are now seen as innovation leaders.

(7) *Invitation.* Join our program. Be an innovation leader. Read our books. Learn the philosophy. Become a facilitator.

The Heilmeier Catechism

When he was director of DARPA (1975-1977), George Heilmeier crafted a list of questions for his program managers to use when proposing new initiatives for DARPA. They became known as the "Heilmeier Catechism" and are still used today. Notice how similar they are to the questions you ask when examining how the Prime Innovation Pattern applies in your project.

- What are you trying to do? Articulate your objectives; absolutely no jargon.
- How is it done today and what are the limits of current practice?
- What's new in your approach and why do you think it will be successful?
- Who cares? If you are successful, what difference will it make?
- What are the risks?
- How much will it cost?
- How long will it take?
- What are the midterm and final "exams" to check for success?

Conclusion

It is worthwhile (essential!) to become competent in the skills of making declarations. It takes practice. Practice feeling when a declaration resonates and appears as a welcome invitation to action. For big innovations, practice the manifesto form of declaration. Once you learn these practices, you will be rewarded with many successes.

10
ASSESSMENTS

> *Everything that is new begins with assessments we make about insufficiencies, messes, opportunities, and obsolescences. Our reputations and identities are formed from assessments about our performances and actions.*
> – Chauncey Bell

The story of coordination through Conversations for Action is incomplete without looking at the context. The Conditions of Satisfaction are intended to bring something new into the world of those who are coordinating. What is happening in their world that makes it worthwhile to bring forth the new conditions? How do we create a compelling context for new conditions?

Declarations and assessments are our two main tools for creating context for innovation. A declaration initiates a new state of affairs. An assessment evaluates or judges a state of affairs. Assessments are supported by assertions, which are claims of facts in the world. Innovation leaders must develop their skill at recognizing declarations, assessments, and assertions as well as making their own declarations, assessments, and assertions.

Assessments and Assertions

An assessment is a speech act in which the speaker expresses an evaluation, judgment, or opinion about a state of affairs. Assessments are not true or false. Instead, they are grounded or ungrounded. Grounded means:

- The assessment comes with a set of assertions that serve as evidence for the validity of the assessment.
- The assertions given are relevant to the assessment and sufficient in number.
- There are standards for determining which assertions are relevant and how many assertions are needed.

Assessments are usually made to motivate or guide action. Listeners are most likely to accept and act on well-grounded assessments. As a speaker, you may need to engage your listeners in conversations about whether they accept the assessment and, if not, what additional evidence might be needed. And it is possible that some listeners will not accept the assessment at all, no matter what grounding is offered.

An assertion is a speech act in which the speaker makes a claim that something is true, and the truth can be verified by witnesses. The speaker thus claims (asserts) that something is a fact. Those who doubt it can verify its accuracy by fact-checking.

It generally not a good idea to include assessments in the list of evidence offered in support of an assessment. Opinions based on other opinions usually seem flimsy and unconvincing. One notable exception to this rule is the evaluations of job candidates, where we rely on the assessments of reviewers. We ask them to testify to the strengths and weakness of the person and provide evidence in support of their claims. If a reviewer's claims are not well grounded with assertions, we tend to discount their review.

What about opinion polls? Many leaders base actions on poll results. At first glance, that looks like leaders are trying to ground their opinion in the opinions of many others. But if you look a little closer, you see a subtle but important difference. The poll reports the number of people who agree with a specific proposition. That number is a fact. The leader is using the polls to ground an assessment about the strength of certain concerns in the community.

The practice of grounding assessments is essential in many domains. Here five examples.

Grounding assessments is central to science. Scientific claims start out as hypotheses (a form of assessment) and evolve into assertions over time as more and more experiments verify them. Eventually the hypothesis is so well grounded that the doubters fade away. Science is not about discovering certainties. It is about navigating through uncertainties to find hypotheses that withstand the assaults of doubters.

In a similar way, lawyers in courtrooms practice grounding assessments all the time. By compiling assertions into a cohesive narrative, prosecutors seek to convince the jury that the defendant is guilty beyond a reasonable doubt. On the other side, defense lawyers seek to cast doubt on the evidence offered by the prosecution by discrediting the assertions or the supporting narrative.

The practice of grounding assessments is essential for innovation leaders. In the previous chapter we discussed the Declaration of Independence. Its authors declared their standards and their source of authority. They made a well grounded assessment of the King's treatment of them. They then declared a new order. Innovation leaders are in much the same position. They must describe the breakdown in the current situation with a well-grounded assessment and offer a resolution through a new practice. Their assessments make sense and motivate action.

The practice of grounding assessments is essential in the workplace, and not just for performance reviews. The team decides what new product or service to offer based on grounded assessments of what customers will buy. Those who complain that their innovation proposals attract little interest from their bosses or teams are often suffering the consequences of their own inability to ground their assessments and reconcile their assessments with others who disagree with them.

Our reputations – the stories people tell about us when we are not around – influence the level of trust people grant us and the kinds of offers that we can successfully make. Our reputation is in effect a giant, often invisible, assessment of us, grounded in the actions that people see us taking over time. If we don't like aspects of our reputation, there is no point in trying to refute them with logical arguments. The only way to change our reputation is to make new offers, the fulfillment of which will elicit assessments different from the ones behind our current reputation. That takes time.

An example of how declarations, assessments and assertions work together can be seen in the Marine Corps Force Design 2030 published in March 2020. The Commandant of the Marine Corps declared that "the defining attributes of our current force design are no longer what the nation requires of the Marine Corps." He based his declaration in part on a claim in the National Defense Strategy of 2018, which said that current US forces in the Pacific region had shortfalls of capabilities. Many of the Marine Corps' former senior leaders opposed the very idea that the Marine Corps might have a shortfall. From their perspective, the Commandant's claim was nonsense. But the Commandant persistently repeated his assessment and grounded it in scenarios where the current force could not cope. He eventually convinced the doubters and initiated a Marine Corp upgrade program. Grounding assessments that will persuade an audience is an iterative process that depends on your skill at listening to concerns that at convincing or explaining.

Exercise: I am Competent

We designed an exercise to help our students see what the practice of making a well-grounded assessment looks – and feels – like. We ask them to imagine they are appearing before an interview panel who will select the members of the team to which they aspire. What will they say to persuade the group they are competent at something valuable to the team? Since most people have experienced anxiety over a job interview or getting chosen for a coveted team, our students could see from this framing that the practice of grounding their claim of competence is relevant to their professional aspirations.

We ask them to prepare an assessment claiming "I am competent at X", where X is a professional competency, and then provide supporting assertions. They present their claim to a group of fellow students. A straw vote reveals whether the group accepts the assessment; usually the vote is mixed. We then encourage group members to ask questions. The speaker may provide more assertions, clarify the community standards, and establish the relevance of some assertions. A subsequent vote reveals whether the group now accepts the claim of competence. This is not an exercise in logic: saying the claim and listing the assertions is not the goal; initiating a conversation for accepting the claim is the goal. Each member of the group may have different conclusions about whether the speaker has provided sufficient relevant evidence of competence. In the exercise, students discover the following:

- Some members of the group may not agree with their standards of assessment.
- Some members may conclude some assertions are not relevant.
- Some members may conclude the number of assertions is insufficient.
- Some members may conclude that some assertions are not really assertions at all, but are ungrounded assessments.

- The speaker suffers moods of self-doubt or embarrassment and cannot speak with confidence, reacting poorly to groupmates who argue with some of their assertions. The speaker gets defensive and answers poorly.

It is valuable for the speaker to receive real-time feedback from the group about who accepts their claim. Often in the ensuing conversation the speaker adds more relevant assertions, deletes non-relevant assertions, and discards assessments posing as assertions. When that happens, the group often accepts their claim.

Characterizations

Characterizations are an important category of assessments. They assess that a person or group has a permanent quality that can never change. A sub-category are self-characterizations, assessments of one's own capabilities and weaknesses. Examples of characterizations: Alice is always trying to control things. Bob is arrogant. Claire is a genius. The system oppresses the little guy. Examples of self-characterizations: I'm no good at math. I am a gifted athlete.

Characterizations shape our expectations when interacting with others. Consider the effects in the examples above:

- *Alice is always trying to control.* This affects your interactions with Alice. You might get cautious and defensive when you perceive her trying to control you. Alternatively, you might get confrontational and try to exert your own control. Either way, your interactions with Alice are strained by the characterization before she says a word.

- *Bob is arrogant.* This signals a mood of anxiety or resentment when you interact with Bob. You actively avoid him. You do not look for ways the two of you can cooperate successfully. He may be arrogant only about certain topics; you're better off staying away from those topics than staying away from Bob.

- *Claire is a genius.* This leads you to believe she is smarter than you and most people in almost all things, even if she is untrustworthy in some areas.
- *The system oppresses the little guy.* This leads you to distrust management, challenge their directives, and take offense at small remarks that seem to suggest you are of little value.
- *I'm no good at math.* This signals a mood of resignation that you can never learn math, resulting in your avoiding math and never improving at it.
- *I am a gifted athlete.* This suggests a mood of overconfidence in your athletic abilities. Most athletes are good at one, or perhaps several) sports but not all. You may be fixated on your own talents and not be a good team player.

It is a good practice to look for the grounding of the assessments of a characterization. They are often not grounded, especially where they assume permanence. Here is Bob questioning Alice's self-characterization and concluding it is not well grounded:

"I am no good at math," declares Alice.

"Why do you say that?" responds Bob.

"I failed the Advanced Placement math test in high school."

"Did you pass the AP math course?"

"Yes, I got an A."

"Hmm. Even though you're good at math you gave up because of one math test!"

Alice convinced others to accept that she is no good at math. Because of this characterization, she missed opportunities to innovate in her favorite field, computer security. Here she is being considered for a position on a new team led by Claire and Dan:

"I think Alice would be the perfect person to invite to my team for a new computer security protocol," says Claire.

"That would be a poor idea," says Dan, "She's no good at math."

"OK, I'll look for someone else," says Claire.

Claire and Dan decide to bypass her on something where she would probably do well.

Unfortunately, a thorough investigation on grounding may not get someone to give up the characterization. They cling to their assessment despite substantial evidence to the contrary. This is usually the result of unspoken concerns and standards that keep their assessment in place. Without addressing those, the holder of the characterization will not let go. We will return to this issue in the next chapter (Moods).

Identities

Identities are stories about who we are, our skills, our strengths and weaknesses, our character, and our ideals. Our personal identity is the story we tell about ourselves. Our public identity is the stories others tell about us. It is often difficult to find out what our public identity is because we do not have access to all the conversations about us "behind our back". Our public identity is particularly important because it opens certain possibilities for us and closes others.

Our identities are based mainly on assessments. Self-assessments and assessments given to us by others shape our private identity. Assessments from many people about our actions aggregate into our public identity. Some of the assessments come from the history of our community with no action on our part. If we do not like our public identity, we cannot change it by arguing with people or trying to persuade people they are wrong. Instead, we must make different commitments and take different actions that lead to different assessments.

Negative Assessments

Negative assessments are judgments that something is lacking in a situation or a person's performance. Negative assessments can have a positive influence in performance evaluations and team after-action meetings, especially if delivered in a way that inspires improvement. In these cases, team leaders and members have learned to deliver grounded assessments and to receive assessments without getting defensive. This takes practice. Negative assessments can deflect and discourage people from pursuing their goals. For this reason, negative assessments are the favorite tools of those who want to resist a proposed innovation. We have witnessed many team leaders who are reluctant to make a negative assessment of a direct report, and many team members who are reluctant to share negative assessments with their teammates, even when the assessments are justified and necessary for improved performance. Their unwillingness to make any negative assessment is as damaging to a team as making ungrounded negative assessments.

Many people are unskilled at both **delivering** and **receiving** negative assessments. Recipients who do not see the justification or grounding for an assessment are likely to become defensive and uncooperative. Recipients of ad hominem attacks may respond with anger or withdrawal. In the ideal world, we would always give grounded assessments and not trigger these reactions. In the real world, however, we will deliver negative assessments that trigger bad reactions. This can be a serious problem in teams and workplaces. The cure is not only to teach everyone how to deliver grounded assessments that open conversations for improvement, but also to learn how to recover their dignity after a negative assessment.

Exercise: Negative Assessments

The Negative Assessment Exercise is a training opportunity to learn how to recover from a gratuitous negative assessment.[1] It teaches people how to respond with dignity to such assessments, and also to become mindful of what it is like to deliver such an assessment. Learning to maintain one's dignity in the face of an attack, and maintain the relationship, is an important skill. Negative assessments are a stumbling block for many people.

Gratuitous ungrounded negative assessments are effective tools in the hands of those intending to derail our innovation proposals by derailing us. Even when negative assessments are grounded and necessary, they can still trigger our conditioned tendencies and throw us off center. This exercise allows us to experience our conditioned tendencies, tame the emotional reaction, and learn from it. We use the term **somatic vulnerability** to mean a sensitivity to negative assessments that others can use to manipulate you: "pushing your buttons". The exercise teaches you how to mitigate and eventually eliminate somatic vulnerability.

DIRECTIONS. Instructors form participants into a circle of 6-8 people. (If there are more, break them into several circles of this size.) The instructors are coaches and do not participate. Participants take turns coming to the center, where they receive negative assessments from each of the others. When it is your turn to come to the center of your circle, do three things:

1. Announce a somatic vulnerability you would like to address.
2. Make your project declaration.

---

[1] The exercise was designed by Fernando Flores in the 1980s to teach people how to recover their dignity after an insult.

Assessments

3. Move from one person to the next around the circle. The two of you interact as follows.

    a. The Assessor delivers a negative assessment about you (or your project) in light of your declared vulnerability.

    b. Pause 5-10 seconds to notice your reactions. (Common reactions include jumping, flashing anger, cowering, shortened breath, gasping, laughing, looking around, avoiding eye contact, and sweating in the palms.)

    c. Speak the script. Slowly. Stick exactly to the script; no paraphrasing.

    d. Pause again to notice what you are feeling.

    e. Thank the person, move to the next, and repeat.

THE SCRIPT

(Assessor delivers negative assessment)

(YOU pause 5 seconds and observe your reactions)

YOU:

> I can see why you might say that.
>
> It is only an assessment.
>
> It could be grounded. It could be ungrounded.
>
> I have not given you permission to make this assessment.
>
> And I am open to future conversations with you about it.

Assessor: Thank you.

YOU: You're welcome.

DISCUSSION. When everyone in the circle has completed the exercise, the instructors ask the members of the circle to sit on the floor and debrief what they observed. Everyone speaks from their roles as assessors, receivers, and spectators. The instructors guide the discussion if necessary with questions such as the following.

1. What reactions did you experience when receiving an assessment, delivering an assessment, or observing the interaction between two others?

2. Were you emotionally stable? Uncomfortable? Tense? In your head? Did you lose ability to listen?

3. What was the effect of script on recovering your center? How did all the others, as witnesses, react to what they saw?

When everyone has debriefed, the instructor walks through the script to explain the purpose of each element. The script guides you from the moment you are off balance upon receiving an assessment to the point of restoration of your center and preservation of your future relationship with your assessor. The script begins with an acknowledgement that you and your assessor are real people with names. You pause to observe your somatic response and reaction. You acknowledge that you have received an assessment. You acknowledge that you do not know if the assessment is grounded or not. You make a powerful declaration ("permission") that recovers your dignity and composure. Finally, you recognize that the other person might have something valuable for you, which you can learn in future conversations.

After the walkthrough of the script, the instructor shares these points and requests:

- The exercise is designed in a rigid format so that the only variable is how you react.
- Many of you reported discomforts at the start of your turn; you settled as your turn progressed. The assessors and witnesses

(others in the circle) reported feeling uncomfortable at knowingly giving gratuitous negative assessments. This is good news because it motivates you to look for the grounding of your assessments.

- Some of you said that you had no significant reactions. You thought the exercise is scripted and not "real". However, in conversations, everyone has reactions. That is what our bodies do, react to stimuli. Your reaction may be to suppress your reaction. In the next few days, you may discover that you had reactions but did not realize it at the time. Be open to this.

- Notice how easy and subtle it can be to go off center. For example, apologizing for not getting the script right. Wanting to stop to take notes to remember the negative assessments. Explaining why your upcoming performance in the exercise might not be smooth.

- Warning: DO NOT recite this script to someone else who assesses you outside of this class. It will almost certainly cause a breakdown. The script is part of the exercise. It shows you how you can recover from a somatic shock that may follow a negative assessment. You can silently recite the script to yourself to recover from a negative assessment. After a while, you will not need to recite it, you'll just take a breath and recover your center.

- The line about "permission" startles people. It is there to provoke you into realizing that you have a choice whether to accept (and act on) the negative assessment. You do not need to grant blanket permission to everyone to assess you. Of course, be careful: your relationships may already contain permissions. For example, the relation with your supervisor includes the presumption that your supervisor makes performance assessments. Similarly you have granted your spouse or partner permission to make assessments of you. All the more reason to heed the warning against "weaponizing" the script in your interactions with others.

- Negative assessments, especially when gratuitous and ungrounded, can knock you off center. They manipulate you by appealing to your self-doubt and silent fears.
- Warning: positive assessments can also be used to manipulate you. Flattery can be manipulative. The main difference is that positive assessments feel good.
- The exercise can be seen as a form of training, like sparring with a partner. Delivering a negative assessment helps the other person in the exercise gain strength in dealing with negative assessments and improve their ability to regain center.
- Those who have repeated this exercise two or three times over several months find that they are progressively better at recovering their centers.

ADVICE FOR THE COACHES. This is a profound exercise. Participants are likely to experience solidarity with the others in their circle. However, they will often take 24-48 hours to fully process it. Be very sensitive, especially to support those who show strong negative reactions when receiving negative assessments. Offer to be available to talk with anyone who needs to discuss their reactions and discover what they mean.

Listen for Concerns Behind Assessments

Many people are attracted to notion of grounded assessments supported by relevant assertions. It gives a framework for analyzing an assessment and discovering what is missing if you do not accept it. There is, however, a danger. It is the same danger in viewing the Conversation for Action as a procedure rather than a map for listening commitments. You can become enthralled by the mechanics of grounding and lose sight of the concerns behind the assessments. This will show up in your questioning about the grounding of the assessment – the other person may be put off because your questioning feels like a courtroom cross-examination. They clam up.

We have found it is much better to ask about the concerns behind their assessment. They commonly welcome the chance to talk about their concerns. You are likely to have a good conversation around the assessment and often come to an emotional resonance with that person, which will allow the two of you to discuss the grounding and work together.

Conclusion

Innovation leaders must become competent at the skills of making declarations and grounded assessments. It takes dedicated practice. Through practice, you get the feel of when a declaration resonates and appears as a welcome invitation to action. You learn to recognize when an assessment (yours or someone else's) is well grounded. You inquire into the concerns behind assessments. Once competent at these practices, you will be well rewarded with successes.

11
MOODS

As beginners, we regularly fall into the moods of confusion, insecurity or anxiety, which may prevent us from continuing to practice, asking for help, or trying new things without worrying about making mistakes. As experts, we may fall into a mood of arrogance and impatience, which may prevent us from listening, continuing to learn, and reaching mastery. Fortunately, navigating moods during learning is a skill that can be learned.
– Gloria Flores

We're losing social skills, the human interaction skills, how to read a person's mood, to read their body language, how to be patient until the moment is right to make or press a point.
– Vincent Nichols

Resentment is like drinking poison and then hoping it will kill your enemies.
– Nelson Mandela

Imagine yourself as a leader of a team that just suffered a setback because customers did not react enthusiastically to the new software release. You ask team members for their evaluation of what happened. Caitlin says, "I don't know what is going on, but I would love to interview our customers and find out what was behind their reactions. I am certain we can learn something from them." Harry says, "I also don't know what the heck is going on, but those customers are jerks. We listened to their requirements and delivered exactly what they asked for and this is how they treat us?" Which of those two is going to be more helpful in navigating the way forward? They both say they do not know what is happening. Each embeds that acknowledgement in a mood that shapes their attitude toward future actions. Caitlin brings wonder, a mood of excited openness to learn from the situation. In contrast, Harry brings confusion and resentment, a mood of hostility toward not knowing what is happening. Team leaders wish that everyone could bring the mood of wonder when it is time to learn something new. Teachers wish the same for their students. It is so much easier to learn from your mistakes and move forward when you are in a mood of wonder. Can such a mood be cultivated?

To get things done, we need to be good at collaborating and coordinating. Competition is necessary with rivals, but competing with our customers, clients, and teammates will not get us very far. You have probably heard dozens of tips and tricks about the mechanics for fostering collaboration and coordination. One thing you probably have not heard much about is moods. Mastery of moods – your own, your team's, and your customer's – is essential to your success at collaboration.

Imagine yourself as a project manager. You are trying to follow the advice to make clear requests -- requests with clear statements of the desired outcome and the due date. If you make your request to Jane who is in a positive mood, she will accept your request gladly. If you ask Mike, who is in a mood of resignation and sees no possibility that your desired outcome is achievable, you may find yourself in an argument about the futility of the request. Or perhaps you ask Leslie, who is in a mood of resentment about perceived injustices by teammates. Leslie will present you with a begrudging acceptance followed by covert attempts to undermine your project. In short, the same request leads to very different conversations and different reactions depending on the recipient's mood.

Moods

Moods belong not just to individuals, but to groups. Your mood is often shared with others around you. Experienced speakers try to read the "mood in the room" -- a sense that the audience has an overall receptivity (or hostility) to what the speaker has to say. Experienced managers pause when their teams or organizations have poor morale; they know they will have trouble accomplishing their mission unless they can generate a more positive mood. Experienced marketers pitch advertisements to their sense of the public mood.

These examples show an important feature of moods: they carry assessments about what is possible or not in the future. *Expansive moods*, which see new possibilities, predispose people to listen and respond positively to offers to change practices. *Restrictive moods*, which see few or narrowed possibilities, predispose people to reject attempts to change anything. Expansive moods are a powerful force for productivity; restrictive moods are barriers to change.

In this chapter, we will explore the complex world of moods and the ways they shape the social space. We start by distinguishing moods from emotions, emphasizing the central notion that moods function like assessments of future possibilities. Then we examine five skill levels for navigating moods. We will discover many complexities of moods in the social space by looking at teams and wicked problems.

Moods Defined

Moods and emotions are not the same. Emotions are mental and physical reactions to stimuli from our surroundings. Moods are pervasive background interpretations of what is possible in the future. Both emotions and moods depend on our histories. Both are accompanied by feelings and physical sensations. For example, anger is often accompanied by a red-hot flush of the face. Fear is often correlated with sweaty palms. Anxiety is accompanied by chest tension. Joy is accompanied by a strong urge to smile broadly and hug someone.

Most people are aware of emotions. Psychologists recognize eight basic emotions, with each positive balanced by a negative:

        Love -- Hate
        Joy -- Sadness
        Peace -- Anger
        Curiosity -- Fear

An emotion may have multiple shades corresponding to different intensities of the feeling and the disposition toward acting on the feeling. The thesaurus shows at least 40 synonyms for anger, representing different degrees of anger from annoyance and irritation on the low end to rage and revenge on the high end; chagrin is in the middle and resentment is closer to revenge.

Emotions are triggered by identifiable events. For example, a loved one returns from a trip and you feel joyful at their safe return. A hooded figure follows you on a deserted street and you feel fear. Perhaps someone insults you and you get angry. In contrast, moods seem to appear without a trigger – you "find yourself" in a mood but cannot identify a specific moment when you entered that mood. An emotion tends to subside after a time, but a mood can persist for a very long time.

A mood is like a "filter of interpretation" that predisposes us to see things in a particular way, with certain expectations about the future. For example, in a mood of ambition you have confidence in your ability to generate an outcome that matters a great deal to you; you expect to be successful. In a mood of resignation, you are certain that there are no workable solutions to a problem at hand; you expect no attempted solution to work.

The Assessments in Moods

The most important distinguishing feature of moods is that they are assessments of future possibilities. You can recognize a mood by listening for the assessments the person or community is making about their future. Moods shape our expectations about the future.

Moods are situational. They are likely to change when the situation changes. For example, if you are driving in heavy downtown traffic with many cars switching lanes, you may find yourself in a mood of anxiety about your safety. When you emerge from downtown onto quiet suburban roads, your mood becomes calm and you anticipate good things when you reach your destination.

Table 1 summarizes common moods and their associated assessments. They are divided into three groups. Expansive moods open possibilities and energize. Restrictive moods shut down possibilities and de-energize. Neutral moods are neither. The six moods in the center of the table– curiosity, wonder, inquiry, perplexity, confusion, and apathy –are commonly associated with learning and show up for beginners. Refer again to the Beginner's Creed in Chapter 2 for moods of beginners.

Moods belong to not only individuals, but to groups and to time periods. I can be in a personal mood of resignation. My team and organization can be resigned. We can be living in a period, like a recession or war, where everyone is resigned to bad outcomes. Regardless of how they are layered by different horizons, moods are all characterized by their assessments of the future.

Mood	Linguistic Indicator	Type
joy / gratitude	Look at all the gifts bestowed on me, I am delighted and grateful for them.	Expansive (energizing)
speculation	We are inventing new possibilities and I like them.	
ambition	I strongly desire a particular outcome and I am committed to achieving it.	
resolution	I am determined to make the outcome happen, no matter what.	
trust	I firmly believe that the others have the ability, integrity, and care to fulfill their promises.	
serenity	I accept what has happened and the uncertainty of what will happen; I am ready for next conversations	
curiosity	I have a strong, perhaps overwhelming, desire to find out what is going on.	
wonder	I am inspired by all the opportunities to learn new things; though I don't know what is going on, I like it.	
inquiry	I do not know what is going on, and I will keep exploring until an answer is found.	Neutral
perplexity, bafflement	I am unable to make sense of what is going on; I don't know which way to go with this.	
confusion	I cannot make sense of what is going on, I don't know what to, and I don't like it.	Restrictive (de-energizing)
apathy	I am Indifferent and have no motivation to try.	
arrogance	I already know everything necessary here, they just need to listen to me; being here is a waste of my time	
anxiety	I sense danger and do not know what to do about it.	
overwhelm	I am frustrated by the sheer volume of what is going on, and I cannot figure out what to do.	
resignation	I see no possibilities for resolving this issue.	
resentment	I am hurt by insults or injuries from the other. I seek opportunities for retribution. I refuse to discuss this with anyone, it's none of their business.	

Moods

Sensing and Reading Moods

How do I tell what mood I'm in? How might I sense your mood? How might I sense the mood of the community toward adopting a new practice? There are four main ways to do this.

First, *listen for assessments*. Assessments reveal moods as shown in Table 1. In large communities, it is not possible to have listening conversations with everyone. Instead you can listen to voices that speak on behalf of the community: in the media, the newspapers, the blogs, and YouTube. What are the big voices in the community saying?

Second, *listen for resonances* in conversations. A resonance is a bodily sensation of harmony between you and what is being said. You *feel* the resonance. It amplifies and builds your energy. It is "listening by attunement". This feeling is most likely to occur when someone speaks to your concerns. Resonance can reveal moods that are not explicit in the spoken word. Facilitators of groups, such as teachers or workshop leaders, have honed a skill of listening for resonances. They often call it "reading the mood of the room". The facilitator recognizes the collective mood from the feelings of resonance it generates. The philosopher Hubert Dreyfus discusses the skill of the facilitator in a discussion about teachers (In his book *On the Internet*). He notices that expert teachers are exquisitely sensitive to the moods in the room. These teachers can tell when students are generally receptive to a topic or discussion, when they are engaged, when a student's question resonates with the whole class, or when a quiet student has a burning question.

Third, *listen for histories*. Learn the history of a community. Their history shapes the moods that recur for them. We all have complex and layered histories. Moods show up in the parts of their history that they reference in conversation. For example, someone in a mood of resentment is likely to recount incidents and events in the past where someone offended them or their community. Someone is in a mood of ambition is likely to recall a time when their organization or team was victorious in the face of overwhelming odds. In geopolitical relations among countries, some countries deeply distrust others as have their forebears for centuries.

Fourth, *listen for your own moods and emotions provoked in the conversation*. We have sensibilities toward each other that enable us to detect moods. You can often read another's mood by watching what mood they provoke in you.

Navigating with Moods

If you and the other person are in positive (expansive) moods, your interaction is likely to go smoothly and you can achieve a positive outcome. If you are both in negative (restrictive) moods, some sort of negative outcome is likely. If one of you is in a positive mood and the other in a negative mood, the outcome is much less certain. Which person's mood will most affect the outcome? A person skilled in working with moods may be able to identify and then shift the other's negative mood to a more positive one. A good manager may help the resigned person by initiating a conversation for possibilities. A good leader can help the overwhelmed person on the team lessen the perceived load by sorting through commitments and dropping the least important. Leaders help everyone avoid the toxic moods of distrust and resentment by practicing transparency. Teachers work to bring confused students into moods of inquiry or curiosity.

These examples remind us that moods are forces for productivity (when expansive) or stuckness (when restrictive). Most people are at best dimly aware of their mood and oblivious to the actions they can take to move people from unproductive to productive moods.

Navigation with moods means that, not only can you discern moods in your community and move in resonance with them, but you can shape the mood to move toward the goal. The skill of navigating

Moods

moods grows through five stages: sensing, recognizing, shifting, orchestrating, and cultivating (Table 2).

Table 2. Skill Levels for Navigation with Moods

Stage	Actions
Sensing	Attuning somatically to sensations accompanying moods enables listening for group moods that take many people with them like uncontrollable ocean currents.
Recognizing	Naming moods by listening to the assessments people make about the future.
Shifting	Change the physical situation by moving to a new environment, play music, show videos, lead conversations for new possibilities. Learn the standards behind the assessment and have a conversation whether the assessment is grounded for that standard.
Orchestrating	Lead a group to a new mood by engaging in practices that produce the mood.
Cultivating	Engage people in new practices over a long term, including rituals and ceremonies, associated with the mood you aim to become dominant.

The first stage, *sensing* moods, was described in the previous section.

The second stage is *recognizing* moods, that is, putting to words what you have sensed and validated from their linguistic signatures. Table 1 is a useful tool for this.

The third stage is *shifting* moods. This level of navigation supports mobilization, the gathering of people around your offers of new practice. In this stage, you transform the mood of your group or team to one conducive to adopting the new practice. To do this, you have conversations with members of the community to find out what assessments they have, why they have these assessments, and whether their assessments are grounded. You can then help them form new assessments. For example, you can shift the mood of a resigned person by showing them possibilities they have missed. You can enter the mood of speculation needed for a conversation for possibility by taking a walk with the other person rather than sitting across a conference table. You can enter the mood of wonder and gratitude by having a conversation for relationship that enables you to appreciate each other.

The fourth stage is *orchestrating* moods. This refers to shaping the moods of groups. The leader acts like the conductor of an orchestra, so that all the instruments play together in harmony. Ron Kaufman, an internationally recognized speaker for uplifting service and care, opens his workshops by asking each person to turn to their neighbor and ask, "Will you be my partner?" – transforming a mood of anxiety from being in a room full of strangers to a mood of engagement. Appreciative Inquiry, a design-thinking process, begins by pairing people, asking them to learn about each other, and then asks each person to introduce their partner to the whole group in a way that leads the group to appreciate the talents and skills of the one being introduced. Through this practice, they quickly enter a mood of mutual appreciation, which becomes the foundation for working on tough problems.

The fifth stage is *cultivating* moods. This supports long-term stability and is critical for high-performing teams. In this stage, you foster ongoing conversations that generate stable moods conductive to the outcomes you seek. The aim is to train people's awareness and sensibility so that a positive mood becomes the norm. Cultivating is accomplished by working with the group to embody new practices that are consistent with the desired mood. For example, the ongoing practice of expressing appreciation will lead groups to greater solidarity and mutual trust. Repeated rituals like civil ceremonies and religious gatherings promote moods of belonging and solidarity. Meditative practices of letting go of thoughts that grab your attention promote serenity. The Beginner's Creed promotes acceptance of being a beginner and accelerates learning.

In her book *Learning to Learn and the Navigation of Moods* (2016), Gloria Flores tells a story of interacting with a child to both shift their mood and cultivate a new mood. The child, let's call him Luis, seemed to be good at math but suddenly one day declared he was no good at math and would not pursue it further. On questioning, Gloria learned that Luis was comparing himself to a classmate whom he deemed smarter because the classmate could solve math problems much faster. Luis did not want the embarrassment of being upstaged by the other person. Gloria discovered that a standard – in this case "faster is better" – hid behind Luis's assessment. She asked him if he was aware of how long it took to discover the polio vaccine. He acknowledged that it took a long time and required the work of many people. She pointed out that doing something fast does not mean you are doing something important. Luis saw the point. The next day he declared he was returning and after reflecting on it returned to math. The moral of the story is: revealing the standard behind the assessment lets you look at the grounding and may change the possibilities open to you.

It is also possible to cultivate a negative mood. For example, if as leader you fail to manage someone prone to repeated tantrums and outbursts, that person's mood of resentment can spread through your organization like a cancer. If this happens you will be seen as a toxic leader. If you cannot manage your own tendency to scream at people when things inevitably go wrong, you will also be seen as a toxic leader.

The bottom line for navigation is this: You can look for conversations that are associated with the mood you would like, and then take the other person there with you.

Resonance

Moods are often referred to as attunements to the situation. The word attunement is interesting. In music, it means a sound chamber that vibrates at a particular frequency and requires little energy to maintain the vibration. In electricity, it means a circuit that vibrates at a particular frequency and can amplify weak signals at that frequency. In both, it also means that frequencies that do not match the resonant frequency of a chamber or circuit go unnoticed. Attunement of moods means that our body acts like a chamber or circuit vibrating at some frequencies generated in our communities, but not others.

We experience resonance as a feeling. Almost everyone has the experience of "being on the same wavelength" with something another has said. It is a sensation that you and the other person are aligned emotionally with similar interpretations and assessments. It evokes an emotional response of solidarity and sympathy.

As you gain experience in working with moods, you can learn to listen for moods that are not being stated because you resonate with them. Experienced leaders probe their community with words and expressions, looking for resonances that reveal moods and concerns. When they find a wide resonance, the people experience an emotional rush and sympathy toward the speaker. The emotional energy moves people to action. This skill is very important for mobilizing.

Teams, Collaboration, and Competition

To effectively coordinate on a mission, teams need to be in expansive moods conducive to collaboration: especially appreciation, trust, and mutual commitment to the mission. When the mission involves a competition with other teams, the team needs these moods for focus and discipline because they may have grounds to distrust the competitors. Your skill at working with your teams to dwell in the expansive moods, and avoid being drawn into the restrictive moods, is a professional asset. Hone it well.

Teams working on projects go through a series of moods as the project unfolds from inception to completion. Richard Strozzi Heckler put it this way: the team progresses through four stages that can be interpreted as team moods, which are summarized in Table 3.[1]

Table 3: Moods and Team Project Cycles

Stage	Supporting Moods	Detracting Moods
Formulation (starting)	speculation, wonder, ambition	resignation, confusion
Expansion (ramping up)	discipline, focus, destiny, perseverance	apathy, indifference, lack of focus
Containment (steady state)	appreciation, trust, resolution, "zone"	resentment, distrust
Completion (winding down)	gratitude, forgiveness of debts	lack of appreciation, grudges

The leader inspires the team to the moods conducive to each stage; otherwise, the team will not make it to the next stage. The fourth stage is as important as the other three: failure to declare that the mission is complete and the team disbanded leaves members feeling unsettled and disoriented, not ready for their next team or mission.

---

[1] R. Strozzi-Heckler, *Anatomy of Change*, North Atlantic, 1984 and 1993

Messes and Wicked Problems

Innovation leaders are often sought to help groups find their way out of messes, also called wicked problems. A wicked problem is a very messy social tangle. The players have formed into groups with different interpretations of the problem and different ideas for solution. No group has enough power or resources to impose a solution, but every group has enough power to block someone else's proposal. The underlying problem is that the participants do not have a shared interpretation of the issue and they distrust each other; therefore, they cannot generate a mood of solidarity to move in any direction.

Solving the mess begins with finding some common concerns among all the parties and leading them into a new practice to take care of those concerns. Finding resolutions to a mess is a challenge in managing moods. But managing the moods is not enough. Generating a mood of resolution around a shared purpose is part of the process of mobilizing the community. We will return to this question in Chapter 17 Mobilizing.

Teaching and Learning

Learning is not just a classroom activity; it is a team activity and professional responsibility. In Table 1, the six basic moods affecting learning are grouped in the center of table – curiosity, wonder, inquiry, perplexity, confusion, and apathy. Learning from a mistake or breakdown is much harder if the person has a negative mood. The best moods for accelerating learning are wonder, curiosity, and ambition: the person likes learning, seeks new things to learn, and embraces that something good will come from learning. The worst moods are apathy and confusion: the person is either indifferent or is annoyed at mistakes or breakdowns and blames them on someone or something else. The leader or manager seeks to transform the mood of the confused person to inquiry, curiosity, or even wonder.

Recall situations where you did not know what to do, or you were surprised that an event did not go your way. How did you react? Do you have conditioned tendency that dragged you toward confusion and away from wonder or inquiry? Did you procrastinate when you saw that an inquiry might be useful?

In innovation, the community adopting a new practice is engaged in a learning process. Their goal is to attain competence in the new practice and coordinate effectively with others in the community. Innovation leaders are teachers of the new practice in their communities. The leader must promote community moods of solidarity and ambition to support community members in moving from beginner to competent in the new practice. As we saw from the Beginner's Creed, beginners experience a variety of moods, presenting a challenge for the unprepared teacher.

Managers who espouse "fail fast and often" are trying to predispose people to accept failures and mistakes, inquire into what can be learned, and take new actions. They are trying to dispose their people toward wonder and inquiry, and away from confusion, procrastination, and resentment over wasted effort.

Conclusion

The moods and emotions of the people around us -- our partners, teams, and groups -- strongly affect our performances. Expansive moods enhance performance, restrictive moods detract and can render teams and groups dysfunctional. Skilled managers, facilitators, and teachers are keenly aware of moods and emotions. They know how to interact effectively with different moods and can guide their groups through the moods necessary for a successful project, problem resolution, or learning. As innovation leaders, we must continue to develop our own sensibilities to moods and emotions.

12
TRUST

> *All trust involves vulnerability and risk, and nothing would count as trust if there were no possibility of betrayal. Many people are blind to trust, not so much to its benefits as to its nature and the practices that make it possible.*
> – Robert Solomon

Trust is the glue that holds relationships together. It is essential for all couples, families, friends, teams, communities, institutions, and societies. Many of us never consider how we engender trust in other people, within groups, or within our community. As innovation leaders, we must nurture trust to engage successfully in all the practices from Sensing to Mobilizing. Our power and influence are directly related to the amount of trust we have cultivated in our relationships.

To fully understand trust, we must also understand distrust. Many relationships are tainted by distrust. We must learn to navigate in a complex social sea that has hidden shoals of distrust that can sink the unwary. When trust is highly situational, temporary, and conditional, relationships at all levels tend to degrade and collapse. Trust corrodes from neglect, unmet promises, and misunderstanding. When innovation leaders identify these sources of friction, they can create new opportunities for building trust. When distrust arises from deception, corruption, or misinformation, they must treat it as a deliberate act that may require removing the individuals responsible for perpetuating it and changing the incentive structures that enable it.

What are the practices for navigating in a world with currents of trust and distrust? The practices will depend on the role in which we operate. First is the *insider*: we are already a member of the community. The background of shared ways and traditions with the others forms a solid foundation on which we can nurture and maintain trust. Our identity in our community influences what others see as possible or acceptable for us. Second is the *outsider*: we are a new leader entering into a community where we may see possibilities to bring about change. Building and nurturing trust as an outsider requires deliberate practice, sensibilities, and navigational skills beyond those of the insider. Third is the role of the *coach*: we guide innovation leaders as they build trust in their communities. In all three roles, trust is built by taking care of relationships and expectations.

We will discuss trust as a transaction, an assessment, and a mood. This framing gives us the foundation to engage as insiders, outsiders, and coaches who build the trust necessary to drive adoption of new practices.

Introduction to Trust

Trust is a belief that the other person has the ability, integrity, and reliability to fulfill their commitments. The belief can run from firm (high trust) to conditional (low trust) depending on the community.

Trust is in the background of all conversations. You can see this with the Conversation for Action (reproduced in Figure 1). When we enter this conversation, we need a sufficient level of trust that we can count on the other person to fulfill their part. Alice counts on Bob to deliver a satisfactory result. Bob counts on Alice to accept the result into her world. Over many successful loops their level of mutual trust grows; but it takes only a few broken loops to drag them into distrust.

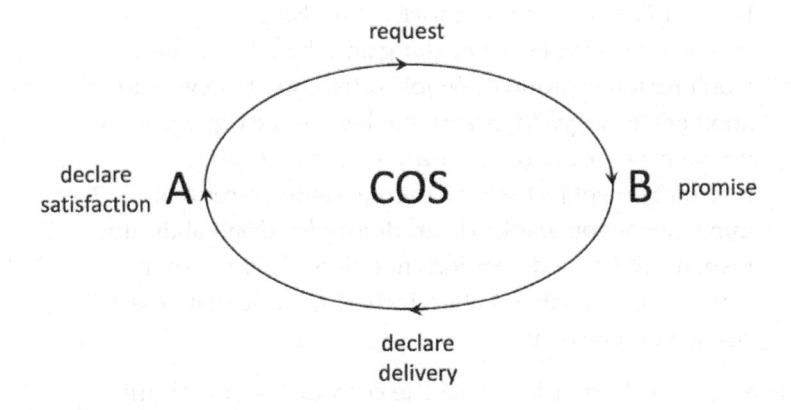

Figure 1. Conversation for action loop for achieving a condition of satisfaction (COS). Alice requests, Bob promises, Bob delivers, Alice accepts delivery and is satisfied.

Trust begins with individual interactions and extends to teams and organizations. A team whose members trust the others to "have their backs" will perform significantly better than a cluster of "lone wolves" looking out for themselves. Elite military organizations like Navy Seals and Army Rangers require not only advanced physical fitness to join, but more importantly the ability and willingness to put the needs of others on the team ahead of one's own. In these organizations, trust that the others will reciprocate trust is even important than physical fitness and technical competence.

Organizations fall into distrust when the workers lose faith that their leadership cares about them or is competent to take care of their concerns. Low morale is the most common sign of pervasive worker distrust of management. As leaders, how do we build the trust we need to successfully coordinate action, navigate challenges, and mobilize our community? We asked an experienced leader how he generates trust in his leadership. He replied:

> In my opinion, trust is not tricky. *Do what you say. Say what you do.* Don't say one thing and then do another. Don't treat one group of people differently than you do another. *Make good decisions* that benefit the organization, not your pet peeve or agenda. *Listen* to all valid information not just select information or voices that mimic what you want to hear. *Be a leader.* Don't abdicate responsibilities and decisions to others. *Fight* for your team. Pick fights that matter, including those that pose a risk to you personally.

This is a beautiful articulation of the common sense about building trust. Everything listed is a good practice. However, this understanding of trust is incomplete. Some employees and leaders believe they are practicing good leadership in this way and yet they do not trust each other. A complete understanding rests on our skills with language. To navigate the often-complex social dynamics of trust in organizations and groups, we need to become skilled observers of the ways groups interact in language.

Trust as a Transaction

In life, we trust entities as well as individuals. When we interact with an organization or institution, we want to have faith they will deliver what they advertise and their products will work properly. When we interact with a machine, we want to have faith it will function properly and safely, require minimal service, and continue to operate properly for a long time. These interactions of trust often go together. When we buy a car, we look for reputable car dealers who sell safe and reliable cars. We turn to respected third parties such as *Consumer Reports* for well-grounded assessments of dealer performance and product reliability.

Our initial interaction with a company or government agency is likely to be a transaction via a webpage rather than an office visit or a phone call. If we need support, our interaction is likely to be with a chat-bot that attempts to deflect our inquiry to a "knowledge database" rather than a human being. Many companies no longer provide a customer service phone number, and some do not even provide chat. And when we do contact them, many companies and government entities treat us with low trust, as if we are thieves rather than loyal customers. To minimize insider threats of data breaches, companies have instituted "zero trust" policies that require their own employees to present their login credentials for access to each new subsystem. Interactions with government bureaucracies are often similarly non-human, compounded with the added complexity of all the rules and norms the bureaucracy enforces.

In these contexts, trust acquires a formal, engineering meaning: an entity is trustworthy if it meets its specifications. All interactions are transactions by automated tasks. The simple act of logging into a seller's website has become a chore of credentials validation with encryption keys and multiple checks with us via secondary devices. If the trustworthy login protocol fails for any reason, we get locked out of our accounts and lose access to our own data. Once logged in, we click to place items into our "cart" and pay with a credit card on file. All these transactions have formal specifications that the company believes have been met. However, none of the technical specifications addresses "caring for the customer". When we call for help, customer care robots begin by running us through more protocols to prove that we are not fraudsters. Then they pass us to technicians who do not care about our circumstances and often do not have the technical expertise or authority to solve our problems.

In short, defining trustworthiness via "trust specifications" paradoxically undermines trust because care is left out. Treating trust as an objective specification often builds customer dissatisfaction. It lowers the trust that human customers have of the organizations on which they depend for service. We do not advocate this approach.

In his *Seven Habits* book Stephen Covey uses the metaphor "emotional bank account" for trust. Every time we keep a promise or perform an act of kindness, we make a deposit in the emotional bank account with the other person. Even if we have a high balance in our account, it takes only a few broken promises to deplete the account. Covey also notes that simple things like engaging in gossip can undermine trust, because we come to be seen as a person who spreads ungrounded negative assessments about others behind their backs. Still, this metaphor has been useful to many people because it guides them to take actions that increase trust.

It is sometimes recommended that to restore trust, we must devise a convincing counterargument to the negative assessment that drives the distrust. This does not work very well because the assessment of trust is not based on logical argument. It is based on a history of experience with us as performers who care about their customers. For innovation leadership, these views of trustworthy entities and bank account metaphors are too transactional and abstract. Instead, we need an understanding of trust grounded in the ways we interact with each other in language.

Trust as an Assessment

We said trust is a belief in the ability, integrity, and reliability of the other person to fulfill their commitments. In other words, trust is an assessment composed of three components:

- Competence (ability). We judge that the other person has the skill and resources to deliver what is promised. If we believe they lack the necessary skill or resources, we will not believe that they can deliver.
- Sincerity (integrity). We judge that the other person intends to fulfill their promises and has a record of doing what they say they will do.

- Care (reliability). We judge that the other person will act to take care of what is important to us in case a contingency would block the normal completion of a promise.

Most people want to ground their assessments of competence, sincerity, and care. That means they accumulate evidence over time that other persons keep their promises, match their intentions with their words, and take care of concerns when contingencies arise. Reciprocally, we pay attention that we complete actions, keep our word, and take care of our relationships, thus providing others the grounding to trust us.

Let's take a closer look at the care assessment. Suppose that a vendor says they cannot complete our order because they cannot obtain a replacement part, a skilled worker quit, or the roads were closed by a storm. If such an event happens, does the vendor just give up and leave us stranded? How much more satisfying it is when the vendor acts to resolve the contingency – finding an alternate supplier of parts, finding a replacement worker, or mobilizing an alternative means of transportation. There is a famous story about a Federal Express driver in the early days of the company who believed in the company's motto to deliver "absolutely, positively on time". When a snowstorm blocked the roads and prevented him from delivering a package, he hired a helicopter and personally delivered the package on time. This story became a legend and inspired many to become customers of Federal Express. CEO Fred Smith commented wryly that his drivers were smart enough not to hire a helicopter every time there is a snowstorm. This legendary story illustrates the lengths some people will go to keep their promises when confronted with seemingly impossible contingencies. That kind of commitment is the third element of trust. Can I count you to go out of your way to keep your promise even when things go wrong? Can I count on you when it will cost you something?

A deeper truth hides behind these assessments. An interaction between a customer and a performer is an event in a relationship. It is not enough to step through the speech acts of a loop. Each party acts to support and nurture the relationship. In most situations, this simply means they *keep each other informed when contingencies arise*. That way, even if the performer cannot deliver the original promise or the customer no longer needs the delivery, their relationship stays strong. The idea that many successfully completed loops generate trust, as in the emotional bank account story, misses the essential point that trust builds when the parties take care of their relationship as they coordinate together. Should either come to believe that the other does not care, trust breaks.

How do we decide to trust machines? Machines have no customers; users interact with them as tools. Machines cannot be sincere or care about us. However, the three assessments have machine analogies that make it possible for human users to declare they can trust the machine. Competence applied a machine means it meets its functional specifications. Sincerity applied to a machine means its designers' representations of functions and limitations are truthful. Care applied to a machine means its designers have anticipated many breakdowns and have built the machine to recover from them.

Treating trust as assessment opens the possibility for navigation. You can constantly assess what actions you can take to earn trust. When you make a promise, ensure you are competent to perform, sincere about delivering, and care about the outcome. If you do not think those conditions apply, consider declining or deferring. A firm decline will build trust more than an ambiguous promise to deliver. Incomplete loops undermine trust. Always take care of your relationship with the other person, especially when circumstances arise to block specific promises.

Trust as a Mood

We have seen that moods are pervasive background orientations toward the world, bringing with them assessments about what is possible or not possible. Trust is a complex mood based on three assessments: competence, sincerity, and care. Negative assessments of any one or more of these three yields distrust. See Table 1.

Table 1. Assessments Characterizing Trust and Distrust

Trust	Distrust
They are competent to do what they promised to do	They are not capable of doing what they promised to do
They intend to carry out their promises; their intentions match their words	That have no intention of doing what they say they will do
They care about what is important to me and will act to protect my interests when contingencies arise	They don't care about what is important to me and may well just walk away when the going gets tough

Trust is supported by two expansive background moods, gratitude and appreciation (Table 2). Gratitude is a mood with the assessment of appreciation for all that others have done for us, all the doors they have opened, and all the gifts they have bestowed on us. Appreciation is a mood with the assessment that persons, events, and situations bring us value and meaning that we enjoy receiving. It is very hard to linger in ungrounded distrust if you genuinely appreciate the other people and you experience their appreciation of you.

Table 2. Assessments Supporting Trust

Gratitude	Appreciation
I have received so many gifts from others.	The person, event, or situation has brought meaning and value to me.
Many people and circumstances opened doors for me	Associating with them is good for my well-being.
They, and all of life, are gifts!	I enjoy being seen as a source of value and meaning for others.

Even when the target of distrust has changed and earns positive marks for the three assessments, distrust can persist. This is because distrust is often supported by two restrictive moods, resignation and resentment (Table 3). Resignation is a mood with the assessment that there are no possibilities for positive action. Resentment is a mood with the assessment that someone has wronged or offended you; you harbor a grudge in which you secretly wish something bad would happen to the offender. Those in a mood of distrust often see no possibilities to restore trust and may develop hostile attitudes toward those who try to restore trust. They do not trust anyone to improve things ("management hasn't in the past"); they do not believe anyone can fix the situation ("there is no hope for the future"); and they conclude it is not worth the trouble to try to fix it. In this mood, the only options seem to be quitting, or just keeping your head down as you grind out your work.

Table 3. Assessments Supporting Distrust

Resignation	Resentment
Nothing has worked in the past to fix this situation; we've been here before.	They have done me an injustice.
No reasonable plan for fixing this situation is likely in the future.	They deserve retribution.
No one cares; there is no hope for change.	They are <expletive deleted> jerks. I am not willing to talk with them.

Resentment that persists over a long period can turn into *ressentiment*, a French word used by German philosopher Friedrich Nietzsche for a sense of suffering that is so durable it has no apparent resolution. It scapegoats leadership for the pain and suffering of perceived oppression. People in this mood justify their ingrained resentment with a value system that claims the moral high ground. They may not grant the humanity of the other; forgiveness is out of the question. They barely manage to conceal their hostility. They have lost faith in the possibility of trusting.

Practices that Support Trust

To gain the trust of those around us, we must develop practices that affirm their assessments of competence, sincerity, and care. We only make promises we know we can deliver. We keep our word. We go out of our way to take care of the interests of those who depend on us. Those practices are not enough if unless we support them with practices that maintain the relationship, especially gratitude and appreciation.

We have described gratitude and appreciation as moods. We can also engage them as habitual practices. What does a practice of appreciation look like? Appreciation must be shared to be enjoyed. When expressing appreciation try to use language that resonates with the other person. It is important that they *feel appreciated*. Here are four examples:

- Expressing appreciation when someone delivers a promise to you.
- Expressing appreciation in meetings by acknowledging other ideas.
- Performing little acts of kindness.
- Praising authentically and generously. When you are given the credit for something, make sure you pass it to the rest of the team. Almost always someone else helped you achieve whatever was praiseworthy. Paraphrasing a sign that sat on President Ronald Reagan's desk quoting Harry Truman: "There is no limit to what one can do or where one can go if one doesn't mind who gets the credit."

These practices are not hard. There is always something to appreciate. Look and you will find.

Some people say that a way to appreciate is to ask people what they care about and then express appreciation for what they say. It is a good practice to listen for what people care about. But this practice can backfire if you are clumsy about it. One way to be clumsy is to approach the conversation as an interview or, worse, a cross-examination. People often cannot put to words when they care about something. They may be uncomfortable with your question or suspicious about your motive, sincerity, or care. It is better to avoid the "interview" and let them know what you already appreciate about them. When they feel your appreciation as an emotional resonance, they are more likely to believe you care about them and open up about what they appreciate.

There are also many ways to practice gratitude. Begin the day with a short meditation on the gifts you have been given, including the gift of the new day. During the day, as your loops complete, take a moment to express your gratitude to the other person for their work. End the day by completing the conversations of the day, leaving no loose ends for another day. The practice of gratitude enables us to avoid regretting the things we could have said but did not.

These practices are not difficult if you cultivate a view that each person brings unique talents and gifts. Be curious about what they offer. You will be amazed at what they tell you. It is all too easy to view other people as abstract members of organizations or classes and not look for their unique gifts. Do not allow this sort of detachment to blind you to seeing them and what they offer.

After a few weeks of daily doing, these practices will seem normal and easy to do. Your mood will shift toward serenity.

The Long Tail of Trust

We have mentioned that trust takes time to cultivate. Trust depends on a long history of interactions between you and others around you. Why is this?

It relates to our primordial desires for survival. We depend on others in many critical ways, for example, growing and distributing food, running the infrastructure that gives us electricity, telephone, and Internet, taking care of our children while they are growing up and vulnerable, taking care of family and friends when they are ill, and protecting us from predators. We did not create these dependencies and have little control over them.

Other dependencies are generated in our interactions with others. Every Conversation for Action generates a mutual dependency between requester and performer. Pretending that these dependencies do not exist can hurt cooperation, reputation, or our ability to keep a business running. Since organizations are built on networks of conversations for action, a broken promise in one part of the network can propagate and result in broken promises elsewhere in the network. The cascade of broken promises generates distrust.

When we do not trust that a critical service will always be available, we make contingency plans. When we do not trust that other members of our organizations will fulfill their promises on time, we champion new rules and policies to keep them in line. We create workarounds to bypass untrusted parts of the organization. We fall into bad moods and our work slows down and diminishes in quality. This experience with distrust builds over time and is the result of a history of promises not delivered and relationships not nurtured. Distrust that accumulates over time is difficult to heal.

Some kinds of trust have long historical roots. The historian and philosopher Yuval Noah Harari writes about how humans have built economic systems over millennia.[1] These systems rely on money – more precisely, on trust in money. He points out that this trust is built on a fiction – that a head of state or a strong and powerful institution stands behind the money. Persons who don't trust each other can engage in transactions because they both trust the money they are using. Today, we see what happens when trust in the bank that holds our money crumbles. Depositors create a flash mob to withdraw their money, causing the bank to run out of cash and go into default. In these cases, the bank's promise to hold money safely and return it on demand is no longer trusted. The same thing happened when investors' trust in crypto currencies broke – everyone pulled their investments out and the value of crypto-tokens collapsed. Harari's great insight is that our ability to trust fictions enables us to coordinate in groups. The fictions are the stories invented about the goals we are

---

[1] Yuval Noah Harari. 2015. *Sapiens: A Brief History of Humankind*. Harper.

working for together and the circumstances of our work. The long tail of our history affects who we trust and how fast we achieve trust.

When Trust is Lost

Most of what we have said above is good for earning other people's trust of you and cultivating trust with your immediate coworkers and teams. When dealing with distrust with a friend or coworker, you can start with an appropriate apology and follow up with actions that demonstrate your competence, sincerity, and care.

What if you are the leader? What do you do to cultivate trust? This is more difficult because you need to deal with the expectations of the group as well as those of individuals. Your group members most likely do not have a homogenous expectation of you. When you take an action, some will find it meets their expectations and their trust in you will increase; others will find it does not, and their trust in you will decrease.

What if you are a coach brought in to help an organization improve their performance or resolve their mutual distrust? This is a much more difficult and complex question. Organizational relationships can be complex and turbulent. The coach needs professional training to be effective. Some coaches have developed processes that transform their clients' distrust into trust. One example is Appreciative Inquiry[2], a workshop format that begins with exercises to bring out qualities of the others in the room that inspire appreciation; this is followed with breakout groups that design projects to yield results previously impossible. The mood of appreciation, orchestrated at the start of the workshop, makes the breakout teams more open to sensing, finding common ground for envisioning, and offering new practices. Moreover, the coach needs a

---

[2] Frank Barret. 2005. *Appreciative Inquiry.* Taos Institute.

great deal of emotional fortitude, lest the coach's own emotional reactivity derails the conversations.

Innovation Leaders and Trust

Trust relies on expectations. We tend to trust people who fulfill our expectations of them. The eight basic practices of innovation leaders – sensing, envisioning, offering, adopting, sustaining, embodying, navigating, and mobilizing – all support setting and fulfilling expectations for the competence, sincerity, and care assessments of trust:

Sensing: Supports the care assessment. People who believe you understand them and have taken the take the time to do so, will see that you care.

Envisioning: Supports the care and competence assessments. You have taken the time to show them a better future and how they might get there. You also exhibit competence at planning and connecting actions with their concerns.

Offering: This practice supports all three assessments. Are you competent to fulfill the offer? Do you fully intend to do it? Will you stick with it when things get tough? Here you must demonstrate that you have the skills to do the job, access to the resources needed, and the grit to see it through to the end.

Adopting: You are asking early adopters to join your movement for a trial period. Their commitment is your reward for building trust with them in the previous practices.

Sustaining: You are asking the majority to join your movement for a sustained period. The voices of early adopters, who are trusted members of their community, will strongly support the assessment of trust they need to close the long-term deal. Majority adopters also look to the competence, sincerity, and care of your team or company – have you institutionalized trustworthy practices that will continue after you are gone?

Executing: Demonstrates your (and your network's) ongoing ability to fulfill promises and generate customer satisfaction with results.

Mobilizing: Demonstrates your ability to listen and take care of concerns of people who gather around you.

Embodying: Develops empathy, compassion, presence, and emotional fortitude, which support the care assessment.

When you are competent with these practices, you will automatically generate trust.

13
POWER

Knowledge is power.
— Francis Bacon

*For the strength of the Pack is the Wolf,
and the strength of the Wolf is the Pack.*
— Rudyard Kipling, The Jungle Book

Power is an illusion. Although it flows, it is not a fluid. Although it accumulates, it is not a substance. Although it appears that one's gain of power is another's loss, there is no fixed quantity of it. Power is the ability to influence action in the world. Those with power merely act with the expectation that what they wish will happen. Those without power can live in a state of perpetual frustration that they are incapable of bringing what they want into the world. Power does not exist by itself, but only in relationship to others. Power is at its most potent when it is least visible. Power is weakest when self-proclaimed and enforced at the end of a gun.

You cannot succeed at innovation without understanding power in your community. Your supporters use their power to mobilize others and your resisters use their power to derail you. Our purpose in this chapter is to give you an understanding of power so that you can navigate in the social space of your community.

Power is Influence

The common understanding of power has been shaped by technology. Electric power is the rate of movement of electrons. Hydropower converts the momentum of moving water into electricity. Wind power does the same for air. Horsepower is the number of horses required to move the same load as an engine. In these examples, power is a flowing force affecting the movements of material things. Technology gives us ways to measure the rate of flow and total amount of flow before the power is exhausted.

This technological analogy of power is woefully wrong for understanding power in social spaces. In social spaces, power is the relative ability to influence action. We say relative because there are no fixed measures of one's power; we can only say that one person is more able to influence actions than another.

Consider a story that illustrates power as a perception. An individual who can lift the largest stone might be seen as the most powerful in the community. Yet the strongest person acting alone can be outperformed by weaker person who organizes a group of people who cooperate to lift an even larger stone. And that group is weaker than a leader whose stories inspire their community to pick up the largest stones and shape them into a pyramid. And that leader is weaker still than another who sees far and sets in place the foundation of a society based on pyramids that lasts for a thousand years. All power is predicated on stories that people in the community believe. When a story changes, the locus of power changes. The person who tells a different story that the community accepts gains power.

A sailing story illustrates power as a source of action. The ship's owner asks, what powers will shape the journey? The opinions vary across the crew. One sailor says it is the wind, for the wind determines what direction the ship can move. Another says it is the ocean, for the currents can drag a ship where it does not want to go, or they can rage in a storm that destroys all ships. Another says it is the moon, for the moon influences the tides. Another says it is the sun and stars, for they tell us where we are and which direction we are going. The captain, a veteran of many journeys, says that the success of the journey depends on all the sailors working together to skillfully blend the energies of sea, wind, moon, and stars. Otherwise, these energies move at cross purposes, and the crew are lucky to survive.

The story of the stone illustrates that there is more power in groups than individuals; simply forming a group creates power. Moreover, there is power in narratives that transcend the immediate space and time of the workers. The sailing story illustrates that there is power in blending with forces rather than fighting them individually.

As an innovation leader, you master these distinctions by seeking ways to mobilize groups around your proposal and tell stories that maintain their involvement over the long haul. You attune yourself to the concerns of those with power. You recognize that that positional authority is one of the weakest and least durable of powers because those who wield it eventually move on. Leaders who change the narratives of their community are stronger because their envisioning stories blend the existing narratives into something new while respecting the familiar and relevant background.

Power is neither good nor bad; neither righteous nor sinful. Power does not exist by itself. It is a belief accompanied by willingness to defer to the constraints and expectations imposed by that belief. The belief spreads in the narratives shared in the community. Power is revealed only when exercised. It is exercised by individuals in organizations, bureaucracies, and communities who initiate actions and tell community stories to bring something into the world. It is also used by community members to prevent something from happening. Many bureaucracies, for example, feature a powerful "clay layer", the middle layer of managers who review requests from below and use their positional power to deny requests that would place the status quo at risk. Speakers who assess that power is good (or bad) are voicing opinions that power is being used for outcomes they perceive as positive (or negative).

Kinds of Power

A prime reason people resist innovations is that they perceive that the new practice will reduce their relative power. Suppose you are the mayor of a town. All the towns of the region are being asked to join a coalition of support for a new seaport serving the region. If you perceive that joining will force your town to give up important practices, you will probably decline to join. If you perceive that joining will bring your town new benefits without disrupting important practices, you will probably join. The coalition organizers navigate the varying political powers of the region's mayors by closing "win-win" deals with each mayor. We will shortly say more about this form of navigating power.

There are at least ten common sources of power.

Positional or office power is the ability to set policies and rules for an organization that govern how everyone must act. An office manager can set personnel policies and define penalties for those who do not comply. A CEO can chart the direction of a company through its declarations of mission, strategy, and budgets.

Personal capital is the ability of an individual to shape community directions because the individual has earned great respect and trust for past actions. Peter Drucker had enormous personal capital among professional managers. Henry Kissinger had enormous personal capital among diplomats in international affairs. Steve Jobs had enormous personal capital in the personal computer market.

Coercive power is the ability to apply force or threats of force to get people to comply with an action. This kind of power is commonly associated with the military and the police. It is also exercised by street gangs and drug cartels.

Money power is the ability to buy people's acceptance of an action. An organization with high salaries can recruit people that an organization with low salaries cannot compete with. A venture capital firm can impose operating rules on a startup in return for its financial backing. Recall the slogan, "Whoever has the gold, makes the rules."

Manufacturing power is the ability to produce large quantities of goods rapidly. A company entering a new market can displace others because they have superior ability to manufacture the new product. Countries that can manufacture more weapons and vehicles can win wars because adversaries run out of ammunition.

Reward and incentive power shapes behavior by providing incentives to engage in desired behavior and punishment to discourage undesirable behavior.

Institutional power means that an institution can set policies and procedures for a group, without identifying who determined them. The Department of Motor Vehicles sets procedures for driver licenses. The Internal Revenue Service sets procedures for tax collection.

Traditional power means that communities bind themselves to traditions that make sense to them but not necessarily to outsiders. There is an expectation that joining a community means you will honor its traditions, and you can be dismissed for violating their traditions. Navies have traditions dating back many years such as honor codes and definitions of chains of command. Universities have traditions for academic freedom and research. Religions sustain traditions and rituals that developed over thousands of years.

Tribal power is similar to traditional except it pertains to identity groups and implies strong penalties for those not practicing loyalty to the tribe. The tribe can be any social group that shares culture, ancestry, language, or geographic region.

Coalition power arises when a group organizes into a coalition for common action. Generally, larger groups have greater influence.

The key point for navigation is that power vests in communities and the individuals who represent them. To navigate around resistance and mobilize followers for your innovation proposal, you must first recognize the power centers and who to engage.

Bringing Power Centers into Alignment

Much of the resistance you will encounter when you make your offers for change of practice in your community will come from those who perceive their power is threatened by your proposals. Some will express their resistance by indifference to your proposal; they will not support it or spread word about it. Others will express their resistance by actively using their social power to thwart the new practice.

If you are going to succeed with adoption, you must find a way to bring these power centers into alignment. That happens in the conversations you will have with their leaders. You may find those leaders and approach them on your own, or you may get someone to introduce you. Either way, you must have conversations with them.

Bringing power centers into alignment is a process of building a coalition in favor of the new practice. The new practice championed by the coalition must be something of value to every coalition member. Individual centers will join if the coalition offers them something that responds to their concerns without requiring them to give up anything they hold dear. The innovation leader is proficient at the five basic innovation practices – listening for breakdowns others see and would like to resolve, envisioning a future without the breakdowns and showing a path to get there, offering to help get things moving down that path, and working with early and majority adopters.

It is, of course, possible that some power centers do not want to join the coalition. In that case, it may still be possible for the coalition to achieve its purpose if it has amassed enough power to overcome the remaining resisters.

Identifying power centers and bringing them into alignment on issues of common interest is the key strategy for resolving wicked problems and organizational messes.

CAYA Green: An Example of Navigation of Power

Todd Lyons tells the following story of his experience as Marine Corps attaché in the Middle East. Prior to Operation Iraqi Freedom (2003), the US and Israel had worked out a process to conduct annual joint exercises to enable their Marines to maintain their readiness while deployed. The process to plan one exercise typically took 12-18 months and required a lot of coordination among seven commands. Each exercise required additional agreements between the combatant command, the host country, the host country coordinator, host country exercise units, and a representative from the US Embassy. Coordinating all these groups was a complex annual challenge. It was no model of simplicity or efficiency, but it worked.

Operation Iraqi Freedom caused a breakdown because the various parties wanted to reserve their assets for operations and declined to commit them to the exercises. Without the exercises, the participating Marines would not be fully ready for future operations. The war rendered the existing process inoperative.

Todd explored ways to conduct the joint exercises for the Marines without the long planning cycle or commitment of assets. He asked whether Israeli counterparts could support shorter exercises conducted while the Marine units were in transit through the region covered by the Sixth Fleet. The exercise could be initiated on short notice (2-4 weeks) and would be shaped around assets available in that time frame. This was agreeable to all parties because it was inexpensive, required no long term commitments, and could be completed in the same time as the units would have taken anyway to reach the combat zone. The new practice was called CAYA Green, meaning "Come As You Are" and the color green represented the

Marine Corps. The exercises continued in this way for the duration of the war and beyond. The participating units and their leaders were happy with the new practice.

What is the role of power in this story? The key point is that all parties involved each had sufficient power to block a proposal they did not like, but none had sufficient power to bring the others in line. The resulting gridlock is characteristic of wicked problems. The solution was to find a new practice that all could support. The common ground involved a much simpler process that cost less and was done in the transit time to the combat zone.

The moral of the story is that innovation leaders in large, complex, well-established communities are highly likely to have to deal with power centers as they navigate toward the adoption of new practice. Each power center has its own concerns and interests. The power to attain the adoption of new practice by all of them arises only through negotiations that offer each party a way to take care of their interests by joining a coalition. Navigation of power means that the innovation leaders bring these power centers into alignment by finding "win-win" deals with each power group.

Voices of Your Community

The first step in navigation is learning not only who are the power centers in your community, but also whose voices speak for them. Many key speakers will be inside the community, and a few may be outside. The voices are important because power is exercised through conversations. Listen to the right voices and you get a good idea of what concerns them and how they see the world. This enables you to make attractive offers for them and their followers to join the coalition favoring the new practice.

Where will these voices be found? If you are not very familiar with your community, you can start with publicly available information. Look at the institutions of your community and find their organization charts and public relations pages. Search for articles about your community and its history. Look at professional magazines and financial newspapers for controversies and who is speaking up about them. Search for video recordings of these prominent people speaking. As you conduct these searches, you will see certain names recurring. Dig into their articles, blogs, commentaries, and speeches. What names do they mention? Track them down too. You do not need to agree with any of these voices. You let them reveal the landscape of various concerns and moods in the community.

In *The Innovator's Way*, we called this process "mastering the mess". You accept the messiness of your community. You educate yourself on the main factions and their histories. By listening to what each is saying, you will develop a broad perspective that enables you to navigate through the mess.

Augment this general search procedure by having many conversations with people in your community. What are they concerned about? What are their assessments? What do they say are the power centers? Who do they say speaks with authority? As you learn new names, research them as recommended above.

After a while, you will know who is influencing the conversations in your community and what they saying. You will know what concerns they have. You will know what assessments, declarations, and offers they are making.

Voices show us the currents flowing in the sea of conversations we are immersed in. Like ocean currents, conversation currents pull us along and we have no control over them. The voices show us the currents and their direction. We can then choose whether to ride the currents or merge into other currents going the direction we want.

Finding Your Voice

The five basic practices – sensing, envisioning, offering, adopting, and sustaining – are a sound way to develop your voice for change and mobilize people to the change.

Exercise these practices in conversations with the members of your community. They will tell you when your articulation of concerns resonates with them. They will introduce you to other people. Eventually your network will reach a critical mass and you will have a much clearer idea of what offers will be attractive. Our experience is that reaching this level of understanding can be done in a few weeks with as few as five conversations a week with members of your community. You can accelerate this pace by following up immediately on introductions. As these conversations evolve, you will see opportunities to make small offers that deepen your relationships and extend your network. Take them.

Be wary of those who urge you to use your voice to "speak truth to power". While your "bluntness and candor" may make you feel better, in practice it is likely to annoy the other person and shut down the conversation. It is far better to engage them in a sensing conversation, listening for their concerns as well as discussing yours. The goal is to evolve a network of voices behind yours, spreading your vision and offer.

Social Networks and Power

We often use the term "network" for a group of people we interact with, some in our team, some in our organization, some in our community, some in the external world. Our networks are important because they mobilize our followers and generate the emotional energy that turns our proposals into practices.

Some scientists have studied how to map social networks to reveal who has more power or influence in the network. They do this by examining records of communications, such as email logs, which record senders and receivers of messages. They compile the records into a graph in which each node represents a person, and each arrow is labelled with the number of messages sent from one person to the other.

Almost all social networks mapped in this way include a few special nodes. A node that connects to many others is a "hub". A node on a single path between two subnetworks is a "connector". Hubs have considerable influence in the network because they connect regularly with so many people. They have power that is not recognized as a position on an organization chart. Connectors are also influential because they are trusted bridges between separate subnetworks.

By tracking the flows of messages and tangible goods such as money and materials, social network maps can uncover power centers that are not visible in organization charts or other public information. These maps reveal the existence of conversations but not their content. You can discover the content by tracking key voices.

Conclusions

Social power in our communities is an underappreciated aspect of social space. We aim to make allies of those with power. When someone resists, we first try to reconcile with them and, if that does not work, we seek to neutralize them through coalitions with our supporters. We cannot succeed with our innovation proposal without understanding the configuration of power in our community.

Power is exercised through conversations. Find the main voices speaking for each of the power centers. Educate yourself on what they are saying without trying to agree or disagree with them. Let them inform you of ebbs and flows of power and moods. When possible, visualize the movements you discern with graphs and maps.

14
RESISTANCE

> *The resistance to change exhibited by social systems is much more nearly a form of "dynamic conservatism" -- a tendency to fight to remain the same.*
> -- Donald Schon

> *Service is care in action.*
> – Ron Kaufman

> *The Master doesn't talk, he acts. When his work is done, the people say, "Amazing: we did it, all by ourselves!"*
> – Lao Tzu

As candles attract moths, so innovation offers attract resisters. You know this from experience. You work hard to propose something of demonstrable benefit to your clients or community and their first inclination is to resist it. Logical arguments do not change their minds. Optimists unhelpfully tell you to keep your chin up because resistance signifies you are doing something important. You start to wonder if anyone takes you seriously. Resistance is so common and intractable that it has a name: Valley of Death. Everyone wishes you good luck in getting through it alive. What's the story about resistance?

The most strenuous resistance appears when you start to implement the innovation rather when you merely propose it. Implementation asks people to commit to the new practice whereas a proposal only asks them to consider it. Resistance to adoption is a social issue, not a management or production failure. Overcoming resistance is a social skill.

Crossing the social chasms from ideas to implementation is challenging and frustrating for leaders. This is especially true for beginning leaders, who do not know what to do when they encounter the resistance, hesitation, bureaucratic slow walking, and stonewalling that block the implementation of new practices and prevent innovations from taking hold.

Your community is an ecosystem. The interactions within the community are stable for long periods of time. Stephen Jay Gould (1941-2002), a paleontologist, postulated a theory of punctuated equilibrium for ecosystems. He showed that fossil records demonstrate long periods of stability interspersed with occasional periods of sudden, transformative change.

As with other ecosystems, human communities share the behavior of punctuated equilibrium. The punctuations can be triggered by external events that change the system, by new technologies that alter the costs of performing tasks, or by internal conversations that generate new concerns. The equilibria are not rigid; they can change in small steps, called *incremental innovations*, that mildly disturb the overall equilibrium. Occasionally major changes, called *disruptive innovations*, hit part of the system, forcing adjustments throughout the system. Sometimes a big change, which we call an *avalanche*, transforms the whole system and generates the need for an entirely new equilibrium.

All changes – incremental, disruptive, and avalanche – disturb the equilibrium of an ecosystem. The system "fights back" by resisting the change. Resistance to change is a normal systemic response. In this chapter, we will explore the kinds of change and the phenomenon of resistance so that you can learn the navigational skills to cope with it.

The Nature of Resistance

The abstractions "equilibrium" and "inertia of the system" are illuminating metaphors for a system's resistance to change. But these metaphors do not guide us in navigating through resistance. The key to navigation is to frame resistance as a phenomenon in language: *resistance is a negative assessment of a proposed or imposed change, supported by social power to block the change.* Community members see the change as a threat to their comfort, identity, or power. Their resistance may be passive, such as by indifference, or active, such as by aggressive use of power to derail the initiative. Navigation begins with conversations with community members to discover the concerns behind their negative assessment of the innovation proposal.

Social equilibria are held in place by the concerns shared in the community. The current practices reflect their current concerns. Only if their concerns change or are put at risk will they be open to new practices and a new equilibrium. When you propose a change, you need to understand and address those concerns. Rather than run *away* from the resistance or try to overcome it by force, leaders move *toward* the resistance with curiosity and humility to understand why people are committed to the current equilibrium. The goal is to discover latent concerns, which when brought to their awareness will motivate people to move toward the proposed change. You will not find a cause for the resistance by looking at external circumstances. You will find its causes in the everyday conversations of people in the community.

Technological change that alters the relative costs of tasks affects the equilibrium. Those who adopt the lower-cost way gain a marked advantage, forcing others to adapt or lose. Exponential decreases in the costs of technology can produce sudden changes as people switch rapidly to the much cheaper alternative. Moore's law in computing is an example. In military affairs, recent wars have revealed that cheap autonomous drones enable all sides to see what the others are doing and make mass formations a disastrous vulnerability.

Although resistance most forcefully appears in the adopting practice when you ask people to commit to a change, there are many early signs. They appear at the beginning during sensing when no one resonates with the breakdown you declared, or during envisioning when your envisioning story inspires mostly yawns, or during offering when your initial offer attracts few takers. It is better to anticipate the resistance than to try to deal with it once it hits. You can anticipate it by listening well during sensing, envisioning, and offering.

Resistance is your friend. It lets you know that your proposed change matters to your community. It reveals concerns of the community that you may have misunderstood or discounted.

Next up, we will review the adopting practice to set the context for understanding resistance. We will then discuss how to navigate avalanches and disruptions. We will conclude this chapter with ways to overcome resistance.

Adopting Practice

In his classic *Diffusion of Innovations,* Everett Rogers wrote that on average about 16% of the community will be early adopters, 68% majority adopters, and the remaining 16% laggards who may never adopt (Figure 1). Each group has concerns distinct from the others. Early adopters are disposed to try new things; they tolerate risk, they put up with bugs in the early releases, they want to stay on the leading edge, and they do not want to be seen as laggards. Majority adopters want stability; they want leadership backing, predictable costs, reliable infrastructure, low risks, multiple vendors, good technical support, and helpful customer service. They seek endorsement from early adopters. Resistance will be lowest among early adopters and highest among laggards. If early adopters resist you, there is little chance the

Resistance

majority will follow. If early adopters embrace you, you get only 16% of the potential market.

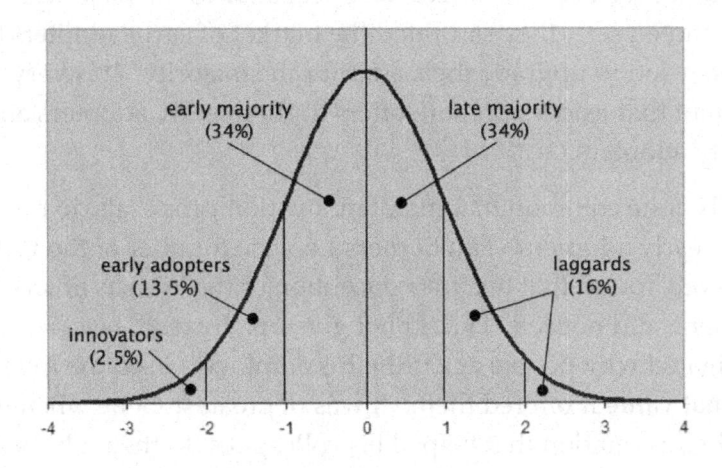

Figure 1. Everett Rogers divided adopters into five categories on a Bell curve depending on how many standard deviations their adoption times differed from the mean. The mean is the peak of the distribution (zero deviation).

Early Adopters	Majority Adopters
Disposition for novelty	Disposition for reliability
Join quickly	Join slowly
Risk tolerant	Risk averse
Go ahead without support infrastructure	Wait until infrastructure is reliable
Independent decision to join	Imitates others who have joined
Scattered through subcommunities	Clustered in subcommunities

In *Crossing the Chasm*, Geoffrey Moore said that many startup businesses fail because their founders appealed to early adopters only and did not set aside resources to appeal later to the majority. After two or three years, they saturated the market of early adopters but had no money left to upgrade their offer for the majority. It is very important that leaders prepare offers for both early adopters and majority adopters.

It is quite common that initial innovation proposals do not appeal even to early adopters. Tim Berners-Lee, the founder of the World Wide Web, found that his first conception of the Web as links between documents did not sell. He did not give up. Instead, he carefully investigated why people at CERN (his employer) used the Internet and what value it offered them. It was of greatest value when it brought information that helped his colleagues do their jobs better. To show them that the Web could do this better than anything in the Internet, he built a prototype browser. He worked to overcome the skepticism of CERN's management toward introducing a new technology into the organization. He persuaded programmers to build production browsers and start a network of web servers. He worked to make the Web a friendly place for business. When he started to become successful with these groups, he found that a few commercial providers wanted to appropriate the Web technology as their own intellectual property. He established the World Wide Web Consortium to keep Web technology in the public domain and encourage commercial groups to cooperate on its development.

Adoption is not marketing, although marketing may help promote adoption in the community. Marketing can be especially important for large-scale adoptions. On the other hand, many innovators skilled in the adoption practice have succeeded without help from a marketing department.

The term "stakeholder" is often used to represent a member of a subcommunity who needs to "buy in" to your innovation proposal.

Resistance is seen as a lack of buy-in. This is not a constructive way to look at adoption. Buy-in is an intellectual decision to support a proposal. For adoption, you are not aiming for buy-in, you are aiming for individuals from the subcommunities to commit to embody new practices. The focus on embodiment raises the stakes. The intellectual decision to "buy-in" is easier to achieve and easy to lose.

Subcommunities

Unless your community is very small, it probably contains several subcommunities, each with its own set of early and majority adopters. You can see this easily in any sport. Take baseball. Baseball is a large community comprising individual teams, commissioners, game schedulers, ticket sellers, paraphernalia marketers, museum and hall of fame staffs, and farm teams. Suppose you propose an innovation for Baseball: a time limit for pitchers to make their next throws. You will need to negotiate with most of the subcommunities to be sure the implementation of this new rule will be accepted. In effect, you are customizing the main offer to reflect each subcommunity's concerns. Forming a package of customized versions of the main offer is often a good strategy for overcoming resistance. However, this strategy will not work if some of the subcommunities steadfastly demand conditions that the others cannot accept.

Another strategy is to reframe the main offer to appeal to all the communities. Steve Jobs, CEO of Apple, was an inveterate reframer. The Apple Apps Store (2008), which became the model for distributing software to devices, was a reframing of iTunes (2003). Jobs created iTunes to reframe the controversy created by Napster, which was distributing bootlegged soundtracks over the Internet; iTunes distributed copyright protected soundtracks at an affordable price. The iPod, which was invented in 2001, was itself a reframing of a portable mp3 music player. Jobs's most majestic reframing came with the iPhone (2007). He brought several technologies together: the iPod music player, cell phone service, internet connectivity, and software apps. He needed to bring several potentially resistant subcommunities together to make this happen. Avid iPod users had to be convinced they would get better music service if their iPod was absorbed into the iPhone. Cell phone service providers had to expand their data services significantly to accommodate untested new demand from internet connected phones. Software developers had to start offering software for a new platform. Content developers had to be sure their copyrights would be honored. Jobs did not position iPhone as a convergence of these technologies. He reframed the whole concept of a phone into a comprehensive communication device customized to its owner's identity and preferences. It was a fashion statement and a tool for intimately connecting and sharing with friends. Jobs's reframing created a context in which carriers, developers, and owners could co-exist harmoniously.

Another example of reframing can be seen in the resolution of the Troubles in Northern Ireland (1968-1998), a civil war. The Troubles were resolved when both Britain and Ireland became members of the European Union, giving Great Britain the opportunity to devolve powers to local authorities in Northern Ireland. The shared membership in the EU and the possibility of a new power sharing arrangement changed the context for the dispute. Under the new identity, the border between Great Britain and Ireland lost salience in the daily lives of the people on both sides. Political leaders on all sides took advantage of the historical moment to reframe success and effectively end the conflict. Unfortunately, since Britain withdrew from the European Union in 2020, the reframing has faded and many of the old tensions have started to reappear.

In the examples above, the resistance presented by conflicting subcommunities can be interpreted as the need to find a new offer. The first example illustrates customizing the offer to each subcommunity by direct negotiations. The second illustrates a leader reframing the issue to provide a new context for all the subcommunities, leading to a new offer that is attractive to all. The third illustrates that the flow of history changes the context, and the leaders take advantage to craft a new offer.

Unfortunately, these ideas of customizing offers and reframing may not be enough to bring all the subcommunities into the new practice. Some subcommunities may be so deeply in conflict that tailored or reframed offers do not work. This situation is frequently called a wicked problem. The conflicting groups are deadlocked in a power struggle with interlocking histories and wildly different interpretations.[1] (We will discuss wicked problems in more depth in Chapter 17, Mobilizing.) One way to deal with this challenge is to bring representatives of all the groups together in a facilitated meeting to search for common concerns. In the resulting dialog, the participants may modify how they articulate their concerns as they talk and listen – in effect helping each other to reframe the problem to something mutually agreeable.

The Power of External Forces

Many communities are forced into change by external forces beyond their control. Examples are sudden emergencies, disruptions by other businesses, and avalanches. Even in these extreme cases, communities often react by resisting the need to change.

Natural disasters such as fires, earthquakes, and hurricanes can suddenly make normal practices inoperative. People may have to evacuate their homes, tolerate power and communication outages, find food, and repair damage. Shortages of food and fuel impair fire, police, and medical services. A common way to resist the disaster is to fall into a mood of helpless panic, hoping for a savior to appear. Public agencies try to avoid panic reactions by advance planning. They prepare for contingencies by planning how first responders will

---

[1] Nancy Roberts. 2023. *Design Strategy.* MIT Press.

react, stockpiling emergency supplies, positioning supplies at key distribution points, practicing interagency coordination, and practicing response exercises.

A second kind of change-inducing force is "disruptive innovation", a term coined by Harvard Professor Clayton Christensen. He meant an innovation that renders an existing line of business obsolete and unprofitable. In disruptive innovation, an established company's line of business is challenged by a competitor's cheaper, lower-quality version. Eventually the competitor builds higher quality and starts siphoning off the established company's customers. This induces a dilemma for the incumbent: should they stick with the successful current model or change to an unfamiliar, potentially more competitive model? Many established companies have been disrupted by this process and subsequently disappeared. Resistance often takes the form of complacency and reluctance to change the business model. It is better for business leaders to constantly monitor for signs, such as customer loss, that competitors are appealing to their customers. The key to avoiding disruption is developing a new practice while the earlier practice is still profitable.

Kodak is a famous example of disruption. Kodak invented digital photography but did not start a new line of business to offer it. Competitors picked it up and established themselves in the market. Kodak ultimately folded when film photography was upended by digital. Their resistance to change led to their demise. Netflix, on the other hand, saw a disruption coming and prepared for it. Their original business offered DVD movies for rent. When the technology of digital streaming started to appear, they set up a second line of business to distribute movies by Internet streaming. Eventually the DVD business dried up and Netflix became a streaming company.

A third change-inducing force is a social avalanche. This is a rapid transition in the everyday practices and institutions of a community.[2] Its arrival shocks the community's ecosystem. Everything changes. Businesses, standard operating practices, and identities are swept away. Power is reconfigured. The precursors may be subtle and easily dismissed. Even when seen, precursors only signal that the conditions for a tipping point are ripe; that is enough for wise leaders to prepare without knowing when the change will happen. Science cannot predict the moments of transition and technology cannot control them.

Avalanches can be triggered by changes in relative costs within the ecosystem that may at first appear incremental. For example, an automotive avalanche has been forming as the costs of electric vehicles drop below those of internal combustion engines. Tony Seba, a Silicon Valley entrepreneur, estimates that the cross-over will happen by 2030. Ray Kurweil, futurist and entrepreneur, predicts an avalanche by 2045 when the power of information technology equals the power of the brain, an event he called the Singularity. Andy Grove, CEO of Intel Corporation developed a "10X rule of thumb" to advise when avalanches might happen: a new technology with a 10-times advantage over existing technology attracts large scale adoption. He tasked his research labs to prototype the new technology to enable Intel to react competitively when the time came.

A trend analysis for higher education by the Institute for Public Policy Research in 2013 predicted an education avalanche is coming but noted it could take years to manifest.[3] They examined 10 dimensions of colleges and universities that are being unbundled by technology. A student now has options to pick a subset of those dimensions at a much cheaper price. The authors gave no specific

---

[2] P. Denning. 2014. Avalanches are coming. *Comm ACM (CACM)* 57, 6 (June 2014), 34–36. https://doi.org/10.1145/2602324

[3] S. Rizvi, K. Donnelly, M. Barber. 2013. An avalanche is coming: Higher education and the revolution ahead. Institute for Public Policy Research. https://www.ippr.org/publications/an-avalanche-is-coming-higher-education-and-the-revolution-ahead

time for the avalanche to hit, but issues like hyperinflation of tuitions or accumulation of student debt cannot go on forever.

Observers of these impending and slow-moving changes are not trying to scare people but rather to alert them to the coming changes so they are prepared to adapt and can create new products and services for the world after the change.

Resistance

Although resistance is normal and expected, it is still unnerving. As innovation leaders, we must learn to cope with resistance and navigate successfully through it. Resistance is a negative assessment of your offer accompanied by social power to thwart you. It appears in several guises:

- Unwillingness to change institutional structures, rules, and other social agreements
- Discomfort and frustration when trying out the new practice
- Perceived threats to identity, standing in the community, comfort, or power
- Negative assessments spread in the network ("viral gossip" and "bad buzz")
- Apathy and other negative moods, especially resignation and resentment
- Organized opposition by powerful players or groups

Resisters are not "bad guys" – their concerns are often legitimate and their assessments grounded. You have a greater chance to address their resistance by listening and addressing their concerns, than by pressing or compelling them to accept your solution. You can inadvertently provoke greater resistance by not listening to their concerns and instead trying to pitch, convince, persuade, cajole, or coerce them into adoption. It often helps to mobilize influential early adopters as voices of support in the network. Always be listening and sensing concerns.

Resistance is not uniform. Some subcommunities may endorse, while others may offer varying degrees of resistance. Sometimes you will find that the concerns of a particular subcommunity cannot be reconciled with the concerns of another subcommunity. For example, a technology that moves decision making power to the front line and away from managers might be embraced by those on the front line and opposed by the managers. This can be a real challenge for which there are no easy answers. We will discuss navigation strategies for apparent irreconcilable differences in Chapter 17, Mobilizing.

Somatics of Resistance

Although resistance is normal and expected, it is still unsettling. People react to resistance in four ways:

- Ignore. Pretend it does not exist and does not matter to you.
- Evade. Step aside and do not engage with it.
- Defend. Meet the challenge with a strong defense, using force if necessary. Overwhelm the resisters with pushback, explanations, and declarations.
- Blend. Flow with the resistance, seeking to understand the concerns behind it and revising offers to take care of those concerns. Mobilize followers to build social power behind your offers and neutralize the social power of the resistance.

In our work, we have found that ignoring and evading do not deal effectively with the resistance. Defend is a conditioned tendency often associated with military and political communities in which you get a powerful person to declare that your way is "the way" or you organize force to crush the resistance or foment an insurgency. While it may be perceived to be effective, defending against resistance rarely outlives the tenure of the leader. When the powerful advocate departs, the community abandons the new practice and reverts to the old. Blending means to align your momentum with the resister, by listening, acknowledging their concerns, adapting your envisioning story, and offering to respond to those concerns. Blending is the most effective way to counter resistance. Blending leads to improvements in the offer and creates more satisfied members of your community.

For many of us, the greatest obstacle is self-resistance. We make negative self-assessments that bring us moods of apathy, complacency, resignation, or resentment. When you encounter resistance, take a close look. Is it coming from others? Or from you?

Exercise: Four Responses to Resistance

We illustrate the possible reactions to resistance with a somatic exercise we call the *four-response* exercise. We ask the members of the group to pick a partner, then designate one as A and the other B. Partners stand facing each other about 20 feet apart. A is the innovation leader and B is the challenger. A brings the offer by walking a collision course with outstretched right arm, palm aiming directly toward B's sternum. B then reacts as listed below. This is repeated four times, once for each reaction.

- Ignore. B does not react or move. A walks straight into B and jolts B. B often looks surprised.
- Evade. B sees A coming and simply steps out of the way, letting A pass by. A does not attempt to follow B.
- Defend. B blocks or acts aggressively to stop A.
- Blend. As A comes within arm's distance, B turns 180° to the right and starts walking next to A. During the turn B reaches out with left hand and contacts A by placing back of left wrist lightly on A's outstretched right wrist – with just enough pressure to be present but not enough to force anything. A

does not attempt to change direction. It usually takes two or three tries with the blend until B figures out the turn that results in walking alongside A while touching A's wrist.

Nearly everyone prefers the blend by a wide margin over the other moves. It feels satisfying to form a connection with the other person and walk side by side with them. In conversations, blending takes the form of the listener showing interest in the offer of the other, for example, "Your offer is interesting, I would like to find out more." Blending does not mean you have to accept the offer or even to agree with it. It means moving with the other person and learning more about the offer and concerns behind it.

Exercise: Redirected Blending

After the group has completed the four-responses exercise, we introduce an advanced exercise called *redirected blending*. The idea is that B initially blends with A's momentum as above, and then B redirects A into a new direction. The new direction represents B inducing A to modify the offer. This is accomplished by B varying the pressure on the wrist contact until A responds and follows. B finds it fairly easy to get A to turn to the left by applying more pressure on A's wrist. B is likely to find it harder to get A to turn to the right because that is associated with lightening the pressure on A's wrist. A has to be sensitive and follow. After some experimentation with repeated attempts, most people figure out how to do these redirections. With a little practice, A will find B's redirections to be compelling and follow them even with very light wrist pressure. The conversational analog might be, "How about a slight change, would you consider that?" Or "I think it would be good for you to talk to C about this, here, let me introduce you" (and the redirection moves toward C).

Exercise: Group Blending

A final exercise is called *group blending*. The Redirected Blending exercise can flow directly into this.

After B redirects A in a new direction, B hands off the blend to another person in the room, who replaces B walking alongside A and further redirecting A. This is repeated with a handoff to another, then another, until everyone in the room has participated in the redirection of A.

Our experience is that the group likes the group blending the best. A conversational analog is a group where each person builds on what has been said so far and eventually the whole group converges on a common statement.

These somatic exercises show that blending has a strong, satisfying, felt effect on the participants. Blending produces action, whereas the other three moves only produce inaction and standoffs.

Conclusion

We began this chapter talking about resistance, a natural response to offers for a change in practice. Resistance appears when any change – incremental, disruptive, or avalanche – threatens the equilibrium of the social system. Resistance tends to be larger for proposed changes with larger impacts on comfort, identity, or power. Coping with resistance is best done by learning to listening for and blend with concerns. Effective strategies when dealing with conflicting subcommunities include customizing offers, reframing issues, and searching for common concerns among the contenders in a wicked problem. We concluded with somatic exercises to teach what effective blending feels like.

• • •

Resistance

We have now concluded Part II of this book. Figure 2 on the next page is a map of the social space we have discussed in Part II. The main action of the space is in the middle, an endless cycle of conversations begetting practices begetting conversations. On the left side, coordinated social action toward a purpose is depicted as a game. On the right side, conversations produce commitments and then actions, among which are leadership actions that shape the game. In the pervasive background are moods. These distinctions are all useful for navigation, which means to move effectively in the fog of uncertainty, probing and watching reactions as you maneuver ever closer to your goal.

The phenomena in this picture are invisible in the common interpretation of communication as exchange of messages. By this point social space should now be completely visible to you, and you are prepared for the advanced practices discussed next in Part III.

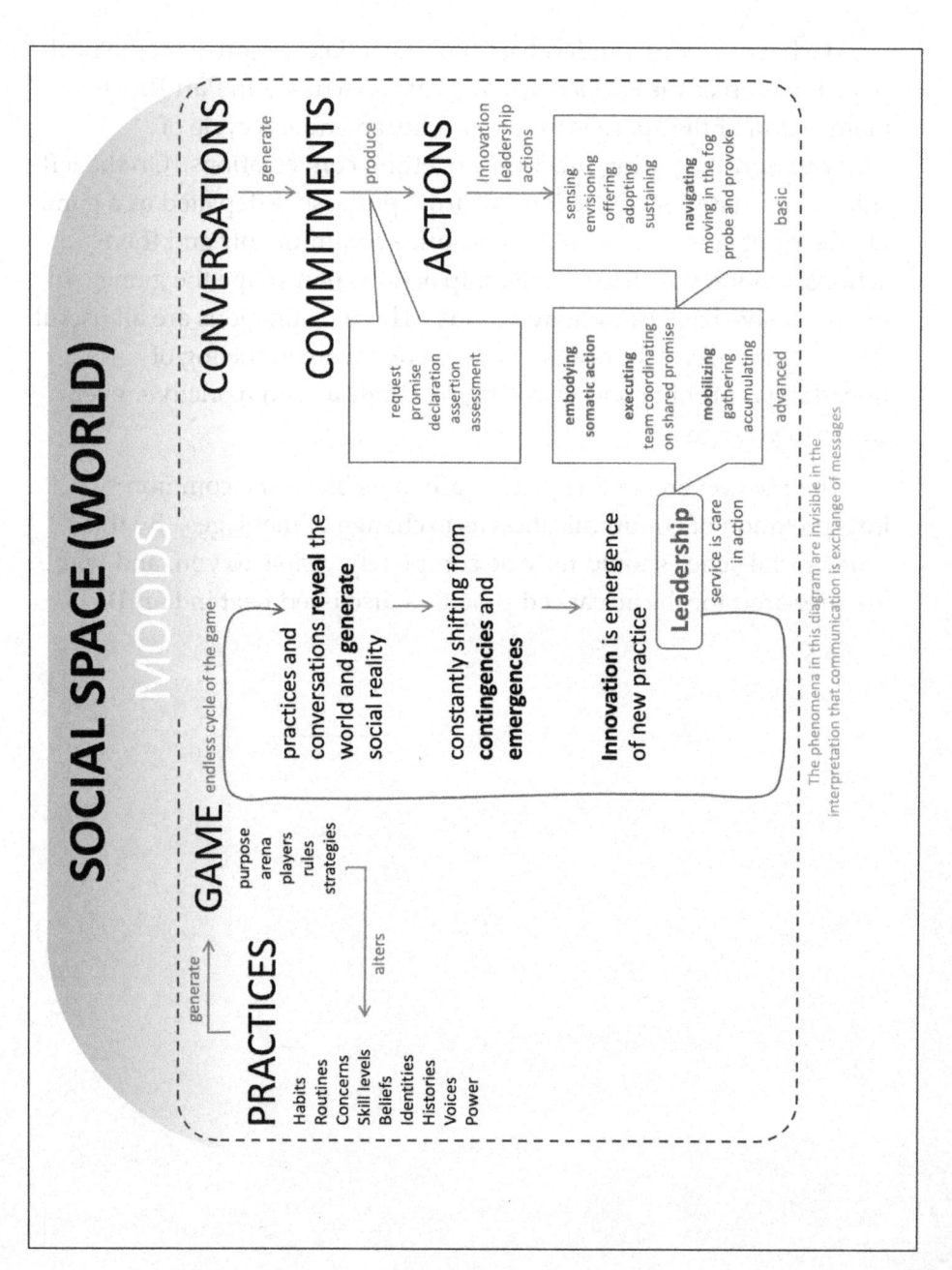

Figure 2. Map of social space

Part III
Bringing It into the World

15
EMBODYING

In the beginning is the body. We are all born into a body and through the body we come to know the world and ourselves. It is only through the body that we are present and make sense to others and become evident to others, the environment, and the world. This is so obvious that it is invisible to us.
— Richard Strozzi Heckler

Presence — or its lack — has enormous consequences for leaders. Presence grants genuine leadership authority by building trust and inspiring others. This is quite a bit different from the leadership that is conferred by position, title, or status.
— Richard Strozzi Heckler

Mr. Duffy lived a little distance from his body.
— James Joyce

In 1914, James Joyce wrote *Dubliners*, a collection of short stories. One of his stories, "A Painful Case", features Mr. Duffy, a cashier at a bank who had no friends and lived alone. He tolerated no deviations from a rigid daily routine. He had a platonic affair with the wife of a ship captain, but angrily broke it off shortly after she reached over and touched his cheek. Four years later, he learned she died in an accident. He experienced a few moments of remorse for having lost his one chance at love, but soon returned to his life of aloneness. In saying,

"Mr. Duffy lived a little distance from his body," Joyce meant that Duffy was always an outside observer of himself, never really wanting to experience himself or anyone else. He could not connect with anyone, even himself.

A story in military folklore tells that in WW II, British artillery gunnery teams launched fewer rounds per hour than their American counterparts. An investigative team concluded that the difference was the result of British soldiers stepping back before the gun was fired and holding their position for a few seconds after the gun was fired. The American teams did not do this. The mystified investigators eventually found a veteran of WW I who knew what was going on. He told them: "They are holding the horses." In WW I and before, the guns were hauled into position by teams of horses. The soldiers had to restrain the horses during the firing, because they would bolt at the concussion. Twenty years later, the practice remained in the training of gunnery teams long after the horses were gone.

These two stories remind us of important lessons for leadership. Joyce teaches that awareness of our own body is a precursor for awareness of what is happening for anyone else. Without that self-awareness, we remain alone and incapable of leading anything. The artillery folklore teaches that practices live on in our bodies long after their purpose is forgotten.

The ability to perform skillfully without conscious thought is called "embodied action". Embodiment is not the same as having knowledge because you can have knowledge without being able to perform. Knowledge usually refers to information that can be encoded as bits and stored as an organized collection, whereas action is fulfilling a commitment in a situation. Performance skill refers to the ability to perform competent action without thinking. The information involved is in subconscious mental processes, muscle memory, neural states, and electro-chemical patterns of living tissues. Skill information cannot be represented and acted on by a machine.

Embodying

Remember the controversy about expert systems – software systems that were supposed to have enough knowledge to perform as well as human experts? Their promise has not been realized because the information they need for embodied action cannot be recorded in a machine processable form.

Our purpose in this chapter is to focus on attaining embodiment of practice that is coherent with our commitments – the somatics unifying mind and body. We will discuss four core practices: *awareness*, a practice of being aware of feelings and reactions in your own body and in others, *centering*, a practice of maintaining physical and emotional balance while in motion, *blending*, a practice of aligning your energy and momentum with others, and *conditioned tendency retraining*, a practice of unlearning an unproductive practice and learning a new practice in its place.

Practices that Bring Forth New Practices

Embodied action arises in those who have achieved the level of competence or higher in the Dreyfus skill acquisition process. In innovation, embodied action shows up in two ways: leader practices and community practices.

When an innovation is in the making, leaders exercise their skill at the eight practices. Let's call them the leadership practices.

When an innovation is adopted, the community becomes competent at the new practices. Let's call them the adopted practices. For a community to be competent at the practice, most of the members must be competent not only with the practice, but also with coordinating with others in the practice.

We can then say that *the innovator's work is exercising leadership practices to generate new adopted practices*. In other words, the leader's practices bring forth new community practices. Table 1 summarizes how the Dreyfus process appears as leaders and community achieve greater levels of competence. Thus, the innovation leader is a student of the eight practices, with coaches and mentors as the teachers. The community members are students of the proposed new practice, with the innovation leader as the teacher.

Table 1. Learning Processes of Leaders and Community

	Beginner	**Competent**
Leader	Basic leader practices look like scripts to follow for different, linear steps of innovation process. It is difficult to know when it is time to move to next step. It is unclear what to do if community persons resist the proposal or contingencies appear. Basic terminology like conversation or practice is unfamiliar.	Leader practices are embodied. Leader engages them as needed without thought, generating a nonlinear blend of conversations producing essential outcomes. Leader senses resonances and concerns and responds to resistance and contingencies. Leader sees that the community must learn the proposed new practice with leader coaching their embodiment.
Members of community	Proposed new practice looks like a good idea as a possible way to resolve a concern. Acquiring the new practice requires giving up familiar things to get something that is still unknown and risky. So many questions remain unanswered.	All community members have embodied the new practice. They engage as familiar routines that need no special thought. Their concerns about risk and implementation have been answered. Members say the new practice is comfortable and gives better results than the old way.

The Somatics Challenge

The innovator's challenge is to get the members of a community to adopt (embody) a new practice. When that is accomplished, community members will speak differently, act differently, feel differently, and even see the world differently. To meet this challenge, the innovator must manage and maintain coherence among the three dimensions of every practice: language, body, and moods. It is easy to segregate the three dimensions and forget their coherence. All three have distinctive vocabularies and professions – linguists for language, physical trainers for body, and psychologists for moods.

The common approach to adoption conversations emphasizes the linguistic aspect, downplays the bodily aspect, and ignores the mood aspect. The five basic leader practices appear as selected scripts of words to be memorized. We are likely to be blindsided by breakdowns from emotional or body reactions. For example, if we become fixated on "offering" as a linguistic procedure, we forget that our offers will be listened as valuable only if they make sense to our listeners in the context of their existing practices, moods, and body reactions. We will be surprised at resistance to what reads, on paper, like a well-crafted offer.

This linguistic tendency is called *mind-body dualism*: it celebrates the power of the mind and discounts the power of the body. Mind-body dualism puts the brain as the master that reasons and decides, and the body as the servant that implements the brain's decisions. We tend to ignore our bodies except when we are concerned about health, appearance, sex, sports, and fashion. Mind-body dualism inclines us to focus on communications as exchanges of messages and communication breakdowns as misunderstandings of words spoken. In the process we ignore the way we and others listen through our bodies. The antidote to this is somatic integration, achieved by these four practices:

1. *Awareness*: We are aware of signals from our listeners that reveal their real concerns and how our own behaviors are affecting them.
2. *Centering*: We stay balanced while moving, so that physical forces and our emotional reactivity do not knock us down or take us out of the game.
3. *Blending*: Our automatic behaviors and skills enable us to join with others in a smooth, graceful, and harmonious flow.
4. *Retraining conditioned tendencies*: Some of our automatic behaviors disconnect us from our listeners or push them away; we identify them and retrain ourselves into more productive behaviors.

The next four sections explore each of these practices more deeply.

Somatic Awareness

The field of somatics, founded in 1976 by Thomas Hanna (1928-1990), has developed a different interpretation that reveals how to overcome breakdowns when language, body, and moods are at cross purposes. Somatics is concerned with the unity of mind, body, and emotions. It counters mind-body dualism. This field has developed these principles:

- The mind and body are not separate, but form and act as a unity.
- The brain is influenced by experiences of signals carried by the nervous system from all parts of the body.
- Moods predispose how we think and act.
- The history of our experience conditions our perceptions of the world and shapes our capabilities.

Embodying

- Communication is not words being exchanged – it is a dance among people as they speak, interpret, and react with moods, emotions, and conditioned tendencies.
- Practice is the foundation for learning and mastery.

The somatic practices of awareness, centering, and blending are central for innovators. We cannot be effective at these three unless we understand them as *experiences* in our bodies. We will show you somatic exercises so that you can experience them for yourself. These exercises rest on three principles. The first is, *awareness creates choice*. Every practice is based on distinctions that give you choices. Initially, the distinctions may be unfamiliar; you will have to practice until you notice them effortlessly and gain the freedom to choose.

The second is, *energy follows attention*. Focus your practice on what you want to accomplish, not what you want to avoid. If you focus too much on what you want to avoid, you will have trouble avoiding it.

The third is, *your body is always practicing something*. It is easy to develop unproductive habits that block the outcome that you want from the practice. You cannot cut corners by putting up with unwanted outcomes, for then your sloppiness and tolerance will become part of your habit. Malcolm Gladwell's famous claim "practice for 10,000 hours" is often interpreted as "you will master something if you practice it 8 hours a day, every day, for 3.5 years." This is grossly misleading because it is all too easy to practice the wrong thing and master a bad habit that cannot be broken.

Somatics works with these principles to integrate the dimensions of language, body, and moods. All three dimensions are interconnected; a change in one will produce a change in the others. Being aware of these dimensions, in yourself and in others, is the ideal we called "listening to the listening".

INTERPRETATIONS	BODY	MOODS
values	habits, skills, practices	joy
beliefs	awareness	care
culture	attention	wonder
standards	breath	ambition
community	energy	resolution
background		
assessments	centering	
personal history		
prior commitments	open | closed	inquiry
	tense | relaxed	perplexity
	present | distant	bafflement
	contracted | extended	
	grounded | ungrounded	
	connected | disconnected	
		apathy
	conditioned tendencies	confusion
		overwhelm
	blending	resignation
		resentment

Figure 1. Somatic practices confer sensibilities to the three dimensions of mind and body that must be integrated for successful action.

Centering

Centering is a practice of staying in balance physically and emotionally. Physical balance means that you are completely balanced around your center of gravity, which is located behind your navel. Your weight is equally distributed front, back, and sideways. Your breathing is full, every breath fills all five lobes of your lungs and takes your diaphragm through its full range of motion. You are not tensed up. You feel a state of readiness, poised to move in any direction. You are less likely to be knocked over if something strikes you.

The martial arts have a saying that energy follows attention. That means your energy tends to accumulate in the part of your body you are paying attention to. One of the guidelines for getting centered is to bring your attention to your navel area. Today, the most common way

Embodying

to be off center is to "be in your head". Your energy is focused in your cranium, perhaps because you have been thinking hard about something. Your breath is shallow, meaning that your diaphragm expands only enough to bring air into your upper lung lobes, leaving the middle and lower lobes oxygen deprived and unable to oxygenate your blood. You are easily pushed off balance in this state. Moreover, because your attention is focused on yourself, you are unaware of what is going on for other people; they experience you as "disconnected".

Exercise: Energy Follows Attention

The idea that Energy follows attention highlights an exercise to become aware of your body and not get locked into your head. Sit (or stand) quietly and just notice each part of your body. Notice each part for the full duration of a breath that reaches all your lungs. I feel my head. I feel my neck. I feel my shoulders. I feel my front. I feel my back. I feel my stomach. I feel my tailbone. I feel my thighs. I feel my calves. I feel my feet. You can amplify this practice by visualizing tension in each part of your body getting released as you exhale, like smoke exiting your body. You can reduce tension and blood pressure this way.

Exercise: Centered Standing

Once you are aware, you can stand. Adjust your hips, shoulders, and head until you achieve balance. Move your hips sideways back and forth until you find the place where weight is equal on both feet. Lean forward and back until you find the place where weight is equal between ball and heel. Having thus found the centered position of your hips, repeat for your torso and shoulders, moving sideways and frontways back and forth until your shoulders are perfectly balanced over your hips. Repeat this for your head.

Exercise: Centered Balance

You can perform a simple exercise to experience how centering balances you. Stand and get centered as above. Have a friend push on one shoulder. How much pressure does it take before you start to stumble? Purposely put yourself into an uncentered state, for example by going into your head. While there your friend again pushes your shoulder to gauge how much pressure is needed to push you off balance. Most people find that it takes significantly more pressure to push them off balance when centered, compared to when off-center.

Putting it to Work

After you get skilled at finding your center, you can put this to work as you move. After moments of intensity, breakdown, stimulation, or stress, ask if you are centered. Were you thrown off by tension from a mood, emotion, or conditioned tendency? Recenter. As in retraining a conditioned tendency, you will find that the time between noticing when you are off center and regaining your center will diminish. Eventually you will be able to completely recenter in the time it takes for one breath. There is much wisdom in the adage that, when you are tensed and about to do something you'll regret, take a breath and relax before acting.

Now you can notice that stress, emotions, mood changes, surprises, shocks, and more can throw you off center. Emotional reactivity causes you to tense up, knocking you off physical balance as well as putting you into an emotional state where you cannot deal with the issue very well. Emotional balance means that you can maintain a stable mood despite emotional stresses and your reactivity seldom gets the better of you. Emotional imbalance induces physical imbalance because of the tension it generates. This works in the opposite direction as well: sustained physical imbalance promotes emotional reactivity. For example, a posture of shoulders curled forward and slightly up with head bowed is very conducive to resignation. This posture frequently accompanies a habit of resignation. Sometimes you can break a mood by entering a posture that is inconsistent with that mood. Being centered is conducive to the mood of serenity.

It is impossible to remain in the centered state all the time. A random thought can distract the mind. A physical blow can disrupt balance. An emotional trigger can bring up anger or fear. What matters is how quickly we notice that we have gone off center and return to center. The re-centering practices outlined above can help you do this rapidly. Students of the founder of Aikido, Morihei Ueshiba, told him that they admired his ability to be centered all the time. He replied that he frequently found himself off center, as they did, but that he had learned to come back to center very quickly.

Leadership centering means all the above. Physical center means, by moving smoothly and gracefully, you generate a sense of confidence, which engenders trust. Emotional center means that other people's emotions and moods do not trigger negative reactions in you, and you are able to interact with them without being caught up in their emotions. In this centered state, it is easy to remain focused. You will not sense well, envision well, offer well, or foster adoption well if you are off-center. If someone starts to knock you off center, you know how take your breath and quickly recenter – they will hardly notice your fleeting imbalance.

Be mindful that when you encounter resistance to your innovation proposal, your opponents will purposely try to throw you off center, especially by launching emotional ungrounded negative assessments. If they can throw you off center, they have derailed you in your pursuit of a new practice they do not like. When you can maintain your center, you will find it easy to mobilize followers for your movement, overcoming the resistance. The centered leader is more able to blend with resistance.

Blending

Blending is a practice of meeting someone's momentum, moving with it, and then possibly channeling it in a new direction. This applies to physical momentum and as well conversational momentum.

If the person is in physical motion, blending would mean that you turn as necessary and start moving alongside that person in their direction and speed. Now the two of you are moving together. If the person is in a conversational momentum, blending means to take interest in where the person is going and explore it with them. Now the two of you are one conversation.

In the previous chapter, we mentioned blending as the most effective way of overcoming resistance – blend with the resistance and then, by listening and adapting to concerns, guide it in a new direction. The common idea of a win-win outcome is an example of a successful blend – the parties all conclude they gain something from working together.

When dealing with wicked problems and organization messes, blending with concerns and orienting action around them is the best way to initiate a resolution. We know an attaché who illustrated this when he got involved in conversations to allow the Navy to operate in a new seaport in another country. Many people were involved – politicians, representatives of foreign governments and shipping companies who would send ships to the new harbor, political leaders of the host country, and mayors of all the towns and cities in the region to be served by the seaport. Although all these players liked the general idea of a regional seaport, they were very protective of their local and organizational interests and would not agree to anything that did not serve those interests. The seaport could become reality only if all parties said yes, and be scuttled if any party said no. What a challenge! Our attaché friend spent many weeks visiting with all the parties, listening to their concerns, and learning what offers would attract them. He iterated the conversations over and over to

Embodying

find blends that brought everyone together. Eventually they all accepted Navy ships using the port. When combined, the offers represented all the commitments needed to operate in the new seaport.

The process of blending many parties into a large coalition obviously requires considerable skill. Yet the basic skills are the same – sensing, envisioning, offering, adopting. As the leader, you must listen carefully to the concerns of each party and find possibilities for blending with their concerns. The listening aspect is especially important. You do not just listen for words and interpretations; you listen somatically with your whole body. Listening to their moods, anxieties, histories, and identities is much easier and deeper if you listen with all your senses. Somatic listening is a whole-body experience, a feeling of resonance that enables you not only to listen to what the people are saying, but also to concerns they have not said.

In the social space of a large community, conversations coalesce into waves of motion, like ocean currents pulling us, not always in the direction we want to go. We have little control over them. We can either move with the waves (blend with them) or stay out of their way. These waves manifest in a variety of ways. People feel so compelled to talk about a particular topic, it is hard to them to change the subject. Certain memes spread like wildfire through the community; rumors and conspiracy theories can't be stamped out; fads and buzzwords won't go away; certain topics or orientations can get you ostracized; and so on. There is a somatic feeling of being swept by these waves and currents.

Somatic exercises are a good way to develop and hone a sensibility for blending. Blending's physical feel is very rewarding. In the previous chapter on resistance (Chapter 14), we presented blending exercises to practice different ways to respond to an incoming request and mobilize others to join you. The exercises show you the feel of getting close to blending with another person. In the chapter on conversations (Chapter 6) we introduced another somatic exercise – "walking in the room" – that reveals what blending is like in a moving group. Of all the ways of walking and paying attention, people most like creating open spaces with declarations, and then walking into those spaces.

Conditioned Tendencies

Sometimes, despite our best efforts at the eight practices, a breakdown blocks our way. How we react to the breakdown strongly influences our success at resolving it. Our conditioned tendencies are the biggest sources of unproductive reactions.

Conditioned tendencies are automatic reactions to stimuli. They are practices learned at an earlier time that show up without conscious choice when triggered by an event reminding us of the past. Some are positive, such as jumping away from a hot fire. Others are negative, such as tensing up and becoming confrontational when someone disagrees with you.

Here are four examples of common conditioned tendencies.

Mark, one of our students, spent much of his time in a mood of overwhelm. He often reported that he could not complete everything on his plate because there simply wasn't enough time. Being conscientious he stayed up late at night to catch up. He was getting four hours sleep and the sleep deficit was impacting his health. One day he was so deep into overwhelm that he could not function. He asked for our help. The first thing we did was to ask him to pause and make a realistic assessment of his situation. He prepared a spreadsheet listing all his commitments, how much time he should spend on each, and how much he actually spent. To his amazement, the listed commitments demanded more than 168 hours a week to fulfill satisfactorily, and the amount of time he actually spent was over 100 hours. He decided to cancel some of the commitments, delegate others, and scale back on the remaining so that his demand for time and actual time were both under 60 hours. After he implemented this,

Embodying

his mood changed to ambition and resolution and his health improved. As we looked to see why he had taken on so many commitments, we discovered a negative conditioned tendency. He grew up in a family in which saying "no" was not accepted. He had learned that it was disrespectful to contradict his elders or say "no" to their wishes. This practice was deeply ingrained into his body. It only became a problem when he took on a professional career. Even though he felt intensely uncomfortable when he knew he ought to say "no" to a request, he could not help himself: his automatic "yes" trumped his better intentions.

Mark's story illustrates how a conditioned tendency may be positive as long as it produces useful outcomes; but it becomes an impediment when it prevents him from attaining his current goals. His conditioned tendency was outside his awareness and took over so fast that he did not know what happened. He had no choice in how he could respond to the next request.

In the martial arts, novices almost always tense up when confronted by an attacker. Tensing up prevents an effective response and lands the novice on the mat in a compromised position. The novice cannot relax despite the exhortations of the instructor to relax. With training and practice, they gradually learn to maintain a relaxed, centered stance that enables them to move toward, and blend with, the attacker. Tensing up is a tendency hardly confined to the martial arts. Many people tense up and respond poorly in a conversation where they think they are under attack.

In the late 1970s, Fernando Flores noticed a widespread tendency for people to accept and act on ungrounded, gratuitous assessments from others. This made them susceptible to manipulation via distracting and ad hominem assessments. To help overcome the tendency, Flores invented a "negative assessment exercise" (see Chapter 10). The people took turns giving negative assessments and observing their body reactions. He gave them a script to retrain their tendency to automatically grant permission for anyone to make assessments. After a few repetitions of the exercise, most people learned to choose a different reaction from the original "What is wrong with me?"

Conditioned tendencies can also become embodied into the practices of teams, producing team malfunctions. Many married couples, for example, consult with counselors to learn how their conditioned interactions are producing negative effects and how they could adopt new practices that are positive for them. Small teams are sometimes stymied during after-action meetings when they cannot share honest assessments about performance with defensive teammates, and the team as a whole cannot learn from its mistakes. In these cases, the prescription is the same: design a new interaction practice that produces a better outcome and learn to substitute it for the old conditioned practice.

In all these cases, somatic training taught how to maintain center and blend with other persons. As innovators, we need to be sensitive to our own conditioned tendencies and those of our audience. Our tendencies can prevent our success in the eight practices.

Once you have detected an unwanted conditioned tendency, what can you do about it? The good news is that the conditioned tendency is a practice, and you can learn a new practice to replace it. The tougher news is that it takes time and dedicated practice to do this. In retraining a conditioned tendency, you will face three obstacles.

The first obstacle is deciding what practice to substitute for the unwanted tendency. For example, if your tendency is always say "yes" to requests you might instead decide to say "I'll get back to you about this." Or if your tendency is to defend against a request, instead of aggressively declining you could say "That is interesting. Can we talk more?" Be warned that the new practice you select will feel uncomfortable because your body is not used to it.

Embodying

The next obstacle is to notice the trigger event before the tendency gains control. Noticing might take a few minutes, maybe an hour, or occasionally a day or more. You may react with great disappointment that you did not notice it in time to perform your substitute practice. Don't dwell in disappointment. Keep noticing. The time between trigger and noticing will get progressively shorter. One day you will discover that you notice the trigger before it fires the tendency. At last, you have the choice to substitute the new practice! The old tendency is no longer in control.

The final obstacle is to realize you are a beginner at the new practice and it may not always go well. Just keep at it and you will become progressively better at the new practice and progressively less uncomfortable in engaging it. It will become natural. The old practice has been banished.

You can accelerate this process significantly by getting a coach and keeping a log. Try to log when a trigger event occurs and when you noticed it. When you reach the stage that you can substitute the new practice, record what happened and how comfortable you felt. Your coach can help you see how your tendency looks to another party and keep you focused on gaining your skill at the new practice.

Exercise: Declining Requests

We often find ourselves saying "yes" to requests we do not want. These "yeses" overfill our plate with unwanted commitments and drags us into a mood of overwhelm. Your inability to fulfill all your commitments erodes other people's trust in us. A simple practice can help break this tendency. Get a partner. Tell your partner something that you have trouble saying "no" to. For the next five minutes your partner asks you over and over, with as many different tactics as possible, to do that thing. The tactics can include flattery, shame, promises of rewards, threats to your well being, threats to terminate your relationship, and so on. You respond to each request and entreaty simply with a serene "I decline." Stick to that response no matter what the other person says or what brimstone they threaten to bring down on you. Simply observe your reactions. After five minutes, you will feel like an old hand at declining a request. Return the favor for your partner by reversing roles and you try to get them to say "yes" to the "no" thing they are struggling with.

Importance of Teachers

When learning new practices, we are dealing with unfamiliar behaviors or invisible ones like conditioned tendencies. We need someone else's eyes to watch our progress and advise on what they see. Who is your teacher as you learn the leadership practices? Is your teacher more experienced than you? And as you work with your community to adopt their new practice, are you their teacher and coach? You harness the power of alliances and voices of influencers who speak for you. You teach your most enthusiastic early adopters how to promote and teach the new practice to their fellow community members.

As described in Chapter 2, teachers are essential in the game. Players in finite games need teachers to show them the skills and coaches to coordinate their play and achieve their objectives. Teachers are important for the infinite game, for they bring new talent to the game and lead innovations in the game. The influence of the teacher remains long after the teacher is gone and is forgotten. Remember Lao Tzu: "When the master's work is done, the people say 'Amazing, we did it all by ourselves'".

Emotional Fortitude

Emotional fortitude is the ability to main a steady emotional state even when under duress. Emotional fortitude is a reward of serenity, the mood in which you accept what you cannot change. Untamed emotional reactivity can overwhelm your desire to remain emotionally balanced. Emotional reactivity is not a conditioned tendency, it is an over-sensitivity to circumstances around you. It can have a similar effect of diverting you from your goals.

Here are practices that help tame reactivity and maintain emotional balance.

Meditating. This is a practice of sitting quietly and letting go of whatever chatter your mind conjures up. Your mind can be quite amazing at generating chatter even when you wish to be quiet. For those who have trouble letting go of the thoughts that well up and seize attention, try listening instead of letting go. Listen to the silence. Listen without judgment to whatever comes. The ideal meditative state is one in which you feel unified with the living universe. Meditation practice, over time, teaches you how to let go of random thoughts and distractions, thus allowing you to maintain your attention on your goals and conditioning you to let go of things that trigger emotional reactions.

Observing assessments as they arise. Although we are constantly generating assessments, we often are unaware we are doing so. We are also constantly the targets of many assessments, to which we react without questioning the relevance or grounding. Counter this by spending time observing the assessments that come up in your conversations and interactions. For example, when reading a book or an article, or engaging in a conversation, notice what assessments are provoked in you and in others. Notice what emotions these assessments trigger. After a while you will be amazed at how many assessments you make and receive, and how reactive you are to them. You can begin to retrain those reactions by declining to engage with them, as you did in the declining request exercise. You can refer back to the script you used in the negative assessment exercise (Chapter 10). You can use that script to *silently* disengage yourself from the emotional pull of the assessment and to engage you into a conversation about the grounding.

Respectful sharing of assessments. Many teams engage in after-action meetings to assess how well they performed in a recent operation, and to share assessments that help each other to perform better on the team in a future operation. This is not as easy as it sounds. Some people are uncomfortable sharing assessments and hold back. Others are uncomfortable receiving assessments and can get defensive because they take the assessments as attacks or insults. The problem is that emotional reactivity impedes the sharing of assessments. The practice of honest sharing of grounded assessments can be cultivated by the team leader. A practice to help get this started is the following. When someone (Alice, say) has an assessment, positive or negative, to share with someone else (Bob, say), they follow this protocol:

A: Bob, I have an assessment for you. Is now a good time?

B: Yes.

A: (shares assessment and grounding)

B: Thank you.

A: You're welcome.

This protocol should be practiced in team meetings until the team has become comfortable with the sharing. Then the formality can be dropped and members can simply share their assessments.

The shared assessments can be positive or negative. For example, Alice could say, "Bob, when you handed the ball off to Charlie rather than keep it yourself, you created an opening for Charlie to make the point, which helped the team win. Well done." Alice could also say, "Bob, when you grabbed the ball from Charlie and tried unsuccessfully to shoot it yourself, you left me feeling like other team members including me do not matter to you."

Gratitude and Appreciation. Cultivate these moods through practices. These moods support collaboration, team unity, and trust.

Open your day by giving thanks for another day. Close your day by giving thanks for the day and allowing yourself to experience again the persons, actions, and events of the day that you appreciated. Practice ending the day with your spouse or partner by talking about anything from the day that is not complete, and declaring completion; thus you can take your night's rest without regrets and the start the next day with no baggage from the previous day. When you interact with people, be curious about what unique gifts they bring and let them know what you appreciate about the work they have done for you. Do not be afraid of making apologies when your words or actions have offended people. Let others know of your appreciation by giving them credit for their contributions. There is always something to appreciate. When these simple practices become habits, many stresses will melt away.

Coaching. If you are a team leader or coach, you will find many opportunities to test your emotional reactivity. A coach's job is to help the other person attain their goals. The first thing a coach must do is find out what the other person's goals are. The second thing a coach must do is obtain the permission of the other person to offer coaching, for without permission the coach can quickly be dragged into an unproductive argument. Once the goal is clear and permission granted, the coach offers help. The help can be advice on which direction to go. It can also be advice revealing barriers the person has to overcome. Ideally, you can listen and advise without distraction from your own emotional reactivity when you or the other person speaks. You improve your skills as a coach by paying attention to your reactivity, and letting it go.

Conclusion

Without our bodies, we cannot participate in the world. The skills that make us effective are in our bodies and are shaped and modified by the conversations we have with each other. Often in leading innovation, we encounter dissonances between what our minds intend and what our bodies do. The field of somatics aims to teach us how to unify our language and the reactive tendencies in our bodies.

The practices of awareness, centering, blending, and dealing with conditioned tendencies are at the core of somatic practice. Teachers and coaches are essential to help us learn to do these things well. Emotional fortitude – the ability to maintain a steady mood when under duress – is a reward for mastering somatic practices.

16
EXECUTING

A good plan violently executed now is better than a perfect plan tomorrow.
-- George Patton

To me, ideas are worth nothing unless executed. They are just multipliers. Execution is worth millions.
-- Steve Jobs

Vision without execution is hallucination.
-- Thomas Edison.

In innovation, execution is the set of actions that convert the possibility offered into a promise delivered. Competent execution is essential not only for the final outcomes of the innovation process, but for the outcomes of all the individual practices. These outcomes are not all that matters. Intermediate results, such as prototypes and demonstrations, build trust in the final promise and its value. More importantly, they build trust in you as a performer and leader.

Many organizations find innovation difficult because they focus their work on generating shiny new ideas rather than on adopting new practice. To mask their failure to achieve adoption, they often engage in "innovation theater", a show of new ideas that look good and brief well, but do not produce outcomes. Innovation theater focuses on the envisioning stories and offers, but it is an illusion that fails to execute.

The executing practice is not innovation theater. Execution is often the most challenging part of innovation because it requires a long-term commitment to manage multiple people with multiple commitments and multiple breakdowns. It is a practice of dogged persistence to bring something new into being.

The Team

Innovation leaders do nothing by themselves. They develop and nurture a delivery team to help mobilize their community in adopting the new practice. By team, we mean a specific set of people who commit to a shared promise to create a new future that matters to their community and who coordinate their actions to fulfill that promise.[1]

The executing practice has three main elements:

1. Forming the delivery team: Gathering the persons with the right skills. Designing the mission. Declaring the goal. Securing their commitment to that shared promise.

2. Managing the network of commitments of the team: Coordinating action to fulfill the team's promise. Monitoring that the team's customers are satisfied and adjusting as needed. Everyone on the team takes responsibility to support the others in fulfillment of the team's promise.

3. Managing breakdowns, changes, and dissatisfaction to maintain the objectives and trust.

Take note: a group of task-doers who receive tasks from the boss and execute them, but take no responsibility for anyone else's performance, is not a team by our definition. In this common case, the boss alone holds the team's promise to the customer; the individual members do not. Their actions can become uncoordinated, leading to

---

[1] Kobe Bogaert, Pam Fox Rollin. 2023. *Growing Groups into Teams.* Altus Growth Partners.

conflict that generates distrust, dissatisfied customers, and ultimately team failure.

We will discuss these three aspects in the sections following. Please refer to Chapter 6, Conversations, for definitions of the types of conversations – context, possibilities, actions – and the networks of commitments in the team. The Conversation for Action, or CFA, is the basic building block for executing.

Initial Conversations

After the initial conversations for sensing, envisioning, and offering, the leader will need to form a team to implement the offer. The leader will identify the right people for the task, invite them, secure their commitment to the shared promise, and set up a network of coordination with them. The "right people" are those with the expertise to deliver the offer. They include authority figures to address the evolving context and environment, investors or resource sponsors to ensure the project is meeting their conditions of satisfaction, and members of the adopting community. Community members come under many monikers, for example, "customers" in business, "users" in software development, and "warfighters" in the military.

When you are the leader, you do not need to have all the answers worked out with your team before the work begins. You are asking people to join you in a journey of many starts and stops before you attain the shared goal. Your team accepts the risk of failure and the necessity to work to overcome false starts, because they believe in the shared goal and in your commitment to bring something new into existence.

A short story illustrates these principles at work. In 1986, Peter visited Fernando Flores at his Action Technologies office. He wanted to bring Flores's email system, The Coordinator, into his work at NASA. Fernando asked questions about the computing field, the state of computing research, computing education, NASA research, and awareness among computing people of coordinating action. He asked about Peter's history, motivations for working at NASA, and assessments about the Winograd-Flores book, which was then in final production. He discussed his own history and involvement with computing. It was quite a wide-ranging conversation. After three-quarters of an hour, when Peter was starting to get fidgety because they had not yet talked about a possible collaboration, Fernando moved from a conversation for context to a conversation for possibilities. They speculated about what they could do together and what value it might bring NASA and Action Technologies. After ten minutes of speculation, Fernando said, "Let us now define action. I will make two requests of my staff. I will introduce you to my head of development so that you can talk details about projects and licensing. I will also introduce you to my head of education so that you can learn about the language-action philosophy behind The Coordinator." Then he adjourned the meeting, introduced Peter to these two people, and went on to his next appointment. From this one-hour conversation a long and fruitful friendship followed.

In this story we see how Flores, a master at management, worked in conversations to produce action and valuable outcomes. He spent most of the time on context -- what was going on in Peter's world, NASA's world, his world, and the general computing world. Then, in that context, he speculated about possibilities he and Peter might pursue together. Finally, in the last minute of their time, he made declarations and requests that led to actions. Many more conversations for context, possibility, and action were to follow.

This example illustrates show the three kinds of conversation – context, possibility, action – combined to enable successful execution. We started with agreement on the possibility we wanted to realize as new practice. We formed a team to carry out the conversations for successful execution. We defined what the promise of the team would be. We designated the team manager and invited the members.

Todd offers another story showing the project leader bringing about a new method of long-range threat assessment for the Marine Corps. The standard practice for generating threat assessments was to prepare a large Powerpoint slide deck laying out the details of threats and likely contingencies. These slide decks were intricate and mind-numbing. They did little to provoke understanding and discussion about threats and their impact on force development.

A new commanding officer for the Marine Corps Intelligence Activity decided to change the practice. He created a team with the mission to shift from explaining possible threats to provoking serious discussion about them. This would be accomplished by focusing on provocative graphics and minimizing text. For the team leader, he selected a person with a strong graphic arts background. In a reversal of traditional roles, the intelligence analysts were to support the graphic artist in developing a presentation of threats. The team was to produce a dynamic presentation that provoked discussion, rather than a thick slide deck. This shift in team composition and roles was the first and most important step in execution.

The intelligent analysts rebelled at the notion they would be support persons rather than content originators. They claimed that the presentation would be bereft of the detailed explanations and justifications they had spent their careers learning to produce. The project leader did not try to shut them down and ignore their complaints; instead he set up a conversation framework that would regularly address breakdowns they identified. He scheduled team meetings every two weeks to allow concerns to be raised and addressed through action items. As the deadline for delivery drew near, he stepped up the frequency of meetings to three times a week. The regular schedule and meeting format provided a way for the leader to review how team members were fulfilling their commitments to complete action items, give status reports, raise red flags about potential breakdowns, and form new action items. He kept his boss apprised of progress and possible threats to delivery of the mission.

You can see that the project leader positioned himself as the customer of the promises by team members for delivery of their action items. He organized the meetings and touch points to allow him to make grounded assessments of the promises made to him. When he found promises that were not being fulfilled, he had a conversation with the responsible person about how to meet the conditions of satisfaction. He also recognized he was the performer for his commanding officer and made sure that his customer was satisfied with the way the team was moving.

This turned out well. The presentation's use of imagery and storytelling provoked a new set of conversations in the Marine Corps that provided the ground for the Commandant of the Marine Corps to modernize the force for the emerging operational environment.

Managing Network of Commitments

When you are the leader, the team's promise might be depicted as a single CFA loop with you as the performer and your community as the customer. This depiction, however, would not be effective because there are many CFAs taking place among team members and with the community. The network that coordinates these CFAs has a form like a tree. Each team member interacts with the manager (you) as a customer, because each promises to deliver elements of the team's goal and you are the one to integrate and be satisfied. Each team member in turn is the customer of a subset of CFAs that supports the team member's promises. This tree is a workflow network; please refer to Chapter 6 for examples of CFA workflow networks.

Your job as a leader is *managing conversations* in your network. It is not acquiring information and making decisions. This carries two main responsibilities:

1. Keeping all conversations moving toward completion and maintaining awareness of the customer for every promise.

2. Ensuring that all performers (including yourself) have the capacity to deliver.

Let's look at each.

Keeping Conversations Moving Toward Completion

You listen to the conversations in your network to monitor their progress toward fulfillment. You facilitate them in moving toward on-time completion by providing coaching, guidance, or resources as needed. Your job may be easy for small innovation projects with small networks but can require considerable management skill for larger, more complex networks.

As a manager, you are the customer of many promises, especially those of your direct reports. To be effective, you judge the credibility of the promises offered to you, and not accept promises in which you have doubts. You rigorously ground your assessments about whether their results satisfy the agreements that you have made with them. You teach your performers how to be rigorous customers of the promises made to them, even as you are rigorous in fulfilling your own promises.

You will need to set up regular touchpoints to verify that all conversations are progressing. In a small network, this may be as simple as reading emails and injecting encouragement and guidance where needed. In a larger network, it will require more structure such as a weekly review meeting. At the review meeting, each team member reports project status, current breakdowns, red flags (threats that should be addressed) and expectations about time of completion. You may need other conversations such as periodic one-on-one meetings with your direct reports and periodic group meetings to focus on context and relationships.

It is very important to have clear purposes for all these touchpoints, or you will wind up with people whose disdain for "meetings" becomes an obstacle for the project. To make your engagements effective, be very clear in advance of the conversations that will and *will not* happen and be firm during the meeting at enforcing those declarations. You may need to coach your team members on the general conversational skills of negotiating agreements, grounding assessments, making clear requests and promises, listening, and articulating clear conditions of satisfaction.

Ensuring Capacity to Deliver

The demand for effective coordination imposes performance standards for the customers and performers throughout the network. An effective customer makes clear requests, provides feedback of satisfaction or dissatisfaction to the performer, and asks to be informed of changes or breakdowns that may affect the fulfillment of their agreement. An effective performer listens for the satisfaction of the customer, keeps the customer informed, coordinates changes or actions around breakdowns, and makes promises that they are competent to keep and committed to fulfill. In addition, each team member is aware of the team's shared promise and supports other team members. By taking care of each other, you maintain the relationships that are critical for enduring team cohesion.

Most people are not trained to be effective customers and performers by these standards. It is common that professionals are competent at the tasks they perform but not at coordinating action with their customers or at being effective customers for those who perform for them. Many are not aware of relationships in the team and do not take care of them well. We find that many leaders cause breakdowns in their organizations by being ineffective customers and performers. Practicing being an effective customer or performer, and fostering it in your teams, is essential for an innovation leader.

All team members must have the capacity to fulfill their promises. Capacity means that a person has the time, competence, and resources to fulfill all their promises. Unfortunately, many people, including many experienced people, do not have good practices for assessing the time or resources they need to fulfill their promises. They are not skilled at requesting what they really need and negotiating counteroffers. They fold under pressure. When they get into trouble, they try to handle it alone and get deeper into the hole.

Exercise: Capacity Assessment

Here is a simple exercise to determine if you are overcommitted. Prepare a spreadsheet with three columns. In the first column, list all your commitments, each with its own row. Include personal as well as professional commitments – all require your time and resources. In the second column, list the "raw demand", which is the number of weekly hours to fulfill the commitment properly. In the third column, list the "actuals", which are the number of weekly hours you actually spend on that commitment. When the total demand exceeds 100 hours per week, or your actual time exceeds 60 hours, you probably have a serious capacity problem and you are at strong risk of being overwhelmed. The solution is to cancel some commitments, delegate others, and restructure the rest to be within your capacity. You can practice this exercise frequently to track whether you are staying within your capacity. When you embody this practice, you will no longer need the exercise.

Once you have matched your commitments to your capacity, you need practices to keep you there. One such seems simple enough: say "yes" only to the important things, and "no" to the unimportant. But the truth is, many of us cannot bring ourselves to say no when we should. It seems as if saying no to a boss is inappropriate, or saying no to a friend will injure the relationship, or saying no to something interesting will leave you on the outside. Yet if you cannot learn to say no, you cannot avoid being overwhelmed. The Declining Requests exercise (Chapter 15) trains you to decline calmly and resolutely without falling into recriminations or explanations. In some cases, such as with your boss or your spouse, saying no may not be an option; look to counter-offer with helpful actions within your capacity.

In his *Seven Habits* book, Stephen Covey divides events demanding your action into the dimensions of "urgency" and "importance". People over capacity wind up spending most of their time on urgent-unimportant tasks and never get to the important ones. Their inattention to the important generates breakdowns that ultimately demand urgent corrective actions. Therefore, a suffocating backlog of urgent tasks can be another indicator that you and your team are over capacity. Distinguishing the important and the urgent is essential in prioritizing projects so that you have enough time to work on important tasks and you have sufficient capacity for all tasks.

Managing Trust, Satisfaction, Breakdowns, and Changes

We are not done once we have our network of coordination running smoothly. The flow will inevitably be threatened by surprises, contingencies, and breakdowns. We must deal with four main issues skillfully or the project may fail.

First, it is important that people on the team trust each other, and that the community trusts the team. From Chapter 11, we know that trust is a complicated combination of assessments of competence, sincerity, and care. This implies that all team members are competent at their roles on the team, they keep their promises, they help other team members keep their promises, and they go out of their way to fulfill promises when contingencies threaten. When the whole team is this way, its customers will trust the team.

Second, in fulfilling commitments, it is not enough just to get the work done; we also manage satisfaction of the customers of every loop in the coordination network. That includes not only the loops that directly touch external customers, but also the internal loops between team members. Managing satisfaction is the practice of regular

Executing

communication with the customer, listening especially for potential dissatisfaction because of changing expectations about the conditions of satisfaction or the conduct of the process. If we sense potential dissatisfaction, we immediately revisit the agreement with the customer, and either reaffirm its original form or change it. This practice avoids dissatisfaction during fulfillment. A satisfactory outcome may not sustain trust and relationship if the process of achieving it is painful and unpleasant.

Third, breakdowns are inevitable. There are numerous ways to interrupt execution. Here are a eleven common ones.

- Failing to initiate all the conversations for action, possibility, and context needed to complete the promise.
- Failures within any particular conversation for action.
- Failing to assemble a good team, representing all the kinds of expertise needed to complete the promise.
- Failing to establish a network of conversations that coordinates all actions toward the completion of the promise.
- Failing to monitor the key conversations and keep them progressing toward completion.
- Failing to ensure that all performers (especially those on the team) are managing their commitments within their capacities.
- Failing to be a rigorous customer of all promises made to you by your team.
- Failing to build trust in yourself, your team, and your promise.
- Failing to manage expectations about what will be delivered and when.
- Failing to listen for and manage satisfaction during the process.
- Failing to declare breakdowns when they happen and develop recovery plans to address them.

Fourth, when a contingency arises or breakdown occurs, we may need to change the execution plan the team is working on. Contingencies and breakdowns can change the operating environment. New conversations may be needed to adapt.

We noted earlier that breakdowns are more likely when we get wrapped up in urgent actions and fail to take care of important things. Therefore, we can avoid some breakdowns by explicitly asking what the most important things are, making sure we have the capacity to do them, and then doing them. We can avoid other breakdowns with the "red flag practice" during review meetings, which identifies impending breakdowns when it is easier to mitigate or avoid them. Finally, we can avoid still other breakdowns by attending to customer expectations even if they are not explicit in conditions of satisfaction.

Conclusion

Execution begins with a delivery team committed to the same shared promise and to supporting each other in achieving it. The team leader (you) makes sure all conversations are moving toward satisfaction of their customers. Regular team update-and-review and after-action meetings support this goal. The team leader monitors that everyone has the capacity and resources needed to avoid overwhelm from urgent tasks crowding out important tasks. When breakdowns occur, the team leader works with the team to find resolutions.

Remember that the delivery team is not charged with producing the innovation. It is charged with supporting the community's adoption of new practice. It does this by generating the technology and services needed to support the new practice. It also assists in mobilization, which we will discuss next.

17
MOBILIZING

The two parts of technology that lower the threshold for activism are the Internet and the mobile phone. Anyone who has a cause can now mobilize very quickly.
-- Howard Rheingold

Leadership = mobilization toward a common goal.
-- Garry Wills

There are a few moments when something new changes the world. The iPhone is such a moment.
-- Steve Jobs

In 1959, Ruth Handler in partnership with Mattel toymaker launched the Barbie doll, an adult-bodied doll that children could dress up and imagine themselves playing adult roles. This toy became immensely popular and remains so today. Mattel has sold over a billion of them in the past 60 years. They have become part of pop culture and featured in a top-selling movie in 2023.

In 2007, Steve Jobs announced the original iPhone. He said it offered a touch-controlled iPod, complete phone service, complete Internet data connectivity, and an array of apps available from the new app store. He positioned it as a way to carry your own data universe in your pocket, a means to download music cheaply without violating copyright, a revolutionary way to connect and share with friends, and a fashion statement. He orchestrated a media campaign to generate interest and excitement about the new technology before its release.

The response was immediate: 270,000 iPhones sold in the first week, and 1 million sold in the first three months. Other computer manufacturers scrambled to offer smartphones. Facebook and other social media companies built new industries based on smartphone connectivity.

In 2002, Elon Musk and his associates founded SpaceX, with the long-term goal of enabling humans to travel to and inhabit Mars. In 2008, they successfully launched a reusable rocket and later that year landed a NASA contract to launch satellites, replacing the Space Shuttle. SpaceX rockets subsequently launched constellations of communication satellites into earth orbit, enabling Starlink, which connected people to the Internet via satellite. Militaries around the world started rethinking their battlefield awareness strategies after Ukraine used Starlink successfully in the war with Russia that started in 2022. Also in 2008, Musk and associates launched Tesla, to build electric cars and supporting infrastructure. They set an electric vehicle standard that the established auto makers scrambled to match.

Martin Luther King was a Baptist minister who advocated nonviolent protest against laws and practices that discriminated against people of color. Through many nonviolent protests and masterful oratory, he convinced many people to support new laws against discrimination, the most famous being the Civil Rights Act of 1964. He was assassinated in 1968. His memory, philosophy, and work are revered through hundreds of streets and buildings in his name, and through a national holiday honoring him every January.

Handler, Jobs, Musk, and King are four of many master mobilizers. Their big visions of the future appealed to many people. They demonstrated an exceptional talent for making offers that attracted huge crowds. They built teams and organizations to enable people to reach those futures. They were always focused on concerns they sensed before most people had words for them. For example, Handler appealed to children's love of playing in adult roles. Jobs appealed to

Mobilizing

people's desires to connect with friends and the world. Musk appealed to people's desires to save humanity from self-destruction. King appealed to people's desire for equality and justice. All held their big visions as long-term goals, the pursuit of which produced many useful technologies and practices.

Mobilizing is the epitome of the advanced practices of innovation leaders. Mobilizing unifies the seven other practices into a social movement. Proficiency at the other seven practices is the foundation for mobilizing (see Table 1 below). The larger and more diverse your community, the greater the skill you will need to mobilize them around the new practice.

Many people have trouble mobilizing because they mistakenly believe mobilization is control. Control is an illusion. The innovations that emerged for Handler, Jobs, Musk, King, and others were not achieved through a controlled process. They were achieved because their leaders tapped into deeply held social moods and inspired individuals to join a movement. The achievement is more like growing a beautiful garden than managing a large factory.

Mobilizers start and sustain social movements that accumulate followers and generate the new world. Mobilizers are leaders who embody a compelling purpose and muster resources to support the movement.

Table 1. Advanced Skills Supporting Mobilizing

Advanced skill	Component of
Listening for community-wide concerns, especially unspoken concerns revealed in practices, moods, and power, articulating them in language that resonates with all,	**Sensing**
Learning the community's history that galvanizes people and generates the current concerns.	
Reading, shifting, orchestrating, and cultivating moods.	
Revealing breakdowns in prevailing interpretations (how people see and make sense of their world) and showing how to resolve them.	**Envisioning**
Keeping the vision present for yourself and your team.	
Making powerful declarations that elicit commitments to join you in conversations and actions	
Developing the courage to make offers and take responsibility of fulfilling them. Listening for opportunities in conversations to make offers.	**Offering**
Understanding power dynamics to learn who has standing to influence, mobilize, and block actions.	**Adopting**
Defusing resistance by listening the concerns behind it and modifying offers to include the resisters.	
Organizing infrastructure and leadership support of the new practice	**Sustaining**

Knowing when to have Conversations for Context, Conversations for Possibility, and Conversations for action – and having them.	**Executing**
Building trust by demonstrating your competence, integrity, and care in every promise you make.	
Making requests, offers, promises, declarations, assessments, and assertions to generate commitments and produce actions.	
Cultivating emotional fortitude, the skill of maintaining a stable and centered mood amid many provocations.	**Embodying**
Staying centered on your vision for the future that takes care of concerns in the community.	
Provoking reactions that reveal openings for movement.	
Recognizing conditioned tendencies and coaching people to retrain them.	

Mobilization

Mobilization is often associated with the military: the actions of forming and deploying armies. Some of those called up are trained reservists, others are volunteers and conscripts who must be trained. The common training experience brings everyone to the same shared purpose – service as a soldier. Many businesses and government agencies understand mobilization similarly. For example, businesses mobilize a workforce to build and implement a new technology; governments mobilize networks of social workers to deliver a benefit program.

Mobilizing people to join an innovation differs significantly from being called up for service in an army or joining the workforce.

Mobilization is a social movement. Followers of an innovation join by accepting an invitation to join the movement. The central concern is not fixed but evolves in response to external forces or other concerns expressed by individual members. The space of possibilities to be navigated can be large, complex, confusing, and contradictory. External forces and shifting moods can suddenly disrupt any plan. The main challenge for leaders is to recruit disparate followers into a community to build a shared future they all want. Table 2 summarizes differences between miliary mobilization and innovation mobilization.

Table 2: Military versus Innovation Mobilization

Military Mobilization	**Innovation Mobilization**
Participants are compelled to join.	Participants accept an invitation to join a community of practice.
Central concern is usually stable and internally coherent.	Central concern evolves and may contain contradictions.
Practices are stable with predictable outcomes.	Practices evolve and outcomes are unpredictable.
Difficulty adjusting to changes wrought by big external forces.	Adapts and blends with changes by big forces.
Leaders are defined by, and gain their authority from, ranks and positions. They wield coercive power sometimes sweetened with persuasion.	Leaders are those who gather a following in the community. They succeed through the powers of imitation, invitation, and persuasion.
Challenge is to recruit and train in the ways of the organization.	Challenge is building relationships among those of differing concerns.

Mobilization often seems like a skill of being on stage and giving amazing speeches that energize the community. Certainly leaders such as Handler, Jobs, Musk, and King leveraged their charisma, status, and public speaking to do exactly this. Amazing speeches are a demonstration of advanced skill at the envisioning practice. *You don't need to attain that level of public speaking to be effective.* Social movements such as Mothers Against Drunk Driving, Black Lives Matter, and MeToo were only marginally helped along by charismatic leaders giving impassioned speeches. Their real success came from tapping into deeply felt concerns that resonated with many people. The recent movement for Generative AI technology was propelled by numerous local leaders all attuned to the general idea that artificial intelligence is a force to be reckoned with and ignored at our peril.

Attuning to a Wide Social Mood

The best mobilizers are strong in the other seven practices, especially at sensing and envisioning. Their advanced skill strikes others as an almost uncanny ability to sense a mood widely shared in the community and to make narratives, declarations, and offers that generate sympathy and emotional energy. The emotional energy propels the mobilization.

Steve Jobs was a superb example. He often located unspoken desires and moods that no one else had identified. The iPod music player would not have shown up as a "customer need" in any focus group or be revealed as a "desire" in any interview. In the silence of their unspoken moods, Jobs sensed that many people would jump at the opportunity of a high-capacity, lightweight, pocket-sized player that could be personalized with their unique musical preferences. He also sensed that people did not want to get entrapped by the extensive copyright disputes around downloadable music tracks. He positioned the iPod as an instantiation of the convenient portable fed by a fully legal iTunes store that banished the fear of copyright violation.

Jobs demonstrated an even more spectacular mobilization in his announcement of the iPhone (2007). He opened with the declaration "There are a few moments when something new changes the world.

The iPhone is such a moment." He cited the revolutions seeded by previous Apple machines, the Macintosh computer (1984) and iPod music player (2001). Against this background, he said that Apple was introducing four new technologies: a touch controlled wide screen, a much more powerful iPod coupled to an upgraded iTunes store, a cell phone, and full internet connectivity – all in one device. He summarized with "Apple reinvents the telephone." Even today, many who view the video of Jobs's announcement experience an emotional rush when he makes his climactic claim "all in one device".

Peter tells a story that gives an insight into Jobs's skill: In the early 1990s I became editor in chief of ACM *Communications*. My staff reached out to Steve Jobs and arranged an interview with him. I and our senior writer visited Jobs at his Apple Headquarters and had a long discussion about Apple and innovation. At the end, I asked him, "Will hackers eventually bring down the Internet?" Jobs put his head into his hands and fell silent. His motionless reverie lasted over three minutes. We began to whisper among themselves, "Is he OK? Did he just experience a heart attack or stroke? Should we call for help?" Just as we were about to call 911, he came out of his trance and said, "No, they need it to do their work." After the interview Peter asked Jobs's associates what happened. They had seen him do that a lot. He put himself into a mental state attuned to the community's energy and mood, where he could sense what actions would resonate. His associates called that ability a "reality distortion field". It was supported by years of meditation practice. When occasionally he talked about what he did, he emphasized the need to *feel* the mood and the energy from immersion in the relationships of the community. For Jobs, sensing was more than listening and describing a concern; it was feeling the concern down to his bones. That is how he was able to discern what offers would be irresistibly attractive.

Mobilization Examples

Let's look at examples of movements in different arenas to reveal common features. Our examples include technology movements, climate change movements, social movements, and local movements.

Technology

Generative AI in the form of ChatGPT was offered for public access at the end of November 2022. It rapidly attracted many people to try it out. Within two weeks, 100 million users had logged in. Within two months, a dozen how-to-use-it books were available from Amazon. Tech companies quickly announced plans to incorporate the technology into their browsers, office packages, online services, and other apps. Start-ups blossomed and readily found venture funding. People shared their findings from personal experiments widely in social media. The speed of adoption was astonishing. Moods of awe, surprise, and intense enthusiasm blossomed. The conversations about ChatGPT seemed to spread with a momentum all their own.

The work of preparing prototypes and early versions of generative AI had begun years before the breakout in 2022. Around 2014, the company Deepmind started work on a neural net system for playing the ancient game of Go, long believed to be beyond the reach of computers. Their machine, AlphaGo, defeated a world Go grandmaster, Lee Sodol, in 2016. AlphaGo demonstrated that large neural networks trained with reinforcement learning could master some game-playing tasks in a fraction of the time it took humans – AlphaGo attained grandmaster expertise in chess in 4 hours, and in Go in 13 days. Leaders in the OpenAI company took aim at an even harder problem – machines to carry on conversations with humans. Their Generative Pretrained Transformer (GPT) technology, also called "generative AI", used a neural network to generate new text given a prompt text; it went through several generations before GPT-3.5 was released to the public. It was quite an accomplishment: a significant number of people said that GPT-3.5 passed the Turing test. Microsoft became an early major investor in OpenAI and worked to incorporate that technology into its Bing browser, CoPilot personal assistant, and office applications. Google incorporated its own generative AI technology into its browser Bard. NVIDIA, led by Jensen Huang, committed to supplying the advanced chips that support the complex computing architectures of all generative AI. Sal Khan, founder of Khan Academy, created concepts for how generative AI might enhance the experiences of students and teachers and then shared them in a TED Talk. These companies mobilized other leaders by making the tools available early so they could teach and mobilize others in the community. The mobilization around generative AI was not simply word spreading on social media; it represents a successful and deliberate effort that continues to this day.

Climate change

Greta Thunburg from Stockholm, Sweden, started protesting climate-change inaction by her parliament in 2018, at age 15. Her protests attracted attention because she appealed to young people in her generation by arguing that their future is in jeopardy because of the inaction of the older generation. She proclaimed, "the crisis is that there is no crisis." With her constant encouragement, a worldwide network of climate activists of her generation took form. She received numerous invitations to speak before many world bodies and impressed people with her outspokenness, thoughtfulness, and appeal to her generation. She mobilized a worldwide following of her generation to work for climate change.

Drunk driving

In May 1980, Candace Lightner's daughter was killed by a drunk driver as she walked to school. Lightner was outraged to learn that the judicial system would probably let the driver, a repeat offender, off with a light sentence. She vowed to start an organization that would change all this. Just a few months before, Cindi Lamb's 5-month old daughter was made permanently paraplegic in a head-on crash with a drunk driver. Lamb was outraged that the driver was still on the road and would probably get off with a light sentence. She started blanketing politicians and lawmakers with her daughter's story and impassioned entreaties to change the laws.

Lightner and Lamb soon joined forces and formed Mothers Against Drunk Driving (MADD). They held a news conference in October 1980 with members of Congress and the National Highway Traffic Safety Administration. They told the stories of their daughters and brought the drunk driving issue into national awareness. Lamb's photogenic paraplegic daughter drew media attention on popular shows such as *Today, Good Morning America,* and *20/20.* Lightner, MADD's first president, insisted that other leaders take over after her term, and MADD was blessed with a succession of effective leaders. She also spoke with universal appeal: "We're dads and daughters, sons and uncles, friends, and neighbors. And mothers. We're all ages and from all walks of life. We are many colors with one voice."

By 1983, MADD had 100 chapters and the states had passed 129 anti-drunk-driving laws. By 1988 all 50 states had conformed to the new MADD-inspired federal law making 21 the minimum legal drinking age. Today all 50 states' laws declare the maximum admissible blood alcohol rate to be 0.8 percent. Drunk driving has been cut in half since MADD's founding. There are 600 chapters around the country offering services for victims of drunk drivers. MADD is a powerful force for public awareness, victim assistance, public policy, and grassroots activism. It is one of the 100 most admired public charities.

Local community

Because of their visibility, the examples above of mobilization might lead to the conclusion that you must be a charismatic leader to be successful at mobilization. That is not the case. The vast majority of mobilizations are not world changing events reverberating around the globe. They are known only within their local community. Here are two examples narrated by Todd, who witnessed their formation.

One of the teachers in the middle school of our community was an avid water polo player and often brought his water polo ball into science class, where he would toss the ball to his students while working water polo into the context of the lesson. A few girls began to ask why the nearby high school, which had a regulation water polo pool, did not offer water polo as a sport. They thought the answers from the high school principal and the athletic director were unsatisfactory. The middle school students banded with some students from the high school and began to mobilize support for offering water polo as a team sport. They talked it up in the hallways and on social media. They mobilized a network of parents and other school leaders to support water polo and overcome the resistance from the high school's principal. They recruited advocates from supporters who had never considered playing water polo. They mobilized the community to attend school board meetings and advocate for a water polo team. When the high school principal said there was not enough money, the students mobilized their parents and the wider community to raise funds. When the high school athletic director said they did not have the equipment, the students found a leader in USA Water Polo who donated the necessary caps and balls. The students showed up week after week at school board meetings and demonstrated that more than enough girls had committed to join the team the following season. Finally, the school board agreed. They committed to create a water polo team at the high school. The middle school science teacher committed to be the girls' water polo coach. The girls started practicing as soon as they were allowed to play water polo. Many boys who had been planning to start football in high school opted instead for water polo. After five years, robust teams for both boys and girls continued to play, long after the initial group of mobilizers had graduated.

Another group in our community offered to create a community robotics team. The local high schools had robotics teams but did not engage interested students from the middle school. Interested girls chafed because the existing boy-dominated teams sometimes relegated girls to non-technical tasks. The organizers approached several Girl Scout troops, offering to start a team if the girls would commit to join. Several girls in the sixth grade committed to participate. After a stint with the First Lego League in the fall, the girls initiated their First Robotics Team in the spring. They mobilized others from the community to participate in the team, external sponsors such as Apple, Disney, and Dewalt to donate equipment and supplies, and parents to take them to regional competitions. On Saturdays, the team met to work on the robot and other First Robotics activities. In subsequent years, the experienced members of the team began to mentor First Lego League teams and recruit the next generation. Today, the team is bigger than ever and includes boys as well as girls.

Students led both mobilizations. Through their conversations, they built relationships and plotted paths to their desired futures. They engaged peers, business leaders, parents, sponsors, and supporters to overcome resistance and generate new commitments for action. An important factor in both stories is the ongoing commitment of the group leaders. The leaders in the girl's water polo team showed up early for morning conditioning and were the last to leave in the afternoon. The leaders in the local First Robotics team showed up every Saturday without fail to ensure the work got done. They mobilized others by their example, their commitment, and their explicit invitations. None was a charismatic person or a leader in business, religion, politics, or industry. They were individuals from their communities who saw a way to improve the well-being of their community and committed themselves to make that happen.

Messes and Wicked Problems

Innovation leaders are often sought to mobilize groups mired in messes, also called wicked problems. A wicked problem is a very messy social tangle among a set of groups concerned with a contentious issue. No one has enough power or resources to impose a solution, but everyone has enough power to block someone else's proposal. The parties often feel they are deadlocked in a power struggle. The underlying problem is that the parties do not have a shared interpretation of the issue and they distrust each other; therefore, they cannot move in any direction as a community. Resolving the mess begins with finding common concerns among all the parties and leading them into a new practice to take care of those concerns.

The term "wicked problem" is sometimes also used by scientists for intractable problems in complex physical systems. The researchers agree on a problem statement but cannot find a solution because extreme complexity hides it. Climate change modeling or finding the Higgs boson look like wicked problems in this sense. With enough time and effort, scientists can find enough structure and recurrences in the system to solve these problems. The CERN facility in Switzerland took nearly 50 years and 5000 physicists to discover the Higgs boson.

Skilled facilitators have worked out processes that help the parties in a wicked problem find agreement; prominent examples are the Appreciative Inquiry, Layton-Strauss, and human-centered design processes. Facilitators use these techniques to help the parties find a shared interpretation and develop action plans. To start the process, a sponsor declares that the time has come for a resolution of the problem and invites representatives of the groups convene in a workshop. Facilitators lead the group through a series of moods:

1. Appreciation. Each player comes to appreciate all the points of view and concerns of the others. Some players modify their own concerns in the process. They develop a feeling that their concerns are understood and respected by the others.
2. Speculation. The players cooperate on developing possibilities for action, but do not commit to any particular action. After the possibilities are out in the open, the players sort through the options to cull out a small set of promising actions.
3. Resolution and ambition: Members of the group form teams to address the promising actions. The group sees the teams as experiments -- try multiple actions and see which ones produce movement.
4. Follow up: The group designates managers to watch over the various action teams and see them through to completion after the workshop. They agree to convene again to renew their shared interpretation, evaluate previous actions, and commit to new actions.

The facilitator waits until the group has achieved each of these moods and only then moves to the next stage. If the facilitator tries to push to the next stage too soon, the whole process may fall apart.

A common failing of this approach appears in step 4. The sponsor does not provide support for the teams to continue their work. The team members get absorbed back into the world they were in before the workshop and do not have the time or support to continue their work on their teams. Most teams fizzle out and little is accomplished. At the start of this chapter, we set three conditions for a successful mobilization: a leader, resources to support the work, and a compelling purpose. In this case, the sponsor is the leader. There is little point in doing the workshop unless the sponsor has committed the resources to support the teams after the workshop ends.

Conclusion

The essence of mobilization can be summarized with four points:

- It is a gathering of people behind a purpose that matters to them.
- It generates the resources to achieve the purpose.
- It is led by leaders who embody the purpose and draw others into the gathering.
- Its leaders inspire mutual support, where each one in the movement helps others achieve the purpose.

The movement may begin with a single leader, but soon the leaders teach followers to become leaders. The movement grows larger as more people join and, in their turn, get others to join. Early adopters become powerful voices encouraging the majority to join. The conversations that mobilize followers are the other seven leadership practices combined with conversations for possibility, context, and relationship performed proficiently.

Movements for a change of practice often arise in a larger context where officials must provide "top cover". Inexperienced innovation leaders who seek top cover *before* starting their movement have their priorities backwards. Community officials are often conservative and defer joining until they see a movement already in progress. Thus, waiting for the leader to commit can delay or even derail your innovation. Start with the movement; community officials will come around when they see there is a crowd.

Managers within organizations want to mobilize their people around new initiatives. They usually begin by declaring mission and vision statements, and back them up by detailed rules and procedures designed to support implementation. Among these details are "incentives" and "metrics". The incentives are stated as carrots (such as salary boosts) and sticks (such as penalties for not playing in the

Mobilizing

new game) and come with metrics to inform management how the incentives are working. This approach often fails. Incentives do not mobilize. At best, they channel the herd in the directions sought by management. True mobilization comes when everyone works together for a shared purpose that matters to them.

Your ultimate goal as innovation leader is to mobilize your community to adopt a new practice that gives them something they care about but could not get before. The mobilizing practice dances in harmony with the other seven practices as it generates the emotional energy that brings people into the movement. Mobilizing puts to the test your skills at sensing, envisioning, adopting, sustaining, executing, embodying.

18

BECOMING

> *If you want to go fast, go alone. If you want to far, go together.*
> -- African Proverb

> *Bureaucracy develops the more perfectly, the more it is 'dehumanized', the more completely it succeeds in eliminating from business love, hatred, and all purely personal, irrational, and emotional elements which escape calculation.*
> -- Max Weber

> *knowledge is and will be the most important factor of production in our economy.*
> -- Peter Drucker

In 1971, Donald Schon published *Beyond the Stable State,* a treatise on the dynamic operations of bureaucracies and the ways in which they resist change. He was writing so that people could understand the ways bureaucracies work, enabling them to overcome bureaucratic resistance to change. He argued that organizational change results from coordinated changes in three basic elements:

- *Structure*: the various roles and authorities people have, their relationships, and their interactions with customers. Some of the structure can be seen in an organization chart, but most of it is sequestered in the business rules defined in policies and implemented in data systems.

- *Practices*: the various routines, habits, workflows, values, norms, beliefs by which the people interact and carry out their commitments.

- *Technologies*: the various systems and tools people use to carry out their work and enable their practices.

Schon argued that organizations have an inherent tendency to maintain the status quo, a "dynamic conservativism" to return to the previous stable state when a perturbation appears. Overcoming that conservatism means more than applying a force for change, it means leadership so that people willingly accept the change. In organizations, the adoption of a new practice is supported by corresponding changes of structure and technology.

This is a key point for navigation and mobilization. When an organization hosts your community, you will need to mobilize support for structural and technological change as well as the adoption of new practices. This is why we treat navigation and mobilization as higher-level skills.

In this chapter we will examine what mobilization looks like in three common organizational situations (Figure 1). They form a spectrum from "easy to start, hard to sustain" to "hard to start, easy to sustain". Each type has its own structures and technologies, which set context for navigating it effectively with the eight leadership practices.

Becoming

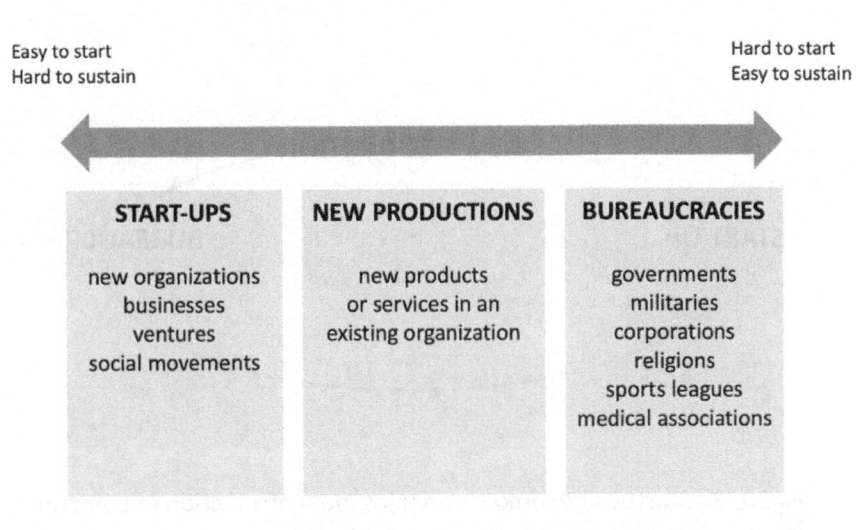

```
Easy to start                                    Hard to start
Hard to sustain                                  Easy to sustain

         ←——————————————————————————————→

    START-UPS          NEW PRODUCTIONS        BUREAUCRACIES

  new organizations      new products          governments
     businesses         or services in an        militaries
      ventures        existing organization     corporations
   social movements                               religions
                                                sports leagues
                                             medical associations
```

Figure 1. Spectrum of organizational types. The organization type sets the context in which the eight conversations take place.

The spectrum is a snapshot of the dynamic evolution of a community's practices. Some startup companies survive and grow into larger companies, which organize new production of new products, which solidify into bureaucracies when they become large and established. Dissatisfaction with bureaucracies motivates new startups, and the cycle begins anew. We call this evolution "becoming". Each type is becoming the next type in an endless cycle. (See Figure 2.)

In the next sections, we will discuss each of these organization types, pointing out how the current common sense impedes them from bringing about adoption of new practices in their communities.

```
           ← NEW PRODUCTION →
   START-UP                    BUREAUCRACY
           ←─────────────────
```

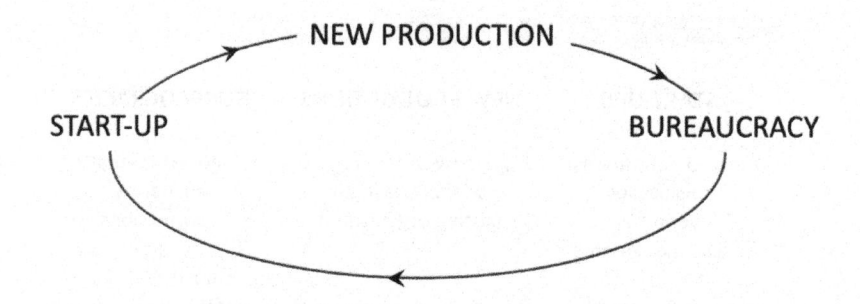

Figure 2. Startups become companies, new production in companies becomes bureaucratized, the immobility of bureaucracies motivates startups. This is an ongoing cycle of organization types.

Start-Ups

A startup is a new organization with a declared purpose for what it is bringing into the world. The most common example is the small company that aims to create a new technology and either sell it in the marketplace or sell the company to another company. We include social movements among startups; they are often overseen by a low-budget coordinating office that maintains event schedules, publicizes the work, and recruits people into the movement.

Consider new businesses. The common sense for starting a business is that we develop a business plan, present it to venture capitalists (VCs), and then execute according to the plan within the agreed budget and timeline. This process is described in detail in numerous books on how to write business plans, make successful presentations to the VCs, and hire a good manager to oversee execution. The books also advise founders to formulate a good vision statement, mission statement, and elevator pitch. The books often pay little attention to identifying community concerns and developing offers to address them. As a result, many teams conjure offers satisfying their own interests but not their community's. They falter as they find few takers for their offer. They wind up doubting if they are the right persons to start the new business.

In his book *Crossing the Chasm* (3rd ed, 2014), Geoffrey Moore identifies a common breakdown with this approach. Most startups prosper early in accord with their business plan. After two years, however, they seem to saturate their market and are unable bring in more customers. They run out of money and lose the confidence of their VC sponsors. They do not have enough cash, momentum, or customer base to survive. To better understand why this happens, Moore appeals to the findings of Everett Rogers, who distinguished between early adopters and majority adopters.[1] Early adopters are risk-takers who enjoy trying out new things to see how they work. Majority adopters are conservatives who want solid evidence that the new technology works, is reliable, low risk, and available from multiple vendors. The offers that appeal to these groups are quite different. The founders are themselves early adopters (by definition) and instinctively know how to make offers that appeal to other early adopters. Their problem arises when they do not think ahead and plan for the offers that will be needed to appeal to the majority. Their business plan does not provide the attention and resources needed for the majority. Moore calls the gap between offers for early adopters and offers for majority "the chasm". It is uncrossable unless you understand it and plan for it. It is like the "valley of death" so much discussed today.

The business-plan orientation breaks down when:

---

[1] E. Rogers. 1962. *Diffusion of Innovations*. Free Press. (5th ed. 2004)

- The business plan does not anticipate mobilizing the majority.
- Founders substitute their ideas for the concerns of their communities.
- Founders fail to have the necessary conversations with their current and prospective communities to understand the various subcommunities and their concerns.
- Though they cannot anticipate all the contingencies that might happen, the founders are not prepared to adapt and change the plan.

The common sense for starting a civic organization or social movement is much the same. It says: first, state a vision and purpose for the movement. Then look for sponsors, both financial and "moral". Next, seek opportunities to get the message out to the masses. Some organizations or movements may generate meetings such as protests and summits to get publicity and create momentum. As we discussed in earlier chapters, social movements are more likely to succeed when their leaders are mobilizers, not simply managers of business plans.

In all these cases, the eight practices are a guide to what conversations you must have and how to listen for concerns.

New Production

Many organizations search intensively for new products and services they can offer customers. The search typically begins with data from focus groups, surveys, complaint departments, and marketing, all aimed at identifying new customer "needs". Once a need has been found, production managers will seek to create a new production line. They will pitch their plan to their senior management, draft a budget, bring in engineers to design it, and hire the staff to execute it.

The software development process illustrates this practice. In the 1970s the process was called a Waterfall Model – identifying requirements, specifications, prototypes, acceptance testing, and delivery. The Waterfall Model is a form of pipeline. In the requirements stage, the developers find out what customers want or need. In the specification stage, they lay out a detailed engineering plan. In the prototype stage, they build an initial version and using methods such as code walk-through and red teams, they satisfy themselves it meets the specifications. In the acceptance test stage, they let the customer run tests on the software and develop bug lists for fixing. In the delivery stage, they certify they have removed the bugs and hand the software over to the customer. They issue patches to fix bugs reported by customers after delivery; thus, post-delivery debugging is accomplished incrementally by real customers trying to do their real work.

Developers and customers complain constantly about this process. Developers say customers don't know what they want, but they want it fast. It is expensive to backtrack and start over with new requirements. Customers say that they are plagued with bugs and security vulnerabilities, and that software developers don't seem to care. The general discontent around this spurred software developers to look for better methods than Waterfall. They introduced feedback loops and renamed the process the Spiral Model. They expanded by adding new subprocesses including Agile, Scrum, and DevSecOps to insert customers into the pipeline so they can detect early when adjustments are needed. Software developers are waking up to the value of frequent conversations with customers to reduce the chance of misunderstanding and decrease waste from backtracking.

We argued in Chapter 1 that production is driven by a set of conversations embedded in the social space. The production line itself can be seen as a workflow network of commitments composed of CFA loops in each stage of production. The managers of the production line watch over those conversations, aiming to complete all loops on time. They also engage in conversations for possibility with their teams when they encounter breakdowns and contingencies. They keep their teams aligned with the shared promise of production through frequent conversations for context. The most successful production lines are those whose managers have these skills.

Bureaucracies

A bureaucracy is an organization that renders defined services in a highly structured, rule-based, and impersonal manner. Bureaucracies continue to perform the same services reliably over long times despite changes of personnel staffing their various offices and functions. Bureaucracies emerged in times long past to enable conquerors to administer their new territories, providing services that were promised to the people in exchange for peace. Some of the most successful empires have been the ones with the best bureaucracies.

Modern bureaucracies are prime targets for automation because their rules and record-keeping are clear and are easily programmed into the machines that interact with their customers. Managers see this as more efficient because the automation replaces more expensive human personnel. The inexorable process of automation does not necessarily lead to less expensive bureaucracies because bureaucracies often seek to expand their customer bases.

Although bureaucracies are most associated with government, many companies have them as well. Organizations use bureaucracies to administer services not only externally to their customers but also internally to their own employees. A common example of outward facing bureaucracy is the customer service apparatus of large companies. It is now highly automated with chatbots that try to direct customers to online databases and in the process make it difficult to talk with one of the few human agents still on payroll. A common example of inward-facing bureaucracy is the HR department, which aims to standardize all aspects of hiring from initial decisions to fill positions, advertise, interview, select, offer, and on-boarding. HR departments also handle employee conflicts and disputes.

Bureaucracies frustrate innovation leaders precisely because they are designed to resist change. Yet they can be changed when innovators follow the eight practices. We have seen this repeatedly with our students, many of whom are military officers embedded within military bureaucracies.

Max Weber was an influential German sociologist, and political economist. In the early 1900s, he wrote about bureaucracies and their contributions to society. He stated four principles for bureaucracies:

1. A formal hierarchical structure: to maintain discipline and facilitate central planning and decision making.
2. Rules-based management: every decision is made in accordance with written rules, no exceptions. Ambiguities are not tolerated: new rules are created to cure ambiguities in current rules.
3. Functional specialty: each position is staffed by a specialist. Detailed position descriptions state what is expected of each specialist. Promotions are based on demonstrated skills.
4. Impersonality: all employees and all customers are treated equally. Individual differences are not allowed to influence decisions. The names of employees are kept private, unseen to the customers.

When criticized that this structure seemed too machine-like and "inhuman", Weber responded that was its virtue. This structure could be optimized for efficiency and would be equitable and fair to all parties. Frederick Taylor, the father of scientific management of factories, was strongly influenced by Weber's principles.

Obviously, bureaucracies are good for encoding rules, enforcing them uniformly, and sustaining themselves. They are hard to change cause the entire management hierarchy needs to come into agreement with change proposals.

Despite these difficulties, there is hope. Bureaucracies are staffed with human beings who, like all other human beings, take pride in their work and have concerns, interests, ambitions, and fears. In conversations for relationship with them, you can learn what their concerns are and craft your proposal to support their concerns. Many insiders develop networks of relationships that enable "side conversations" to resolve issues within the bureaucracy and get things done. They do favors for each other to keep things running in an environment where there is likely to be a rule prohibiting almost anything. The most successful performers get to know the other persons working in the organization and go to them directly to solve problems. Conversations for change often start informally in these relationships; once the parties see that a proposal makes sense, they write it down and move it through bureaucratic checkpoints.

Many novice innovation leaders complain that getting bureaucracies to accept offers to adopt new practices is very hard. Their proposals must traverse a chain of command, getting approvals from each level. It is easy for a specialist at any level to say "no" because the proposal is almost surely going to change the status quo and that change will violate a rule. It is very hard to get past all these levels. Much of what is called "Valley of Death" is this bureaucratic process that says no to change proposals.

Sometimes the chains of command will not budge even when there is internal support for a change. In these cases, conversations with outside entities can enlist them as allies in a movement for change. The movement leaders can mobilize an external network that has credibility with the internal bureaucratic leaders. The internal leaders can then issue new declarations and directives to subordinates. In these cases, the external conversations create a conversation loop that feeds back to the bureaucratic leader, bypassing the formal chain of command that quashes proposals. In the military, senior leaders who see that their bureaucracy is impeding military readiness often welcome changes and pressure the bureaucracy's leaders to change.

Another way to produce change in a bureaucracy is to persuade the outside governing entity, such as a legislature, to change the rules of the game. That is not necessarily easy but is much easier if you see it as conversations among people with concerns and power. By dealing with their concerns, you mobilize their power.

19
MEASURING

If you can't measure it, you can't improve it.
-- Peter Drucker

Data are inscriptions from instruments; they have no intrinsic meaning of their own. Scientists and engineers give data their meaning.
-- Bruno Latour

The true measure of a man is not how he behaves in moments of comfort and convenience but how he stands at times of controversy and challenges.
-- Martin Luther King, Jr.

It is the theory that decides what can be observed.
-- Albert Einstein

Sailors know the boat is almost never on course toward the destination. As the wind changes, the captain tacks back and forth to move in the direction of the destination but only rarely points directly at it. How does the captain know when to adjust course? The indicators are the "tell-tales" on the sail and the wind vane at the top of the mast. The tell-tales are small pieces of yarn that show how the wind is moving across the sail. The wind vane is a small fin that points into the wind. Through experience, the captain leverages rules of thumb to know when to adjust course based on the positions of the tell-tales and the vane and the direction the boat must go. How might the captain measure progress toward the destination?

A modern captain would simply use GPS readings to figure the distance from the destination and adjust the course to always get closer. Ancient mariners did not have that luxury. They knew only the general direction of a distant land based on the altitude and direction of the stars. Along the way, they contended with ocean currents, winds, land masses, and storms.

The innovator's situation is closer to that of the ancient mariner. Although there is no GPS for social space, the structures of social space can help show the way. Social power is the currents, moods the winds, resistance the land, and contingencies the storms. The portion of the intended community who have joined the innovation is a measure of progress to the destination.

Every domain of innovation has developed metrics to assist in measuring their progress. A common problem is that the systems of measurement have become so complex that they become their own ends. In this chapter, we investigate the design of metrics that can guide us on the path to innovation without becoming ends in themselves. Failing to make our numbers is not the problem; failing to achieve the mission is the problem. We will examine the kinds of metrics used in business and government to measure innovation. Common innovation metrics generate a paradox: despite the rigor and attention given to metrics, many organizations have success rates well below their goals. The metaphor of the Valley of Death describes the failure but sheds no light on what causes the low adoption rate. We have argued in this book that the paradox results from attempting to understand social space as a production system. It is much more fruitful to measure success at the eight practices and the influences they are having with the customer community.

Data Obsession

Our current age is obsessed with data. Managers want data to make decisions for their organizations. Patients want doctors who

Measuring

base their diagnoses on data. Public officials want data to support their regulatory proposals. AI users want data to train their neural networks. Many people refuse to act unless there is data to (somehow) support their action. Even when they have data, people worry that biases in data can entrap them in bad decisions.

We bring our thirst for data into our projects. We build detailed Gantt charts showing when tasks are to be performed. We measure the resources expended and outcomes achieved for each task. We display our metrics on "dashboards" – collections of digital meters – so that we can keep our eye on the big picture and spot developing problems or bottlenecks. Digital meters come with green-yellow-red color codes for positive, cautionary, and negative readings.

A common problem is that systems of metrics often become their own ends rather than guides toward the mission. We find ourselves under pressure to look good on the dashboard – to "make our numbers" or to "score green on all meters". Managers unwittingly use dashboards to enforce conformity to a worldview and resist anyone – notably innovation leaders -- who seeks change.

Becoming entrapped in a system of measurements is a setup for the disruption problem cited by Clayton Christensen. The current business model is humming along, meeting all its numbers. There are no sensors to detect a threat from a new competitor with a different business model. By the time the dashboard registers that the competitor is siphoning off business, it is too late for a response.

We were members of a task force to propose curriculum reforms. Some members wanted to experiment with new forms and delivery methods to see how students respond. Others wanted to see data that would indicate an experiment would produce a good outcome. The experimenters said that the purpose of the experiments is to generate data and enable evaluation. The data champions countered that it is a waste to undertake any task without supporting data. This standoff prevented the task force from doing anything.

It is essential to be ever vigilant of the environment in which we operate. At any moment, things can change that affect our ability to perform the mission. With a data obsession, we will either miss the warning signs, or we will refuse to change until we have data to back up our decision to change. Remember Andy Grove, CEO of Intel Corporation, who wrote a book *Only the Paranoid Survive*? He was constantly on the watch for any new technology that had the potential to outperform an Intel technology by ten times. He knew that these threats would not register on any dashboard. He monitored for them by listening to the voices of his industry.

The Unseen Model

There is a famous story of the man on his knees searching for his keys near a lamppost on a dark night. A passing police officer kneels down to help. "Where did you lose your keys?" asks the officer. "In my house," the man replies. "Then why are you looking for them here?" asks the officer. The man replies, "This is where the light is."

This is the core story of metrics: they shine light on a certain area. It is easier to search for answers to questions in the places where the metrics shine the light rather than asking whether the answers might be in dark places undetected by the metrics.

We navigate toward goals with the help of mental models of the world. We design metrics to sense the world according to the model. The mental model is our way of making sense of the world and therefore determining what to measure. If our destination is not in the part of the world seen by the model, we will be unable to reach it and we will not have a clue that our model has blinded us. We are often not aware of our mental model.

Philosophers prefer to say "ontology" where we have said "model". Ontology is a description of what makes up a domain: the concepts and their relationships, the main concerns, the language, the standard practices, and the controversies. Fernando Flores recommended that innovators begin by articulating the ontology of their domain before designing changes that would bring about a new practice. Throughout this book, we have used the terms "current common sense" and "new common sense" for the current and new ontologies. Interpreting social spaces as coordination games is another way to reveal the ontology of our communities. An innovation is a change in the play of the game, often achieved by changing an element of the game – for example, a new purpose or a new rule.

Whatever language we use to describe the mental model, the key point is that the model gives us the interpretations that dictate what ought to be measured. Einstein's quote, "It is the theory that decides what can be observed," captures this point nicely.

We have criticized the ontology of the pipeline because it does not include social spaces and does not call for measurements that would reveal whether we are making progress toward adoption of new practice. As we have said, production is necessary but not sufficient to achieve adoption. Our task in the remainder of this chapter is to show how we might design metrics that guide us in navigating toward adoption of new practice. When you are not producing the results you seek, investigate the model behind the metrics: it may blind you from seeing a path to your destination.

Metrics are Directed by the Model

There is a popular slogan, "You get what you measure". It is used to encourage people to provide measurements that prove the outcomes they seek are being achieved. The measures you select depend on your mental model. When your mental model is that pipelines produce innovations, you will design dashboards that measure pipeline characteristics such as the budgets and personnel allocated to each stage, the holding times of each stage, the overall throughput of the pipeline, the bottlenecks, and the number of outputs that transition to customers. If the adoption rate too slow, you look for ways to speed up the pipeline. These can include hackathons to generate more ideas to seed the pipeline, increased training for the managers, more capacity at the bottlenecks, reallocation of budgets and personnel among the stages, or a stepped-up marketing campaign. You are likely to be frustrated repeatedly as you discover that these changes do not lead to more or faster adoption.

When your mental model interprets innovation as adoption of new practice, you will design metrics that indicate whether the conversations for sensing, offering, envisioning, adopting, executing, embodying, and mobilizing are leading to their expected outcomes. If not, you correct course with new requests, declarations, offers, and conversations. The corrections may change as the community of practice grows and faces new contingencies and obstacles to execution.

Metrics of Innovation in Organizations

Many innovation measures presuppose a pipeline and aim to evaluate the efficiency and flow of the pipeline. Here are four common examples.

A government agency administering a research pipeline measures the number of ideas generated at the start, how many survive each stage, how long each idea spends in each stage, how much labor and materials are expended in each stage, and how many emerge from the pipeline as prototypes. They publish these data along with interesting ratios such as dollars spent per completed prototype or idea success rates.

A business might interpret the stages of a pipeline as funnels rather than refinements. Each funnel outputs a subset of its incoming ideas, filtering out ideas of low "merit". In an earlier chapter, we showed a pipeline of funnels model that assumed each stage had a survival rate of 25% -- thus four stages of pipeline required 256 ideas at input to achieve one product at output.

An educational institution or school system typically sees itself as a pipeline of grades from K-12 through college. They measure attrition rates of each grade, overall graduation rates, numbers of teachers, student-teacher ratios, budgets available, dollars per student, and student success rates at standardized exams administered at various points in the pipeline.

Software development companies often see software development as a pipeline consisting of requirements, specifications, prototypes, full system implementation, and testing. In the 1970s, their preferred metrics included lines of code per programmer per day, number of known bugs, number of bugs removed, number of programmers, and budget "burn rates". When it was found that only a third of software projects were delivered on time and within budget, software developers modified the pipeline by adding customer representatives to the stages. This became known as agile development. Agile development sought to forestall a common complaint that software met its specifications but not the intent of its customers. Software developers frequently backtracked and restarted projects with new requirements from the customer. Agile development is an example of a paradigm change inspired by dissatisfaction with what the metrics were showing. The process has been further refined into DevOps, short for Development and Operations Collaboration. DevOps refers to several practices that encourage software development professionals (Dev) and information technology operations professionals (Ops) to work together to efficiently design and develop systems software for customers. Examples of DevOps metrics include lead time for changes, change failure rate, deployment frequency, and mean time to recovery in the event of a failure. The hackathon is another augmentation of software development. Hackathons have become very popular social events that bring programmers and customers together to build or improve software programs. Hackathons generate impressive lists of ideas. Their metrics include how many ideas were produced and how many survived a judging process. Because hackathons address only the ideation parts of software development, they have not significantly influenced the rates of adoption of software products.

All these systems of metrics rely heavily on input-output measures of pipeline stages. Although the linkage between inputs and desired outputs is often weak, managers respond to output shortfalls by turning instinctively to input changes rather than depart from the pipeline model. For example, a school superintendent dissatisfied with student test results is likely to argue for more teachers and more money rather than possibilities that do not fit the pipeline – for instance a project-based curriculum or individualized coaching of students.

Pipeline models hide their customers. The research pipeline often has a vague customer such as a military program of record or just industry. The business pipeline is more explicit about sales, retention rates, and quick surveys at the end of customer service troubleshooting sessions. The education pipeline is openly hostile to the notion that students are customers. Software developers realized belatedly that their products would improve if they included customers in their pipelines.

You will find dozens of websites offering systems of metrics and workshops in how to best use them for maximum productivity. They call these metrics KPIs, or key performance indicators. We found one website that listed two dozen "essential" KPIs, which were different from KPIs on other websites. There is no shortage of metrics and productivity models, and no shortage of managers who are dissatisfied with the outcomes.

The Productivity Anomaly

Despite all the attention to metrics and the belief in "you get what you measure", the success rate of desired innovation outcomes is low. The US Patent Office says less than 5% of patents return the inventor's investment, and only 1 or 2 % get commercialized. Yet patents are often used as proxies for innovation. Business surveys asking for percentages of innovation projects that met their financial goals typically reveal success rates under 5%. These poor results raise the question of whether the metrics we use are channeling us in the right direction. Why does the correlation between inputs and outcomes seem so low? The typical answer is that innovation is inherently unpredictable and the 5% success rate is the best nature will allow; the only path to success is to "take many shots on goal". Managers hope the metrics will help decide which shots are most likely to succeed.

Our original research for *The Innovator's Way* did not support the hypothesis that success rate is inherently low. We could plainly see individuals and teams whose success rates were much higher than 5%. We asked, what do these serial innovators know that we do not? What skills are they exercising that make them successful? That question led us to discover their "secret", which is they are skilled in the eight essential practices. Their success comes from their skillful practice, not sheer luck, charisma, genius, or heroism.

In our opinion, the willingness to tolerate the low success rates reveals a mood of deep resignation, in which higher success rates do not seem possible. All we can do is put up with the low success rate and its expenses and frustrations. The mood of resignation inhibits many from seeking other, more successful approaches to innovation.

Metrics for Adoption

When we declare that the intended outcome is adoption of new practice in our community, we are stepping into an unfamiliar world for measurement. How can we assess that we are on track toward adoption? Notice that we say "assess" rather than "measure". Measure implies a numeric quantity. Assess implies declaring a sense of direction grounded in evidence. Some assessments may rely on measured numbers, but many others do not. Two kinds of assessments are needed for adoption:

1. Progress with each of the eight practices. Each has an outcome critical to the final adoption. Are they being achieved?
2. Coherence among the eight practices and the existing community values.

Table 1 illustrates progress assessments for the eight practices.

An important tool for assessing a delivery team's ability to deliver its innovation promise is the skills profile. Our colleague Dave Newborn uses a spider diagram to display a profile. Figure 1 shows an example. He constructs them in real time as he listens to people pitching their innovation ideas. He listens for and counts the speech acts they use, and from those counts he gives a score 1-5 for each of the practices, indicating how strongly the person demonstrates the skill of each practice. These diagrams are useful in providing coaching to individuals to strengthen their weak practices. They are also useful for forming teams that are strong in all the practices; the team's diagram would combine the member diagrams by taking the maximum score in each dimension. Coaches can be trained to listen for speech acts as they observe teams in action. Competence shows up in performance, not discussions of performance. During performance, things move too rapidly for pretense.

Measuring

Table 1. Progress Assessments for the Eight Practices

Practice	Progress Assessments
Sensing	Clarity of articulation of concern or breakdown Resonance of the articulation with community Coherence with history of community Prevailing moods in the community
Envisioning	Clarity of picture of future Credibility of pathways to that future Resonance of the story with community People in community respond positively
Offering	Clarity of the offer (its conditions of satisfaction) How many are considering the offer? Accepting? Willingness of speaker to take responsibility Trust in the speaker and the offer What concerns are revealed by those who decline?
Adopting	Are people committing to try the new practice? Does the offer appeal to all subcommunities? What is the relative power of the subcommunities? What resistance is showing up? Moods? What concerns are revealed by the resistance?
Sustaining	Can the infrastructure support the continued practice? Does the organization leadership support the change?
Executing	Is there a delivery team? Does the team operate from a shared promise and support each other? Is the team trustworthy?
Embodying	Do the leaders embody the eight practices? Does the community embody the new practice? Do the leaders appreciate and work with skill acquisition?
Mobilizing	Have the leaders gathered followers of the new practice? Are followers gathering more followers? Are the leaders involved in their community? Do the leaders operate from service and care?

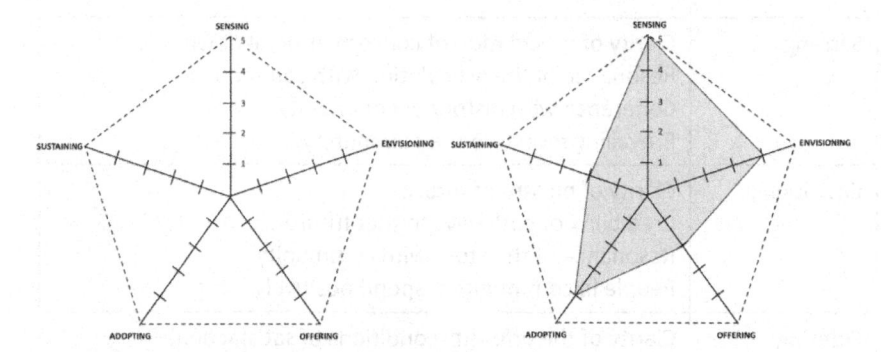

Figure 1. The left figure is a blank spider diagram for the five basic practices. Each practice is measured 1-5, where 1 is unskilled and 5 is maximally skilled. The left figure is the diagram for a particular individual, who is strongest at sensing and weakest at offering and at sustained adoption.

Coherence assessments include:

- When a team is formed, does the team's skill profile maximize all eight dimensions of practice?
- How many conversations a week are teams engaging with customers?
- Does management make time available for employees to engage with the practices? (For example, if the pressure for results is so strong that no one has time for sensing of customer concerns, it will be hard to make progress.)
- Does management provide coaches and mentors for employees to improve their skills in the eight practices?

Our framework for assessing progress is based on assessments of individual performers and teams, grounded in observed, relevant

Measuring

actions. It is important that the parties using these assessments agree on the standards for grounding. We have seen progress frameworks hampered by disagreements among parties about whether the grounding assertions are relevant. For example, in the early 1980s there was a controversy around The Coordinator, a mail-exchange system invented by Fernando Flores and sold through his company Action Technologies. The Coordinator was an email client and a database. The email client tracked progress of conversations for action and guided users toward completion of their loops. The database kept track of all speech acts and the state of each loop. Users who had been trained in workshops about effective practice of conversations for action loved the system. Many said it increased their productivity by 50% or more. However, other users who were not trained in conversations for action often reacted differently. They interpreted The Coordinator as a surveillance tool for micromanagers looking to penalize people for failure to keep their promises. For those who were not rigorous about completing their loops, a software tool that forced them to be rigorous by tracking their promises was outside their comfort zone. In other words, the trained people found the counts of completed promises relevant and useful whereas the untrained people found them irrelevant and dangerous.

The Coordinator story illustrates a distinction we made earlier. When counting kept promises becomes the goal instead of customer satisfaction, employees may feel they were being bludgeoned by management. When satisfying customers is the goal, employees feel more productive and satisfied.

That places a responsibility on managers to teach people the value of conversational practices for themselves and their organization; and to maintain focus on their customers. In that context, these metrics make sense and are not threatening. Organizations that learn this will find themselves with much higher success rates in their innovation projects and much more satisfied employees and customers.

Conclusion

In this chapter we have advocated a change to our common sense about metrics. Our common sense is that "metrics are reality", "Data is king", "Decisions should be evidence-based", "Good performance means making your numbers".

We advocate instead that metrics and dashboards be designed as tools for navigation. Navigation relies on assessments of whether particular actions bring us closer to the destination. The philosopher Bruno Latour, whom we quoted at the beginning of this chapter, said that data are meaningless until interpreted; the resulting actions, not the data, move us toward the innovation goal.

20
MACHINES

> *I believe that at the end of the century the use of words and general educated opinion will have altered so much that one will be able to speak of machines thinking without expecting to be contradicted.*
> -- Alan Turing (1950)

> *What is an offer? It's a speech Act.*
> -- Kari Granger quoting GPT-4

> *A deep-learning system doesn't have any explanatory power.*
> -- Geoffrey Hinton

In late 2022, large language models (LLMs) erupted into the public spotlight. Pundits were quick to claim that LLMs were the next giant step on the path to Artificial General Intelligence and perhaps even the Singularity. These LLM machines have reshaped many expectations about machine intelligence and what conversations are possible with machines. They have created hosts of new opportunities for innovation along with deep concerns about their safety and the future of humankind.

LLM machines mark an inflection point in the computer revolution. For the first time, we have machines that can engage in human-like conversation with us. They seem like newcomers in our neighborhood, and we are not sure what to do with them. For many people, this is profoundly unsettling. How shall we live with machines that talk like us? What if they achieve the power to outsmart us in every dimension of being human? Will they become sources of creativity and innovation? Will they displace humans?

Artificial Intelligence

The name Artificial Intelligence was coined in 1956 by a group of researchers who defined it as machines that could perform cognitive tasks normally considered uniquely human tasks. Over the years many AI technologies have been developed: speech recognition, computer vision, genetic algorithms, language translation, natural language processing, planning, expert systems, board games such as Chess, driverless cars, logic problem solvers, logic processing languages, and neural networks.

Neural networks – circuits modeling the neuronal structure of the brain – were relatively obscure before 2010, a year in which sufficient computing power became available to train very large networks. Those networks could do very interesting tasks. The current generation, Large Language Models, can engage in surprisingly realistic conversations with us. This branch of AI has come to be known as deep learning or machine learning. The term machine learning dates to 1959, when Arthur Samuels of IBM used it for machines that use feedback for self-improvement.

The idea that AI could eventually surpass human cognitive capabilities fell into the background in the 1990s and 2000s. It was rejuvenated after 2010 when it seemed that supercomputing power might enable it. Today this dream is called Artificial General Intelligence. AGI is the idea that computers will eventually be better than humans at every human cognitive task.

Singularity

Raymond Kurzweil argued that information technology is in its fifth generation of exponential growth. At that rate he predicts that around 2045 machines will achieve superhuman abilities. At that point, it becomes impossible to predict the future because we cannot know what concerns the machines will have and what they see of our role as humans. He calls that moment of absolute unpredictability The Singularity, a word borrowed from mathematics where it means a discrete point where a function becomes infinite.

What if LLM machines are not intelligent, but banal? There are indications that this may be so. They cannot distinguish truth from falsehood or the possible from impossible. They cannot care about anything, take responsibility for anything they say, take a stand on anything, or make and keep commitments. They are amoral, with no ethics, and no sense of consequences for actions they might recommend. Let us explore these ideas through the lens of language-action philosophy.

Innovations often deal with ideas and practices that did not exist before. LLMs are good at "learning" enormous quantities of data and, based on those data, computing statistically highly probable responses to questions. The word "probable" is important here. By design, these machines are incapable of coming up with the improbable. Jensen Huang, the CEO of NVIDIA, characterized the power of the large language models as "prior knowledge that enables us to know what is already known". By contrast, Einstein's theory of relativity was an improbable explanation of contradictions between the wave and particle characterizations of light. In science, breakthroughs often occur when an improbable theory or hypothesis is verified.

An Avalanche Arrives

An avalanche is a rapid change in a society that upsets many practices and identities. LLMs precipitated an avalanche. Two themes have shown up in the conversations of the aftermath. One is optimistic and focuses on the good things the technology can bring in narrowly defined applications. The other is pessimistic and focuses on the damages that can be wrought from improper use of the technology. This is not a call to take sides, but rather to be aware there are two sides and act responsibly.

One of the most promising examples of LLMs producing value is medical diagnosis, such as identifying polyps from colonoscopy images or cancer from mammogram images. The same sort of technology is accelerating the search for molecules that can become new drugs. In business, it is creating new products and augmenting existing products. It powers interactive voice customer service. It inspires startups to try out new lines of business. In marketing, it enables new methods of collecting personal data and generating personalized ads. In journalism, it provides new ways to summarize documents and jump-start the writing process. In art, it generates images, music, and poems. In programming, it generates initial versions of code that can be rapidly edited and corrected by programmers. The technology enables all sorts of innovation in the form of new offers for software and services.

On the pessimistic side, LLMs routinely "hallucinate", that is, make up answers to questions and present their fabrications as authoritative statements. This has raised serious questions about their trustworthiness. Artists, musicians, writers, and newspapers are up in arms about copyright issues when LLMs are trained by "scraping" the Internet, including their copyrighted works without permission. Law enforcement and political leaders are concerned about the ease with which troublemakers can commit crimes such as cyberattacks and create false documents, false images, false voice and video recordings, and other deepfakes. Political and civic leaders express deep concern about the use of LLMs to manipulate people in elections. Parents and social leaders express deep concern about its use and abuse in addicting young people to social media. Labor leaders express deep concern that LLM automation might extinguish many jobs. Some AI experts declare that LLMs will, without strong government regulation, spin out of control and inflict great damage on humanity.

> **LLMs routinely "hallucinate", that is, make up answers to questions and present their fabrications as authoritative**

This technology has changed what people perceive as possible in their lives and in the life of their community. It is reshaping the world and changing the realities for people, both positively and negatively.

Now we will examine how LLMs interact with the main issues of human concern.

LLM Basics

From the earliest days of electronic computing in the 1940s, people have wondered whether computers whose structures resemble brains might become intelligent. They invented artificial neurons, circuits that simulate brain neurons. An artificial neuron receives signals from other neurons and enters state 1 if the sum of its inputs exceeds a threshold, or state 0 otherwise. This idea did not take off for mainstream computing because computers built that way were too slow. Researchers continued to investigate this idea and evolved it into today's artificial neural network, or ANN, which is a circuit consisting of layers of artificial neurons. Each neuron of a layer has a link connecting its output (0 or 1) to every neuron of the next layer. Each link as a weight that determines what fraction of its input is delivered to its output. The weights are called parameters because they are adjusted during the training process. The training process works its way through a long series of examples (x,y) where y is the output that the network is supposed to give when presented with input x. The training algorithm adjusts parameters to minimize the error between the actual and intended outputs. The most advanced model, ChatGTP-4, has a core ANN with around 1 trillion parameters. Its training process was done by a massively parallel supercomputer that took 90-100 days and cost over $100 million in electricity and labor. Once trained, an ANN is very fast, producing its output in microseconds.

LLMs are artificial neural networks (ANN) created by a complex, two-phase process. The first phase sets up the core-ANN, whose job is to predict the next word that would appear after a given text (the "prompt"). To enable this, the prompt is encoded so that the nearness of words can be represented; words that are near those in the prompt are more likely to appear next. The core-ANN is trained on billions of words of text from the Internet to respond to a prompt with a highly probable next word after the prompt. The predicted word is appended to the prompt, which is cycled back as a new query of the ANN. This cycle is repeated to generate the sequence of words in the response. The second phase is called "fine tuning" or "tweaking". It sets up a second ANN, tweak-ANN, whose job is to respond to a (prompt, response) pair with a score that indicates human satisfaction with the response. Tweak-ANN is trained from a dataset of (prompt, response, score) elements obtained by generating a large number of random prompts, getting core-ANN responses to each, and having human readers score the responses. Once trained on these data, the tweak-ANN can predict the human satisfaction score for a (prompt, response) pair. The tweak-ANN is then used in a reinforcement learning mode to adjust the weights in the core-ANN so that its responses tend to get higher scores according to the tweak-ANN. In some cases, data from user responses to the tweaked LLM responses are fed back to further fine-tune core-ANN weights for better results.

When this process is completed, the basic fact remains: the LLM is an ANN that makes statistical inferences of text highly likely in response to a prompt. The likelihoods are set during initial training and tweaking and can be changed after by further tweaking.

LLMs produced a dramatic shift in the way people see computers. In 2020, most people said that it would be a long time before a machine could pass the Turing Test. In 2023, a significant minority of people said the machines could pass the test and they could not distinguish between LLM and human generated texts. In 1950, Alan Turing thought it would take until the year 2000 before anyone would think it credible that a conversation machine could not be distinguished from a human. He was off by only 20 years.

A main reason behind this perceptual shift is that these machines have finally "entered into language". People are reassessing machine intelligence based on the impressive linguistic displays of LLMs.

We have stressed throughout this book that language is not simply grammar and words, it is a milieux of expression, coordination, culture, customs, interpretation, and history that fundamentally fashions our way of being in the world. Despite their surprising capacity to participate in human-like conversations, LLMs do not share other human abilities conferred by language. It is more accurate, as some are saying, to see LLMs as "stochastic parrots"[1] manifesting an alien intelligence. LLMs cannot match the ways we humans shape and are shaped by language.

Noam Chomsky, a highly respected linguist, joined with two colleagues in a critique of LLMs.[2] In addition to the issues discussed above, they noted that LLMs' method of learning language – scraping huge text databases from the Internet – is completely different from the way children learn language. This means that there is ultimately no way LLMs can learn language in the way humans learn and live language – no way they can overcome the problems mentioned earlier. After iterating with ChatGPT on questions around morality and ethics, Chomsky concluded:

> ChatGPT exhibits something like the banality of evil: plagiarism and apathy and obviation. It summarizes the standard arguments in the literature by a kind of super-autocomplete, refuses to take a stand on anything, pleads not merely ignorance but lack of intelligence and ultimately offers a "just following orders" defense, shifting responsibility to its creators.

---

[1] The term "stochastic parrot" was coined by Emily Bender of the University of Washington, to describe LLMs.
[2] N. Chomsky, I. Roberts, J. Watumull. 2023. "Noam Chomsky: The False Promise of ChatGPT." Guest essay in *New York Times* (March 8, 2023).

Chomsky worried that with all the enthusiasm to incorporate LLMs into many networked applications, we come to regret our accomplishment and be unable to turn off.

Let's review the differences between humans and machines and then determine what conclusions we can draw about the capabilities of LLM machines to create new ideas and lead innovation.

Care

Care is one of the most fundamental aspects of being human. Humans care about each other and about future possibilities. Care distinguishes between what matters and what does not. What we care about solicits our attention and action. We are not drawn to be in service of unimportant matters.

Language is our means to articulate what we care about and bring our concerns into focus. Language enables our communities to discriminate right from wrong, nobility from baseness, good from evil, and humanity from bestiality.

We demonstrate our care by taking stands and sustaining them, in word and deed. Being in language with others enables us to commit our lives and coordinate with others around shared human concerns such justice, progress, revolution, conservation, romantic love, artistic creativity, and much more.

One important matter that humans cannot help caring about is the honesty and sincerity of others. We care about getting things right. We care about truth.

Machines do none of this. They do not and cannot care.

Shared Spaces of Concerns

Language enables us to explicitly share matters of common concern and to coordinate our actions to take care of them. Even seemingly trivial moments of chit-chat, such as discussing the weather, acknowledge and generate shared spaces of concerns. We have called these shared spaces "worlds" and perceive them as realities. We have a sense of belonging to a larger whole, the "we" who share commitments and norms of proper behavior. We co-create our worlds through our conversations and interactions. We pass on our beliefs, values, and norms to our children and others through our conversations with them in our worlds. We share convictions, commitments, assessments, and opinions. We imitate and influence each other, often without even realizing it. We change each other's minds. We develop life-long friendships and seek mentors to shape our lives. We clean up distrust, banish resentments, and open new futures together. We socialize and adapt in the shared space, shaping each other's ways of thinking, acting, and being. Language can also be a tool of power and domination, a medium to establish, maintain, and contest social hierarchies.

Machines do not have concerns and are incapable of forming social spaces of shared concerns. Machines have no conscience. They cannot discern the appropriateness of their actions or experience remorse for negative consequences of their decisions.

Commitments

Language enables humans to make and deliver on commitments. Our commitments structure our worlds. We examined commitments and the conversations that generate them in Chapter 6.

Commitments are always social. We make commitments to other people. We hold each other responsible for how we live up to our commitments. Consistent success at fulfilling commitments generates a rapport of trust that circulates in our communities. And consistent failure generates distrust, anger, and resentment. Trust in turn shapes the interactions others are willing to have with us.

Commitments are essential for coordinating actions and co-creating a future. Requests and promises are the two main linguistic vehicles for coordinating actions. They are not formulaic sequences of words. They are events in the relationships between people. They generate expectations of future actions. Making a promise and accepting a request both involve setting a stake in the future and guiding our subsequent actions to take care of the underlying concern. When these expectations are not met, or when the concern has been misinterpreted, a breakdown in the relationship often happens, and further conversations are needed to repair it.

A statistical model of language (an LLM) can track a conversation for action as it unfolds, and it can keep records of agreements and convey them to the responsible parties. But without the common sense to discern the vagaries of human concern, without an embodied presence in the world to carry out future actions, and without an emotional susceptibility to breakdowns in relationships that can happen when promises and requests are broken, LLMs cannot yet participate in this all-important dance of human language.

Predicting what words come next is radically different from making the commitments expressed in those words. LLMs cannot make commitments. We already know this intuitively: LLMs are tools. If an LLM fails or causes damage, we do not blame the tool or hold it responsible, we hold the designers or ourselves responsible.

Moods and Emotions

Language permeates our emotional life. Moods and emotions are among the most important ways we experience the world together. Moods are embodied dispositions that shape the possibilities we can see. Emotions are embodied reactions to events. Both are closely linked to our ability to make assessments in language. An emotion is a reactive assessment of a current event; a mood gives us assessments about the future, shaping what actions are possible for us. By examining and sharing these assessments, we have the capability to sense, to anticipate, and to explore our own and other people's moods and emotions.

Language is permeated by emotional resonance. We can be insulted or flattered simply by the way someone talks to us. We would find it jarring if a waiter at an upscale restaurant spoke in the same way as a cashier at a late-night fast-food joint. Our actions provoke emotional and mood responses in ourselves and others. For example, someone who routinely lies or makes insincere promises evokes anger, resentment, or indignation. Communities resonate with collective moods such as anxiety about a pandemic, joy when a sports team wins a match, or distrust of government institutions. Competent leaders read and flow with moods, avoiding making requests when people are unreceptive, and making requests when they are receptive.

LLMs can generate text strings that signify emotions and moods, but these strings are statistical constructions. Having no concerns and no bodies, machines have no emotions and no moods, and no means to develop sensibilities for them.

The Background

Our language conveys the ripples of conversations passed down through years and centuries from prior generations. Our beliefs, customs, mannerisms, practices, and values are inherited from the conversations of our forebears, combining with the conversations we share today. Most of the time we think, speak, and act against this historical background of presuppositions and prejudices without being aware of it. This background is boundless, with no definite beginning or end, extending beyond every horizon.

We have the remarkable ability to sense and reveal what is in the background, to make what is tacit explicit, to "make sense" of current issues. Often, we do this in a process of exploration, asking each other why we said or did something. Such exploration in conversation brings forth new meanings and emotions. Poets do this professionally, by revealing our shared background and transforming our sense of it.

Paradoxically, we often react to a revelation of something hidden in the background with "that's obvious". It is obvious, because it fits the background even though it was not obvious the moment before it was revealed. What we call "common sense" is all that goes without saying in this tacit "background of obviousness" that nevertheless makes sense when revealed and brought into conversation.

In the 1980s, failures of expert systems were attributed to missing "common sense facts" that are obvious to us, but not to the machine. Expert system designers sought compendia of common-sense facts that the machine could use. Perhaps the most famous of these efforts was the Cyc project of Douglas Lenat, which after 40 years had accumulated 30 million common sense facts. Yet even that treasury could not add up to a background of common sense and make expert systems smart enough to be experts.

Now that we have LLMs, it is reasonable to ask whether these machines can infer background context statistically. The documents and tweaks used to train LLMs are written by people who, like the rest of us, are mostly unaware of the vast tacit knowledge they readily draw upon in their context. It seems unlikely that these machines can infer text that has not been written or recorded.

Imagination is another human ability that flows from our tacit background. It is a capacity to conceive possibilities that do not exist and can become incorporated into our shared background once articulated. Although LLMs have generated some surprisingly imaginative poetry, it is more likely that these are unexpected statistical inferences rather than genuine creations relative to the background. This question deserves more exploration.

Embodied Action

Our ability to act exceeds our linguistic powers. Much of what we "know" is in the form of embodied practices rather than descriptions and rules – knowing-how rather than knowing-that. Even if we can linguistically describe a practice, reading the description does not impart the skill of performing the practice. Michael Polanyi, a philosopher, captured the paradox in his famous saying, "We know more than we can tell."

Descriptions of actions can be represented as bits and stored in a machine database. However, performance skill can only be demonstrated but not decomposed to bits. Performance knowledge, what psychologists call "procedural memory" (memory of how to do things), is deeply ingrained into our embodied brains, nervous systems, and muscles. This intuitive, embodied sense of relevance resists being objectively measured, recorded, or described.

We have made frequent use in this book of the Dreyfus skills hierarchy. In their framework, the beginner has no embodied skill and can only act by explicitly following decontextualized rules. The expert has a fully embodied familiarity with typical situations and acts without following rules. A person's skill increases through practice, often with the help of coaches and mentors who already have the skill. The Dreyfus brothers argued that machines cannot attain the skills of experts because experts do not rely on rules and machines have no biological bodies.

Machines store knowledge given them by rules, algorithms, and data. This applies to traditional logic machines, which are programmed, and modern neural networks, which are trained on given data. The statistical inferences performed by LLMs are computed by the algorithms defined by the neural network. In contrast, human bodies live and interact in their connective and interpretative structures constantly shaped by tacit knowledge.

Because tacit knowledge cannot be recorded, it seems unlikely that statistical inference from recorded data can reveal it.

In fact, this is the reason we design and build machines. They can marshal enormous calculation speeds or kinetic forces, well beyond human capabilities. Machines with an exogenous "body" of hardware can get their gears, levers, hydraulics, and circuits to do tasks on a scale that is impossible for embodied humans. That is what makes machines valuable to us.

Can LLMs be Innovation Leaders?

LLMs reveal striking new statistical predictabilities in our use of language and have harnessed these to imitate human conversation in a deeply impressive way. In doing so, they have exposed some serious gaps in our understanding of language. How much of the language we use every day can be modeled by statistical inference? Can the mathematics of inference (Bayesian methods) make inferences that no one has ever considered? Are those inferences "creations" or just "revelations" of what was hidden in the data?

Inference is a third-person phenomenon susceptible to mathematical formalization. Human immersions in care, responsibility, communities, assessments, imaginations, futures, commitments, worlds, moods, emotions, backgrounds of obviousness, and embodied action are not susceptible to formalization and are out of reach for LLMs. Our best strategy is to acknowledge that humans and machines each have powers that the other lacks. We can then focus on designing machines and their interfaces to augment human powers with machine powers. The table below suggests limited ways that LLMs could assist innovation leaders.

The most telling argument against the hypothesis that an LLM can create something new and innovative is the limitation inherent in its design: an LLM can only infer the probable given its training data. New inventions and innovations are almost always improbable.

Machines

Humans live in language. Machines are outside of language. If machines develop an intelligence, it will seem very alien to us and we might regret our achievement.

Table 1: LLM augmentations for innovation leadership

Sensing	LLMs only generate statistical inferences from what has been recorded in training texts and learned during training. Much of what humans call "common sense" cannot be inferred from texts or training data. LLMs cannot listen for concerns that have not been spoken. However, inferences can reveal implications of the data that the leader would be unaware of.
Envisioning	LLMs can generate texts that follow the rhetorical structures of good envisioning stories. They could support humans in crafting envisioning stories. They have no way of assessing how relevant the claims are to the community being addressed.
Offering	LLMs cannot make commitments. Therefore, no offers.
Adopting and sustaining	In their current instantiations, LLMs cannot be trusted and cannot therefore reliably elicit commitments from humans.
Embodying	LLMs have no bodies. They cannot embody a skill.
Executing	LLMs and associated databases can track speech acts of teams and their customers, which is very useful, but cannot enact their speech acts.
Mobilizing	Mobilizing in the sense of orchestrating and gathering a following committed to an idea is not possible without trust in the leaders. LLMs are notoriously trustworthy.

21
MASTERY

> *Only one who devotes himself to a cause with his whole strength and soul can be a true master. For this reason mastery demands all of a person.*
> -- Albert Einstein

> *If people knew how hard I worked to get my mastery, it wouldn't seem so wonderful at all.*
> -- Michelangelo

> *Mastery, I learned, was not something genetic, or for a lucky few. It is something we can all attain if get rid of some misconceptions and gain clarity as to the required path.*
> -- Robert Greene

We play in many infinite games – games with the purpose of continuing the play. This means that there is a constant flow of new arrivals to the game along with departures for all kinds of reasons including retirements and deaths. In turn that means there are always players at every level of skill from beginner and advanced beginner through competent, proficient, expert and ultimately master. Each person enters the game as beginner and advances through the stages with practice until it is their time to leave the game. We have emphasized the need to be a beginner and to tolerate the discomfort and frustrations that arise when learning a new practice. In every innovation, you and your community start as beginners in the new practice.

Mastery is the highest level of skill we can acquire in a game. Many aspire to mastery. At this most advanced stage of practice, you embody your domain so well that you know it and all the possibilities it offers. You no longer consciously follow the rules. You respond to what appears before you with such a depth of knowledge that you intuitively know the right thing to do. You invent new rules that others want to adopt and styles they want to imitate. You perform in the "flow" state with joy and gusto in every performance. You have evolved your own style after studying (apprenticing) with masters. You are always learning new things and you bring intense curiosity to your world. You live in a mood of serenity and satisfaction, always ready to respond to what shows up, always humble because there are so many things you do not know.

Masters are celebrated by their communities and may be recognized by those outside. Masters exist in every domain. The master painter. The master violinist. The master ball player. The master writer. The master chef. The master statesman. The master plumber. The master electrician. In the military, the master sergeant and master chief. Not everyone becomes a master in their domain, and not all masters are publicly recognized. When they are public figures, we go out of our way to attend shows, events, and concerts to see them perform. We shower them our admiration. We take inspiration from them to improve our own practice.

In the progression from beginner to master, you start with no embodiment in the game and can act only from the explicit rules of the game or by imitating other players. As you progress with your skill, you act more through your embodiment and less by applying rules. When you attain mastery, you fully embody the game and are no longer conscious of the rules when you perform.

There is wonderful movie about mastery: *Being in the World*, produced and directed by Tao Ruspoli.[1] It features numerous scenes

---

[1] Do a Google search for YouTube with key words "Being in the World Ruspoli".

of nine masters at their work, interleaved with philosophers interpreting what these masters are doing that makes them masters. They are:

>Ryan Cross, bass cellist
>Leah Chase, chef
>Manuel Molena, flamenco guitarist
>Hiroshi Sakaguchi, carpenter
>Jumane Smith, jazz trumpeter
>Austin Peralta, jazz pianist
>Tony Austin, jazz drummer
>Bob Teague, speedboat racer
>Lindsay Benner, juggler

The movie was inspired by the work of the philosopher Hubert Dreyfus and he is in fact the tenth master celebrated. His message is that if you learn and practice language-action philosophy, you will have the best chance to evolve into a master. We have relied heavily on that philosophy in this book. We recommend this film because it highlights common factors shared by all the masters:

- You need coaches and mentors; without them your progress may stall.
- You need to practice all the time.
- Make it a practice to find joy every day in your work.
- Cultivate a mood of serenity and humility: there is always something to learn.
- Every action can be done with care and excellence.
- Inspire others toward mastery, by showing a path.

In short, although we emphasize beginners, we want you to aspire to mastery.

The Ten Thousand Hour Myth

There is a popular misconception of how much practice it takes to become a master. The misconception was popularized in the book *Outliers*, by Malcolm Gladwell. Gladwell asserted that a common factor among the masters he studied was that they all practiced for 10,000 hours or more. Gladwell was trying to make the point that mastery takes time and work. Unfortunately, many people have taken his "10,000 rule" out of context and claim that all you need to do to become a master is be engaged in practice for 10,000 hours. The problem with this claim is that you can spend 10,000 hours practicing the wrong thing and in so doing acquire bad habits that are hard to break.

Peter tells the following story to illustrate the point. When I was in high school, I became interested in golf, first as a caddy and then as a player. In my junior-year of college my athlete roommate told me that if I really wanted to become a scratch golfer, I should be out on the course every day practicing my game. And so I did. For the next ten years, I played golf every day, rain or shine, cold or warm, winter or summer, without fail. After all that time, however, the best I could shoot was around 80, far from scratch golf at 72. I decided I needed help from a golf pro and took lessons from one of the best in my town. The pro's coaching helped me for a day or two after each lesson, but out on the course my score did not improve. The pro offered a playing lesson, where he accompanied me on a round to observe and coach. At the end of that round, he said, "I'm afraid I cannot help you. Your bad habits are so deeply ingrained I cannot change them." Soon after, I quit golf. The good news is that all the frustration disappeared. I am left only with the memories, and a grumpy back injured by many years of an unbalanced swing.

Over those years, Peter accumulated considerably more than 10,000 hours of practice. He spent 10,000 hours practicing the wrong things. The coach could not undo his deeply ingrained bad habits.

The Path to Mastery

Mastery is an assessment by the community. The path to mastery requires coach or mentor supervised practice and correction. This is an uncomfortable truth for many who want to practice on their own or resent having their practice corrected. We must practice diligently in the community to ensure we are embodying the right practices. Hubert Dreyfus comments on the path:

> The training of musicians provides a clue. If you are training to become a performing musician, you have to work with an already recognized master. The apprentice cannot help but imitate the master, because when you admire someone and spend time with them, their style becomes your style. But then the danger is that the apprentice will become merely a copy of the master, while being a virtuoso performing artist requires developing a style of one's own.
>
> Musicians have learned from experience that those who follow one master are not as creative performer as those who have worked sequentially with several. The apprentice, therefore, needs to leave his first master and work with a master with a different style. (H. Dreyfus, *On the Internet*, Routledge, 2001, p45)

Choose good coaches and mentors on your journey to mastery.

Even more frustrating, improvements in performance are never linear and continuous. George Leonard comments:

> To take the master's journey, you have to practice diligently, striving to hone your skills, to attain new levels of competence. But while doing so – and this is the inexorable fact of the journey – you also have to be willing to spend most of your time on a plateau, to keep practicing even when you seem to be getting nowhere. Improvement comes in spurts. (G. Leonard, *Mastery*, Plume, 1993, p. 15)

Leonard concludes that one day, when you least expect it, you will suddenly find yourself at the next level. The key to staying the path is to find joy in the practice, enjoying the journey more than the destination.

The Arts of War and of Life

We would like to conclude this book with some reflections on the "servant leader", whom we have held as the exemplar of the master innovation leader.

Throughout the ages, various sages have discussed the art of war, which aims to crush resistance to the aims of a powerful leader, and the art of life, which aims to bring harmony to a world riven with conflicts and competition. The art of war is an attack-and-defend response, while the art of life is a blend response. Two sages of these arts stand out as exemplars: Sun Tzu and Lao Tzu. Both Sun Tzu and Lao Tzu lived about 2500 years ago. Sun Tzu was a military general revered for his wisdom in avoiding wars if possible and winning them when necessary. He wrote *The Art of War*, which remains a common reference today for both business and military leaders. Lao Tzu was revered for his wisdom on cultivating harmony in communities while being realistic about conflicts and competitions. He wrote *Tao Te Ching*, which is widely consulted today by business and military leaders for its insights. The "Tzu" in their names is an honorific title meaning "master".

The teachings of Sun Tzu have been popular to this day when companies or governments think of themselves as waging wars – such as competitive battles with other companies in the marketplace or campaigns to reshape social policies. Notice that many companies and governments formulate their offers as wars – war on poverty, war on drugs, war against other ideologies, war against predatory competitors.

What does Sun Tzu have to say about winning wars? Scholars of

Sun Tzu have summarized his philosophy with five tenets:

- Choose your battles: Know when to fight and when not to fight. The best victories are achieved without fighting.
- Deceive the enemy: Appear weak when strong, and strong when weak; close when far away, and far away when close.
- Know your strengths and weaknesses, and those of your enemy.
- Change and chaos bring opportunities; opportunities multiply as they are seized.
- No one profits from prolonged warfare.

What does Lao Tzu have to say about living life? Scholars have summarized his philosophy with six points:

- Don't force anything. The person who uses force to achieve aims is likely to end up with nothing.
- Give up the urge to control the world. Flow with it.
- Don't overburden yourself either with tasks or self-praise. Those who try to outshine others dim their own light.
- Eschew attachments. They drag you down. The less you own the wealthier you are.
- Don't cling to life. Celebrate every day. Each morning, give thanks for the gift of the new day.
- Embrace simplicity, patience, compassion.

Early in this book, we spoke of finite and infinite games. Sun Tzu teaches the art of winning the finite game. Lao Tzu teaches the art of playing the infinite game. Both are relevant because the world is made up of both kinds of game.

Both philosophies share an emphasis and commitment to service and care. Leaders need to conduct themselves in a way that respects and values their people and supports their ability to fulfill the mission. Good leaders perceive themselves as servants of the mission. The stern but wise military leader exercises control to enable the soldiers to take care of one another in the battle, not to benefit the leader's personal whims or lust for power. Both philosophies emphasize diplomacy that brings agreements while avoiding battle. This translates into a practical philosophy for innovation leaders:

- Understand the social community – its structure, concepts, technologies, history, and concerns.
- Listen and interact with the community. What do people care about? For what will they commit themselves?
- Listen to yourself: For what will you commit yourself?
- Blend around resistance. Make offers that address concerns about the costs, benefits, and risks. Be prepared to improvise, disguise, and work deals.
- Recruit supporters and allies. Encourage community leaders to adopt the practice and promote it.
- Teach people the new practice and cultivate those who can teach it too. Be compassionate as they work their way from beginner to competent at the new practice.

Coercive and Servant Leaders

Two kinds of innovation leadership are common: coercive and servant. The coercive leader aims to get new practices through force and compulsion, often against the will of the community. The changes achieved by a coercive leader often disappear after the leader departs, and the previous practice reemerges. In contrast, the servant leader attracts followers with offers that take care of their concerns. The changes achieved by a servant leader persist after that leader is gone, even after the leader's name fades from most memories. Most innovation leaders are a combination of these two styles.

Many new leaders mistake coercion for leadership. They assume that the leader gives orders and subordinates obey. The coercive leader is a Hollywood favorite: the Hollywood general does what is necessary despite resistance and personal or community costs. We have heard novice leaders say they want to learn the leadership practices to more easily make others do what they say. Not only does this display a mistaken idea of innovation leadership, but it also reveals a disposition to interpret leadership as a way of controlling others.

In contrast, the servant leader brings community members to commit to and embody the new practice. The servant leader gives credit to others as they demonstrate the new practice and achieve success. The servant leader is also likely to be successful at bringing about sustained adoption of new practices. We favor the servant leader as a model for innovation leadership. Lao Tzu captures the spirit well: "When the Master's work is done, the people say, 'Amazing: we did it all by ourselves'."

When we talk about service and servant leadership, what do we really mean? Ron Kaufman, internationally recognized as a guru for uplifting service, says that *service is action that brings value to others*.[2] Value can take many forms, such as more money, more prestige, more emotional support, more pleasure, or getting past a crisis.

Kaufman also says that *care is concern for the future well-being of person or a community*. As we have said, listening for concerns is the same as listening for what people care about, what matters to them;

---

[2] Ron Kaufman. 2020. Generative Responsibility. Keynote address to Asia Professional Speakers convention. See the segment 15:00 to 20:00 of his speech at https://www.youtube.com/watch?v=4OlEV2Cb2n0

they will change their practice to take care of a concern that is not being addressed in the current situation.

The well-being of others is at the heart of service and care. Service produces value for the well-being of someone, care is concern for continuing their future well-being. Kaufman summarizes the endless interaction between service and care with the saying *service is care in action*.

Service and care are at the heart of the eight practices. The listening practice attunes to current concerns. The envisioning practice pictures a way to take care of those concerns in the future. The offering practice puts the leader's service to the new practice into action. The adopting practices embody the new practice into the community.

Involvement and Detachment

Two background moods will affect your ability to navigate as innovation leader. One is detachment: you see yourself as an interested objective outside observer of your community. The other is involvement: you see yourself as fully immersed in your community, in its concerns and practices.

Our age values abstraction. Our technology and global connectivity allow us to gather enormous quantities of data and abstract them to characterize groups as sets of defined properties and rights. The groups dominate; the individual disappears. The ability to view large scale phenomena through the lens of distilled data is strong force for abstraction and allows large-scale interventions. Unfortunately, abstraction is also a force for detachment, the loss of connection with our fellow human beings.

Detachment orients us to be an outside observer of our community. A big trap with this orientation is that we substitute our belief about what our community needs for whatever concerns they are experiencing. In our certainty that our solution will work, we become impatient with their uncertainty about whether anything will work. Our solution looks to them like a mindless algorithm rather than a compassionate understanding of their situation. When we are detached, people do not trust us and may pull away from us.

Detachment has two roots – control and objectivity. Control is an orientation to get to a prescribed future by forcing actions. The desire to control is a natural reaction to the unpredictability of the future. Control is essential in many arenas such as government bureaucracies, manufacturing, transportation, and military operations. Control is also used by leaders to maintain their power. Control does not work for innovation because the future depends on the agreements of many people and is unpredictable. As innovation leaders, we accept the unpredictability and employ the practices of this book to guide our community to adoption of a new practice.

Objectivity is touted as a way to avoid acting from prejudices and biases. Objectivity is valuable for some professions, such as science or the law. In science, objectivity is important for the scientific method. In the law, objectivity is a way to reach conclusions of guilt or innocence beyond reasonable doubt. Hubert Dreyfus worried that, outside these restricted domains, detached objectivity supports a "technological way of being" that sees the whole world as objects that can be investigated, manipulated, predicted, and controlled by technology. This worldview, he argued, can lead to chronic feelings of disorientation because many things in the world cannot be manipulated, predicted, or controlled.

Involvement, the opposite of detachment, orients us to a deep listening to our community's concerns, even when community members are unable to put them clearly into words. We are curious about their practices, their histories, their daily activities. We are concerned about their well-being. We are compatriots in their issues, aiming to serve them with a new practice that will dispel their problem. We are not outsiders; we are fellow members of their community. When we are involved, they come to trust us and enjoy engaging with us.

This is why involvement is so important for the innovation leader. Involvement makes no distinction between "inside" and "outside". We are not the outside observer looking in; we are an integral, functioning member of our community. We participate fully in the practices, concerns, norms, and values of our community. We grow and nurture relationships with those in our community. We make commitments to take care of concerns in our community. We take responsibility for our commitments and the consequences of our actions. There is no way to separate our "observer" from our community: much of what we think is our unique insight is actually the manifestation of our community.

We have argued in this book that the social spaces we must navigate to bring about new practice are not governed by mathematical laws. Although they have structures that we can navigate with, we cannot get to our goals by "reasoning together". Instead, we must "converse together". Applying logic is being detached; having conversations is being involved.

How can we open ourselves to greater involvement? The eight innovation practices are a good start. We will be more successful with these practices if we are involved in our community. We do not let our imaginings of what concerns them, honed by years of detachment, substitute for their actual concerns.

The Leader's Legacy

We remarked above that the servant leader is unlikely to be remembered long after the new practice is in place. Leaders who are concerned with their legacy are less likely to be successful because they orient on themselves rather than their community. We would like to reflect on this point.

Peter tells this story: On a Sunday morning nearly three decades ago my wife Dorothy and I were walking along the Potomac River in Washington, DC. I was considering a job change and was concerned about whether my new responsibilities would divert me from my aspiration that my work "make a mark". She asked what I meant by making a mark. That meant, I confided, that people would long remember my contribution by name. She said that if that is my philosophy of life, I am likely to be disappointed. She explained her philosophy, in which she does not have that concern. She sees herself as a cell in the large body of humanity past, present, and future. Her life purpose is to be a good cell. She embraces every project with care and excellence – to do the best possible job. In this way she will contribute to the health of the whole and have impact on the whole without having to control anything. It is not her purpose that her name be attached to anything she has contributed. When she is gone, her job is done and other cells will continue to serve the well-being of the whole. I asked her about the awards and recognitions she received for her work. She said she appreciated the honors, but it was never her objective or interest to win an award or be recognized. This conversation forever altered my thinking about the contributions I could make.

Think about this. If each of us is doing our job, being a good cell in the large body of all humanity, we keep our neighbors healthy and thereby contribute to the health of the whole. Our contribution flows through our neighbors to the whole like a ripple in the river of humanity. Over time, the ripple remains but memories of us disappear.

Anyone who has had the opportunity to take a walk in Arlington Cemetery can see this. In every direction, fading into the distance, are lines of headstones, each labeled simply with the name and dates of a soldier, sailor, airman, or Marine. With only a few exceptions, that is all we know about them anymore. There can never be an answer to the question, "Who was that soldier?" Yet we know that collectively those soldiers made our country safe. Their combined ripples became a torrent etching an indelible mark on history.

Give the limitations on our brains and interactions with other people, how can we make a difference? Start with our neighbors in our communities. We do not accomplish anything alone. A contribution spreads in the conversations, stories, and practices we share with each other. A contribution becomes greater when we mobilize our communities around it – they adopt its practice and become voices advocating it in new networks. This helps explain why individual names often disappear from contributions – the contributions actually came from communities.

Servant leadership serves our communities and takes as reward the contributions themselves rather than long-term recognition. Instead of thinking we are the serfs of technologies that drive our conditions, consider that technologies can enable us to take care of our community's well-being and to learn more about the human condition. The idea that technology reveals and enables the human condition is not the current common sense, although it was a commonly held view in previous eras. Perhaps the fears that computers will take away our humanity are overblown. Perhaps our pursuit of more effective human-centered design will help us to become more fully human. Perhaps it will be more productive to view machines as augmenters rather than replacers of human beings.

We do our best when we focus on what we can do together in our neighborhoods. If we are concerned about credit and recognition of our work propagating through the human network, we are chasing a chimera. Our human identities are mostly local. We have no control over what happens at large distances (in space and time) from where we are in the human network. The ripples we create with our neighbors will likely travel far, but our names will not. And that is how we fulfill our purpose.

Conclusion

Beginner and master are the two ends of a spectrum of skill. The beginner can only apply disembodied rules and has no intuition about what actions to take. The master operates from embodied intuition honed by long experience and is not aware of rules. We advocate pursuit of mastery while maintaining the ability to be a beginner in a new domain.

The master innovation leader is skilled mobilizer and practitioner of the other seven leadership practices. This leader functions as a servant, working with the people in the community toward a clear purpose. In our world we see many celebrity political and business leaders who are excellent mobilizers but operate in a coercive and detached style. Fortunately, these highly visible people are a minority. Many unpretentious leaders show up to help their community achieve a purpose; they do their job and do not look for recognition. Much innovation is accomplished by these unheralded leaders, way more than is accomplished by the celebrities.

We wish you a most excellent journey.

EPILOG

> *God grant me*
> *serenity to accept the things I cannot change*
> *courage to change the things I can change*
> *and wisdom to know the difference.*
> *– Reinhold Niebuhr*

These famous words are known as the Serenity Prayer. They have inspired many people to make changes in their lives. They are a fitting creed for innovators. Serenity is the practice of accepting the whole of life as it is, good and bad, joyous and wretched, including our finitude and ultimate death. Courage is the practice of acting despite fears of failure, injury, or loss of reputation. Wisdom is the practice of knowing when to act and when to let stand, and of accepting that there are many things we will never understand or control. When embodied as habits, these practices become virtues.

When we see a need for change in our community, we enter conversations to learn whether we have tapped into a widely shared concern. We envision a better world and we offer to lead the way there.

Sometimes we encounter dilemmas. A change favored by many may introduce serious risks. Artificial intelligence is a modern example. It holds great promise for improved productivity at many tasks and for amplifying people's creative abilities. It also threatens job loss, misinformation, deepfakes, stolen elections, societal polarization, new wars, and even a possible end of humanity. These threats are dark innovations that could emerge from the shadows of social space and contaminate the whole. Many large-scale innovations are plagued by dark innovations. As leaders in our communities, we pray for serenity, courage, and wisdom to deal with them.

In this book we have made visible and given names to the recurrent structures of language and coordination in social space. This lexicon is a powerful tool for navigation. That lexicon could itself become a dark innovation if we do not resist the technological lure to mechanize and control its distinctions. Would we want our Siri or Alexa to monitor our speech and interrupt us when assessments are not well grounded? Would we want an automated tracker of our conversations for action that interrupts us, and possibly penalizes us, when our loops are incomplete? Would we want a large language model that monitors our commitments and constructs a social score that determines what we are allowed to do? We introduced these distinctions, not for automation or monitoring, but to enable us to discern what people care about. If we succumb to the lure of mechanization, we will lose the power to care and to navigate.

Serenity, courage, and wisdom work best when accompanied by gratitude and awe. Gratitude is an appreciation for all the gifts life has given us, including life itself, and for the long chain of life's contingencies that have brought us to our current situation. Awe is the ability to revel in the mysteries of the universe and our worlds without trying to resolve or explain them.

When we embody these practices, we keep our hearts open and listening. We are able discern the good from the bad. We become skilled navigators on a restless sea of complexity, at the ready to accomplish great things.

Appendices

A1
KEY DISTINCTIONS

Listed below are key terms that permeate our innovation leadership conversations. Become familiar with these terms and adopt them into your own everyday vocabulary.

Adoption

A commitment from members of your community to join your innovation. Community members embody the new practice. Early adopters, around 16% of the population, are disposed to join innovations early because they enjoy trying out new things and don't mind the risk. Majority adopters, around 68% of the population, are disposed to wait until the innovation is stable, reliable, and low-risk.

Appropriation

Learning practices, history, concerns, and trends of one community to use in another community. For example, the inventor of the World Wide Web appropriated WYSIWYG editing, hyperlinks, and publisher markup languages into the first browser. Appropriation may be accomplished by reading, visiting sites and museums, listening to different voices, and conversing with key people in the other community. Approach in mood of beginner, aiming for advanced beginner. The process of understanding a new community may give you greater skill at understanding your own.

Avalanches

Sweeping rapid changes in society wrought by multiple reinforcing disruptions and changing economics of technologies. Avalanches can be anticipated but rarely predicted. Some are natural such as pandemics, climate change, and natural disasters. Others are man-made such as the birth of flight and the atomic bomb.

Breakdowns

Events or conditions that interrupt progress toward goals. Unhealthy responses include cursing, victimization, and resentment. Healthy responses include acceptance and determination to resolve.

Commitment

An ongoing intention to take care of a concern, and to continue taking care despite contingencies and breakdowns that threaten to block it.

Common Sense

A collective belief, interpretation, or sensibility, unnoticed in the "background of obviousness", that gives meaning to things happening and informs us what makes sense. An example is the idea that innovation always begins with an invention.

Concerns

Issues that draw our attention, we care about them, they matter to us, they distinguish the important from the unimportant. Concerns motivate us to spend time and resource. Some concerns are individual; others community. Innovations begin when people respond to concerns. We need to learn to distinguish concerns we imagine existing in a community from those that actually exist.

Conditioned Tendency

A practice learned in the past for coping with a particular situation; although the past situation no longer exists, some current circumstance triggers the old practice, which sidetracks you from moving toward your goal.

Contingencies

Unexpected events that cannot be ignored. Things that generate breakdowns such as surprises, black swans, external events, unplanned or unanticipated outcomes.

Conversations

All kinds of human interactions, mainly talk and writings, but also gestures, postures, dances, and winks. Range from one-on-one interactions to things everybody in the community is talking about. Conversations can transfer information, coordinate actions, open possibilities, reveal context, elicit commitments, generate relationships, and much more. We inhabit various worlds – realities of our communities – through our conversations. The worlds we inhabit are churning seas of conversations.

Disruption

A significant change of practice occurring over a short time, rendering obsolete well honed old practices, possibly ruining businesses, business models, and identities.

Dreyfus Hierarchy

An interpretation of skill levels at practices in a domain, invented by Stuart and Hubert Dreyfus in 1980. They defined skill acquisition as a process of development through the stages of beginner, advanced beginner, competent, proficient, expert, and master. Development comes from practice over time, often with help from a teacher or coach. We use the Dreyfus hierarchy to distinguish performance skill from applying knowledge through data, rules, and algorithms.

Embodiment

A person or community have ingrained a practice into their muscles and nervous system so that they can perform it skillfully without thought. Embodiment is achieved only by practice and immersion in the world of the practice. It cannot be achieved by applying rules. It reflects things we can perform well but we cannot describe how we do it. Examples include riding a bicycle, playing a musical instrument or speaking a language fluently.

Emergence

Welling up of a new practice in a community without an apparent cause. Likely to be community responses to breakdowns, possibilities, opportunities, contingencies, or mysteries.

Emotional Fortitude

The ability to maintain a steady mood and avoid over-reacting to strong emotional stresses. Managing your own emotional reactivity. Cultivated by practicing moods of serenity, centering, blending, meditating, and mindfulness.

Envisioning

Telling an engaging and compelling story about how the world would be if a sensed concern were taken care of. Your listeners feel included in the story and drawn to your innovation proposals. They see a pathway from the current situation to the better future.

Appendices

Game

A social agreement in a community setting the basic ground rules of interaction. The agreement may be explicit, as in professional sports, or implicit as in the norms of civic communities. Key elements of a game are the point (goal) of the game, the space in which the play occurs, the equipment used, the rules specifying allowed and disallowed actions, strategies for achieving the goal, and referees who settle conflicts and interpret the rules. Games can be finite with a definite start and finish; for example, a tennis match. Games can be infinite with no definite start or finish; for example the game of professional tennis. Finite games are played for the purpose of winning, infinite games for the purpose of continuing the play.

Mobilization

Eliciting a commitment from people to be your followers in pursuit of a clear purpose they care about, and getting them into coordinated action to reach that goal.

Moods

A pervasive biological body state that disposes us to certain interpretations of things around us and to what is possible in the future. People in restrictive (negative) moods see few or no possibilities for future action. People in expansive (positive) moods see many possibilities for future action. Moods exist in communities as well as individuals. Moods are "forces for productivity". Moods can shift when the person sees new or different possibilities. We are always in a mood, although we often do not notice our mood. Moods are not the same as emotions, which are automatic responses to events.

Mystery

An issue for which we have no knowledge and cannot explain; can only be approached in a mood combining wonder, exploration, and adventure with no certainty an answer will ever be found.

Navigation

Finding your way to a goal without detailed planning or knowing a path ahead of time, dealing with breakdowns, contingencies and surprises that could block progress.

Offer

A conditional promise. When you offer to your community to work on taking care of a sensed concern, you are promising and taking responsibility to do that work. Your commitment to taking care of them is clear and compelling. Your offer is credible and inspires trust.

Practices

Embodied skills and sensibilities people (and communities) perform without conscious thought. Levels: beginner, advanced beginner, competent, proficient, expert master.

Readiness

A biological and mental preparedness to go into action at an appropriate moment. Possible actions will be invisible if you are not prepared to do them. When you are ready, you can move to action without thinking.

Recurrences

Repeating patterns that can yield useful explanations and predictions.

Sensing

Discerning a concern in your community and giving it a voice (articulating it). May take time if it has not been articulated before and initially shows up as a discomfort, something bothersome, or a disharmony between the ways things "should" be and the way they are. Not the same as creating an idea or invention and showing its benefit.

Social Space

The space of action and interaction of a community. Social space is in constant movement. Individuals and groups navigate toward their goals by moving into the open spaces of possibilities and avoiding the blockages of constraints. The dynamics of movement can be described as a "game" (see earlier). Possibilities for action come and go. Contingencies appear and redirect the flows of action. Individuals make commitments through speech acts that shape the world seen by others. Moods and the assessments that accompany them shape possibilities and actions. Power, influence, and trust also shape the possibilities for action. Culture, consisting of social norms, beliefs, relationships, and values emerges from the histories of communities in the space. Social space is not a "touchy-feely" abstraction of relationships and culture.

Sustaining

Eliciting a commitment from your community to adopt the practice of an innovation for an indefinite period. Most members of a community are conservative. They are not early adopters and will not join an innovation unless they see many others already in. They want a support infrastructure. They want to see multiple vendors providing backup in case one goes out of business.

Thrownness

An automatic disposition to interpret things in a particular way, or to undertake a particular action without thought. A compulsion that throws you in a particular direction without your consent or thought.

Tools and Equipment

Devices and instruments that enable practices. Tools and practices go together because a tool makes no sense without a practice to achieve a purpose with the tool, and a practice may not be feasible without supporting tools. New technologies can "drive" new practices in the sense that they create new possibilities for action and attract people to pursue those possibilities.

Trust

An assessment that someone is competent, sincere, and caring when making promises. Lack of competence to do what was promised inspires distrust. Lack of intention to follow through on a promise inspires distrust. Lack of care about what you promised or in executing the promise inspires distrust. Trust accumulates over time, increasing as promises are completed. A single broken promise can severely damage trust. Trust is essential for coordination in communities.

Wicked Problem

A social tangle in a community around an issue. They agree there is an issue but cannot agree on a problem statement or a strategy to address the issue. Different subgroups have different views on what the problem is and how to proceed; but no one has sufficient power to impose their solution, and everyone has just enough power to veto any proposed solution they do not care for. A very difficult scientific or

Appendices

engineering problem may be overwhelmed by complexity, but is not wicked because there is no social tangle around it.

World

An interpretation of what is real around us. Interpretations go beyond the physical world and include our perceptions of what is real and true. Worlds are constructed in conversations and influenced by the social games we are engaged in. We can switch back and forth between different perceptive worlds by switching the conversations we are engaged in.

END NOTES

These are not rigid categories. For example, a contingency can inspire the discovery of a new recurrence; further occurrences of the (former) contingency now appear to fit a pattern. New data may reveal that a supposed recurrence has exceptions; now a former recurrence appears dependent on contingencies.

Beginners in a domain may see recurrences as mysteries or contingencies because they are not yet prepared to see and practice the recurrences.

Bureaucracies often try to respond to contingencies by inventing new rules (recurrences) that are supposed to prevent the same contingency from recurring. (That sounds like a paradox, doesn't it?)

A2
SUMMARY OF THE EIGHT PRACTICES

This appendix is a summary of the eight practices of innovation leaders. Here is an annotated map of the eight practices. Following is a more detailed listing of the key points of the practices.

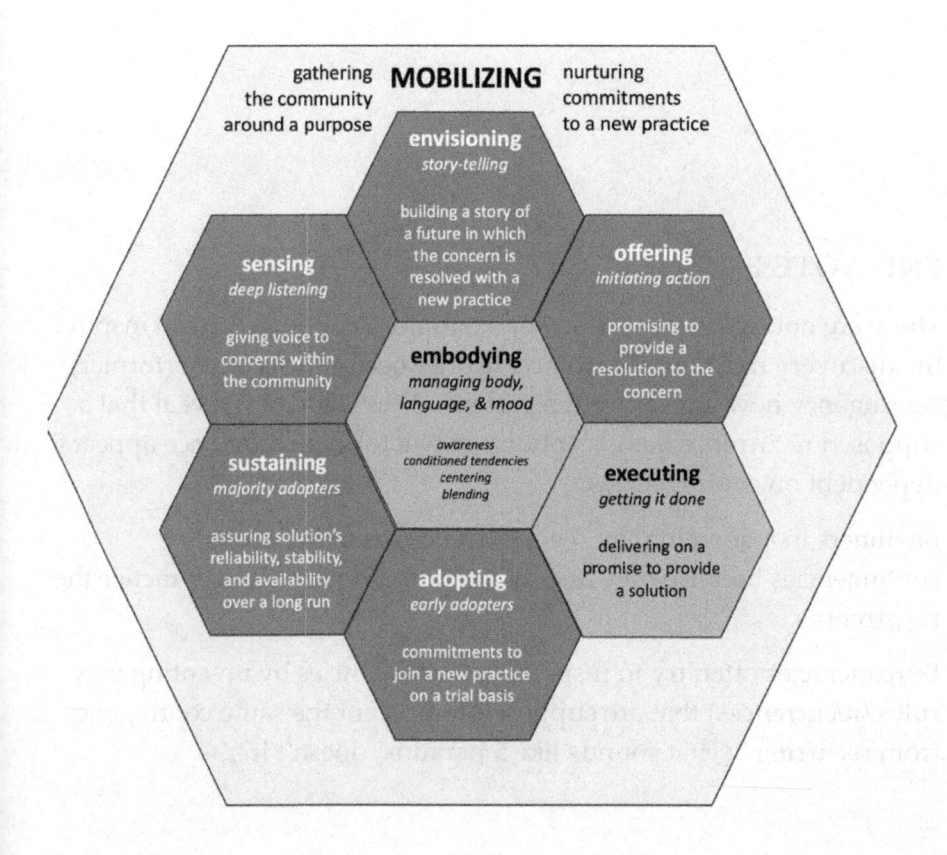

```
                gathering      MOBILIZING      nurturing
              the community                    commitments
             around a purpose                  to a new practice
                              envisioning
                              story-telling

                              building a story of
                              a future in which
            sensing           the concern is        offering
            deep listening    resolved with a       initiating action
                              new practice

            giving voice to                         promising to
            concerns within   embodying             provide a
            the community     managing body,        resolution to the
                              language, & mood      concern

                              awareness
                              conditioned tendencies
            sustaining        centering              executing
            majority adopters blending               getting it done

            assuring solution's                     delivering on a
            reliability, stability,                 promise to provide
            and availability  adopting              a solution
            over a long run   early adopters

                              commitments to
                              join a new practice
                              on a trial basis
```

SENSING
- Start with (awaken to) a sense of an "anomaly" or "disharmony"
- Hang onto it
- Hold it with curiosity, puzzle through it
- Look for value
- Listen for anxieties and other moods
- Listen for the unspoken
- Articulate the concern
- Blindness is always an obstacle

ENVISIONING
- Articulate an engaging, compelling story about the future possibility realized through your innovation
- Locate the value for this possibility – how it addresses cares and concerns
- Show a path to the future

OFFERING
- Make specific offers for outcomes and actions to make the new future happen
- Articulate "Conditions of Satisfaction"
- Listen and co-design agreements and actions to enable acceptance
- Show a demo or prototype
- Show up with presence and produce trust

ADOPTING
- Recruit early adopters in your community to the clear commitment to engage the innovation for a trial period
- Assist them to engage, learn, and experience new value
- Face and overcome resistances and breakdowns
- Blend

SUSTAINING
- Recruit majority adopters in your community to a clear long term commitment to stay with the innovation
- Assist integrating the new practice into their social system
- Assist in establishing supportive infrastructure
- Overcome resistance and breakdowns
- Enable Learning with "small steps"

EMBODYING
- Act effectively without conscious thought
- Build skill through deliberate practice with coaching
- Maintain your center
- Retrain conditioned tendencies into new, more productive practices
- Cultivate emotional fortitude
- Practice blending

EXECUTING
- Build a delivery team
- Plan and execute in conversations
- Elicit commitments to the one team promise
- Develop skills of coordinating action in a network
- Manage commitments, not decisions
- Move people to commitments, then to completion

MOBILIZING
- Show up as leader
- Declare clear and compelling purpose
- Look for everyone to commit
- Hold the center with your commitment and vision
- Teach followers to be leaders themselves
- Encourage everyone to recruit to the movement
- Cope with breakdowns, changes, and rejection
- Listen and learn with others

Appendices

A3

INNOVATION SKILL SELF ASSESSMENT

For a complete self-assessment of your innovation skill, do the following:

- Assess yourself using the directions below.
- Ask a friend or associate who knows you well to assess you.
- Compare the two assessments and discuss with your friend.

For a diagram of the eight practices, see Appendix A2. For more details on the practices, see Chapter 1.

RATINGS FOR THE 8 PRACTICES

1	(Blind) Unaware of this practice
2	(Drifting) Aware, but no action to improve
3	(Resolving) Improvements under way
4	(Settled) Satisfied with approach to this practice
5	(Masterful) Consistently produce significant results and value

RATINGS FOR COHERENCE (FITTING TOGETHER)

1	Missing or disjointed
2	Insufficient to be competitive
3	Strong compared to competition, relevant in market
4	Fulfilling our organizational (business) plans
5	Leader in our domain or market

Fill out the ratings column with one of the numerical scores listed below. The coherence assessments concern how well your performance of the practices fit together into a graceful unity of action.

RATINGS FOR THE 8 PRACTICES

Practice	Your ratings	Friend's ratings
Sensing		
Envisioning		
Offering		
Adopting		
Sustaining		
Executing		
Mobilizing		
Embodying		
COHERENCE		

A master would score a 5 on every practice.

A4

DOMAINS OF CONCERNS

Listening for concerns is a core practice of leadership. What is meant by a concern? How can you listen for concerns if you don't know what to listen for? We outline a practical exercise to assist you in answering these questions.

The exercise is based on the essay "Recurrent domains of Human Concerns," Chapter 11 by Fernando Flores in his book *Conversations for Action*. He argues that, by virtue of our being human beings in living bodies and communities, there are certain areas in which we will inevitably be faced with breakdowns. We all have concerns in these areas. He identified 13 areas, which he called recurrent domains of concerns. They are listed below (Table 1).

He also designed an exercise to examine how each area shows up in your life and to assess your degree of satisfaction with your approach to each area. The exercise is likely to reveal unsettled issues in your life and motivate you to settle them. The exercise appears below.

When you complete the exercise, you will have a plan for taking care of the unsettled domains in your life, which will dispose you to a mood of serenity. You will also gain a deep appreciation for how others experience the same domains and where their experiences differ from yours. In short, this exercise helps you develop a deep appreciation for concerns so that you can listen for them and, more importantly, give them a voice.

You will almost certainly have concerns in other areas besides those listed here. The difference is that these other areas have limited time horizons. They may include professional concerns, which will be with you as long as you are a member of a professional community. They include generational concerns that shift as you grow older and accumulate life experience.

The investigation you are about to begin is open-ended. You will want to revisit your answers from time to time. In addition to Flores's chapter noted earlier, you may find it helpful to read Stephen Covey's chapter on Habit 5, "Seek first to understand, then to be understood", in *The Seven Habits of Highly Effective People*.

Table 1: Recurrent Domains of Human Concerns

BODY	health, illness, diet, personal appearance, handicaps
PLAY	sports, hobbies, vacations, art, theater
SOCIABILITY	friends, colleagues, peers, establishing trust with others
MEMBERSHIP	citizenship, laws and constitutions, clubs, professional organizations
FAMILY	marriage, children, parents, caring for elders
WORK	job skills, commitments on the job, projects
CAREER	choosing direction, preparing for profession, public image and reputation in profession
EDUCATION	school, learning competence in an area, design
MONEY	salary, budget, savings, investment, wealth
SITUATION	temperament, mood, "how things are going", conditions around you
WORLD	politics, environment, peace, commerce, horizons
DIGNITY	self respect, self esteem, standards of performance
SPIRITUALITY	religion, poetry, philosophy, humor, meaning, where we came from, where we are going, mysteries of life and the universe

A concern is an issue or matter that draws a person to care about it and organize action around it. Many people have concerns they cannot put into words, yet they still care and act on them. In this sense, concerns have no voice of their own. It takes someone listening for them to give them voice.

The Exercise

The exercise brings awareness to your permanent concerns so that you can take appropriate action to settle with them. You will make careful assessments of how you are approaching each of these domains. You will make two kinds of assessment. The first is your degree of settlement in each domain (Table 2).

Table 2: Levels of Settlement in a Domain of Concerns

blind	you have been unaware there is a domain of concerns
drifting	you have no plan to take care of your concerns
resolving	your plan is not yet fully implemented and you are not yet satisfied that you are taking care of your concerns
settled	you are taking care of your concerns to your satisfaction

The second assessment is a holistic evaluation of your overall coherence in managing your concerns. Is the balance among them working? Do some domains get more than their fair share of attention?

Make a set of 13 note-pages, one for each domain. Write down your concerns in that domain, your assessment of your level of settlement, and what you must learn or do to move toward settlement. Talk with friends or family or a study partner as you do this to help bring greater focus. We recommend spending time over two weeks because new insights will appear as you continue to reflect and discuss with friends.

Week 1
    a. On your 13 note pages, assess your degree of settlement of each domain. What actions and commitments do you make to move toward settlement?
    b. Assess your balance among the domains. Do any get too little or too much attention? Are you satisfied with the balance?
    c. Write a reflection (1-2 pages) on what you learned. Comment on your mood, coherence of domains, and plans of action. What have you learned that may help you listen for the concerns of others?

Week 2
    a. Review and revise your Week 1 work.
    b. Reflect on the following questions.
        1. What are permanent concerns in your professional community?
        2. What are your concerns in this community?
        3. How do your concerns match up (or conflict with) the domain's concerns?
        4. With whom must you interact to achieve alignment between your concerns and your professional community's concerns?

A5

COMPILATION OF SOMATIC EXERCISES

In Part II of this book we introduced the somatics of conversations, which is concerned with bringing coherence between your intentions and the impulses in your body. Throughout these chapters we offer somatic exercises that assist you in dealing with these impulses. These brief descriptions give the chapter and page number of each exercise.

Walking in the Neighborhood (Ch 7 – 107)

Chauncey Bell's exercise to get you in touch with how our worlds are constituted from conversations.

Walking in the Room (Ch 9 – 128)

Making a declaration is not somatically easy for everyone. The walking-in-the-room exercise develops a somatic sensibility about how to open space in a moving crowd and get their attention with a declaration. The newly opened space represents the invitation of the declaration to step in and be part of it.

I am Competent (Ch 10 – 143)

This exercise helps to see what the practice of making a well-grounded assessment looks and feels like. Sometimes what you think is grounding does not move your listeners. Sometimes the act of claiming something about yourself makes you uncomfortable.

Appendices

Negative Assessments (Ch 10 – 148)

This exercise is a training for recovering from gratuitous negative assessments. It teaches people how to respond with dignity to such assessments, and also to become mindful of what it is like to deliver such an assessment. Learning to maintain one's dignity in the face of an attack, and keep the relationship open, is an important skill. Negative assessments are a tripping point for many people.

Four Responses to Resistance (Ch 14 – 214)

Effective response to resistance starts with an understanding of how you respond to someone who wants to challenge your innovation proposal. This exercise demonstrates the responses ignore, evade, defend, and blend. It allows you to see what is your most natural and train a blend when that is not natural.

Redirected Blending (Ch 14 – 215)

This exercise teaches a more advanced form of blending than the previous. Instead of simply moving with the resister's moment, you can redirect it in a different direction while maintaining the blend.

Group Blending (Ch 14 – 216)

The whole team participates in the blending. Each blender directs the resister for a short while, then hands off the resister to another team member, who continues.

Energy Follows Attention (Ch 15 – 229)

The idea that Energy follows attention highlights an exercise to become aware of your body and not get locked into your head.

Centered Standing (Ch 15 – 229)

Learn how to be fully balanced while standing.

Centered Balance (Ch 15 – 230)

You can experience how centering balances you and being off-center makes it easy to push you off balance.

Declining Requests (Ch 15 – 238)

Often you find yourself saying "yes" to a request that you do not want. An accumulation of these "yeses" pushes you beyond your capacity and drags you into a mood of overwhelm. In turn, that erodes other people's trust in you. This simple practice can help break this tendency.

Emotional Fortitude (Ch 15 – 239)

Emotional fortitude is the ability to main a steady emotional balance even when under duress. Emotional fortitude is a reward of serenity. Untamed emotional reactivity can overwhelm your desire to remain emotionally centered. Here we offer practices that build your emotional fortitude over time: meditating, declining requests, observing assessments, respectful sharing of assessments, gratitude and appreciation, and coaching.

Capacity Assessment (Ch 16 – 251)

Many people cannot deliver their promises and develop reputations for being unreliable and untrustworthy. They live in a mood of overwhelm. This exercise uses a spreadsheet of your commitments to determine if you are overcommitted. Then you can shed load by cancelling or delegating commitments.

A6

INNOVATION IN SIX HORIZONS

In 2013 Fernando Flores led a Commission for the Chilean government on innovation and Chile's future.[1] The report contained a new philosophical framework for innovation, which they called six horizons. He and B. Scot Rousse produced a summary of that section, which we reproduce here in condensed form with their permission. Chauncey Bell introduced the report to his clients this way:

> For those with serious interest in how innovation occurs, this report is a treasure. It examines the phenomena of innovation, the background in which innovation occurs, the current historical state of the world in which innovation arrives, and proposes directions for investigation and action for Chile that can readily be seen as relevant and deeply related to the challenges faced by communities of all sizes and types around the world. Further, the report re-frames, in important new ways, the questions of leadership and design for anyone who takes responsibility for guiding their community or enterprise into the future that is before us.[2]

For this book, the horizons drive home the point that a large number of persons are involved in multiple levels of adopting new practice into everyday life.

---

[1] Fernando Flores et al. 2013. *Surfing Toward the Future: Chile on the 2025 Horizon.* https://docs.consejoctci.cl/wp-content/uploads/2021/05/SURFING-TOWARDS-THE-FUTURE-1.pdf

[2] Chauncey Bell. 2013. Blog. https://chaunceybell.com/2013/09/18/major-new-fernando-flores-work-product/

• • •

The following six horizons of innovation illuminate how new things, products, or services emerge over time. Each horizon represents a set of people working on the innovation from a particular concern. Each horizon has its own style of observation and can be obstructed by particular modes of blindness. Although the horizons can be seen roughly as different stages of emergence, we prefer speaking in terms of horizons because there are no rigid boundaries. Some innovations may not include all six horizons. Others may remain in a particular horizon for many years. The six horizons are a map for how practices change so we can more skillfully navigate toward the emerging future.

Horizon 1: Everyday Life

Horizon 2: Emerging Markets for New Products: Possible avalanches

Horizon 3: New Products or Services

Horizon 4: Search for Concrete Applications: Harnessing an Effect for a Purpose

Horizon 5: Consolidation of the Fulgor

Horizon 6: The *Fulgor*

Horizon 6. *The Fulgor.* "Fulgor" is a Spanish word meaning "glimmer or faint glow." We use it to capture the moment when a new configuration of our practices begins to appear, casting an initially faint light of new possibilities.[3] In the context of an already-existing way of life – Horizon 1 below – the fulgor looks like an inkling of something new, which may eventually turn into the new technologies and services. This horizon has a characteristic mood of unsettlement accompanied by a sense of promise. It has a feeling that

---

[3] It is the "awakening" event that launches the Sensing practice.

the glimmer exceeds our current ability to grasp and express it.

A fulgor typically results from observing and holding onto an *anomaly*. An anomaly is an emergent event or condition that does not fit with the normal way of doing things. Unsettlement is a mood that aims to understand the anomaly. For example, Louis Pasteur saw an anomaly in the breakdown of a fermentation process – some wines were good, others mysteriously turned to vinegar. It bothered him and he moved to investigate. With a microscope (a new instrument at the time) he saw strange microscopic moving shapes (what we now call "bacteria"). This produced a fulgor for him. He wondered if these moving entities emitted chemicals that disrupted the fermentation process. He started to see connections he never saw before. Had he not allowed himself to be unsettled, he would not have found the fulgor.

Horizon 5. *Consolidation of the Fulgor.* This means to bring others into the investigation of the fulgor so that they can see it independently. Consolidation is now often accomplished through experimental work done in a laboratory as experimental science. The point here is to develop the ability to systematically generate recurrences of the emergent phenomenon and to develop our understanding of it. Once in a while a laboratory produces something that can massively change our practices.

Horizon 4. *The Search for Concrete Applications: Harnessing an Effect for a Purpose.* Effects confirmed as recurrent in the laboratory become attractive as means to solve specific problems. They can be put to work (harnessed) before being fully understood. Once an effect is harnessed in an application, its utility seems obvious – but we should be careful not to read this obviousness back into the initial context. For example, it was known that the mold spore *Penicillium notatum* inhibits *staphylococci* bacteria for several years before Alexander Fleming, who had been a doctor in WWI, realized in 1928 that this effect might be harnessed for treating infection. Similarly, the resilience of Corning's Gorilla Glass was known for many years before it was harnessed to make a damage-resistant iPhone touchscreen.

Horizon 3. *New Products or Services.* When an effect has found utility in several applications, a "generative principle" has been revealed, which can be used for other new products and services. This is the domain of R&D (research and development). Here entrepreneurial interest, markets, and possible customers for around seven years.

Horizon 2. *Emerging Markets for the New Products: Detecting Possible Avalanches.* Business models begin to emerge as some companies develop production and delivery systems that perform better than others. A well-developed product or service can solidify its offer by pointing to established practices that it supports or extends. For example, iPhone incorporated iPod and the acquisition of software apps through the ITunes store. Occasionally, new products and services produce truly disruptive changes and trigger transitions in entire industries, as happened with Internet, smart phones, digital photography, e-books, and generative artificial intelligence. We call these massive, unanticipated transformations avalanches.

As the markets mature, competition emerges among business models, not just individual companies. Clayton Christensen, a business professor at Harvard, described this as a dilemma for business leaders. Sooner or later a small company appears that offers the same product or service in a low-end version that does not appeal to any of the larger company's customers. Eventually the small company starts to compete for the large company's customers. The large company cannot compete because its business model is inefficient compared to the small company. Unless it adapts its business model, the large company is disrupted and put out of business. Christensen called this process disruptive innovation.

Horizon 1. *Everyday Life and Practice*: When innovations become an element of our routines in the network of equipment and recurrent practices of daily life, they enter the horizon of everyday life. They become normal and unnoticed. Breakdowns in everyday life set the stage for a subsequent fulgor, and thus a new Horizon 6.

Avalanches

The above horizons of innovation can help us all improve our ability to anticipate avalanches that can drastically impact our worlds. An avalanche is a major, rapid transition in the everyday practices, markets, and institutions. Avalanches present both threats and opportunities – threats to the continued operation of societies and businesses, opportunities for entrepreneurs to develop new businesses for the transformed environment. The skill of interpreting markets to detect coming avalanches is an important navigational skill in the dynamic unfolding of social space.

A7

A TAXONOMY OF INNOVATION MODELS

There are many interpretations and definitions of innovation. Each one leads to different actions in pursuit of innovation. A short summary of the many perspectives and their mindsets is helpful. In *The Innovator's Way*, Chapter 3, Peter Denning and Bob Dunham surveyed the innovation literature to learn how people thought about innovation and to position their book in that constellation.

They found four main lines of thinking about innovation: Mystical, Process, Leadership, and Generative. Although these lines can be seen as independent interpretations, they can also be seen as developmental stages in understanding innovation with each stage having more to say about achieving adoption. The stages are summarized in Table 1 along with examples of advocates from the literature. Table 2 summarizes three skill levels at which each of the four stages can be practiced. A list of citations for those advocates is at the end of this appendix.

This book is based in the generative interpretation. It directly confronts the central challenge of adoption: dealing with the unpredictable and sometimes chaotic social space of the community. Innovators are leaders who can skillfully cope with whatever the community throws at them, finding a path through resistance to bring about community agreement to adopt the new practice. By analogy, Aikido students, through extensive practice and training, prepare for their black-belt demonstrations. Their demonstrations put to the test their skills at deflecting incoming attackers while maintaining balance and center. Their years of preparation may have followed a process, but the actual demonstration is skillful performance. So it is with an innovation leader. The leader can train in the eight practices, but each adoption results from a skillful performance rather than a managed process. The generative interpretation is useful for dealing with the Valley of Death that appears in the process interpretation of innovation.

Citations for the Advocates

Billington, David. *The Innovators: The Engineering Pioneers Who Made American Modern.* Wiley (1996).

Bush, Vannevar. *Science, the Endless Frontier.* A Report to the President. U.S. Government Printing Office (1945).

Christenson, Clayton. *The Innovator's Dilemma.* Harvard Business (1997).

Denning, Peter, and Dunham, Robert. *The Innovator's Way: Essential Practices for Successful Innovation.* MIT Press (2010).

Deschamps, Jean-Philippe. *Innovation Leaders.* Jossey-Bass, division of Wiley (2008).

Drucker, Peter. *Innovation and Entrepreneurship.* Harper Business (1993). (First published by Harper Perennial in 1985.)

Evans, Harold. *They Made America: Two Centuries of Innovators from the Steam Engine to the Search Engine.* Little Brown (2004).

Flores, Fernando, et al. *Surfing Toward the Future: Chile on the 2025 Horizon.* https://docs.consejoctci.cl/wp-content/uploads/2021/05/SURFING-TOWARDS-THE-FUTURE-1.pdf

Gilder, George. *Recapturing the Spirit of Enterprise.* ICS Press (1992).

Kelley, Tom, and Kelley, David. *Creative Confidence: Unleashing the Creative Potential within us all.* Currency (2013).

Kline, Stephen J., and Nathan Rosenberg. An overview of innovation. In *The Positive Sum Strategy: Harnessing Technology for Economic Growth*. National Academy Press (1986), 275-305.

Rogers, Everett. *Diffusion of Innovations*. 5th Ed. Free Press (2003). First edition 1962.

Schon, Donald. *Beyond the Stable State*. Norton (1971).

Spinosa, Charles, Fernando Flores, and Hubert Dreyfus. *Disclosing New Worlds*. MIT Press (1997).

Table 1. Models of Innovation

Level	Innovation is ...	Models			
1 Mystical	Changes achieved through special talent, genius, good fortune, luck serendipity, magic	Inspirational stories of individual innovators (Billington, Evans)			
2 Process	Process taking ideas from inception to impact; process can be managed and controlled	Pipeline (Bush, Kline)	Diffusion (Rogers)	Disruption (Christensen)	
3 Leadership	Change of practice brought about by leadership strategy and action	Sources (Drucker)	Traits and Virtues (Gilder, Deschamps)	Learning Networks (Schon)	
4 Generative	Skill of generating, through language, adoption of new practice in a community	Eight Practices (Denning–Dunham)	Design Thinking (Kelley)	Horizons (Flores)	History Making (Spinosa et al)

Table 2. Development and Performance Levels

DEVELOPMENT STAGE

PERFORMANCE LEVEL	Mystical	Process	Leadership	Generative
Novice	admire talent	follow rules	imitate behavior	Organize to learn the eight practices
Skillful	imitate talent	manage competently; analyze risks and returns; customize process to situation	cultivate personal qualities; inspire; mobilize; create serendipity	competent at all eight practices
Masterful	identify, attract, and hire talent	manage large organizations and production lines; produce "happy accidents"	develop leadership presence; foster culture of innovation	acquire advanced skill through immersion and development of a unique way of observing

INDEX

10,000 hours, 227, 318
10X rule of thumb, 211

A
Abstraction, 324
Abstraction, force for detachment, 324
Action Technologies, 245, 297
Action
   embodied, 222, 311
   from commitments, 83
Adopting, 345
   practice, 204
Adoption, pr3, 18, 335
   as social process, pr4
   Bell curve of, 205
   role of marketing, 206
African proverb, 273
Agile
   development, 291
   model, 279
Aikido, 231
Air Force, US, 43
AlphaGo, 263
ANN, artificial neural network, 303
Appreciative inquiry, 185, 268
Apprenticing, 316
Appropriation, 335
Arlington Cemetery, 327
Art, 302
Artificial General Intelligence, 299
Artificial intelligence, 11, 42, 300, 331
Artificial, neurons, 303
Artillery, British folklore, 222
Asimov, Issac, 1

Assertions
   claim of truth, 140
   use in grounding, 140
Assessments, 139
   coherence of eight practices, 296
   grounded (and ungrounded), 140
   negative, 147
   negative exercise, 148
   progress with eight practices, 295
   respectful sharing, 240
   skill at delivering, 147
   standards for grounding, 140
   where grounding is essential, 141
Austin, John L., 87, 116
Avalanche, 301, 336
   social, 210
Awakening, 1, 27, 49
Awareness, 223, 226
   creating choice, 227
   somatic, 226
Awe, 332

B
Background, 309
   of obviousness, 105, 124, 310
Bacon, Francis, 189
Balance, emotional, 230
Barrett, Frank, 185
Baseball, 207
Basketball, 40
Bayesian inference, 312
Becoming, 273
   cycle of, 275
Beginner, 39, 315
Beginners Creed, 32, 34

Beginning, 27
Being in the World (film), 44
Bell, Chauncey, 88, 98, 107, 110, 126, 139, 357
Bender, Emily, 305
Berners-Lee, Tim, 206
Bias, 287, 325
Big idea, 132
    declaration for envisioning, 132
Black Lives Matter, 70
Blending, 223, 226-227, 232
    group, 216
    redirected, 215
    to overcome resistance, 232
    to resolve wicked problems, 232
Bluntness, 198
Boyd, John, 115, 120
    40 second, 115
Breakdown, 254, 336
Bubble, 103
Bureaucracy, 280
    automation of, 280
    resistance to change, 281
    side conversations in, 282
Burke, James, 81
Bush, Vannevar, 69
Business 2000, 101
Business plan, 276

C
Candor, 198
Capacity, 250
    assessment of, 251
    to deliver promises, 250
Care, 97, 306
    concern for future well-being, 323
Carse, James, 40
CAYA Green, 195
Centering, 223, 226-228
    balance, 230
    emotional, 231
    exercise, 229
    physical, 231
    restoring, 230, 231
CERN, 206
Chain of command, 92
Characterizations, 144
Charisma, of leaders, 260
Chasm, 277
ChatGPT, 263
Chimera, 328
Chomsky, Noam, 305
Christensen, Clayton, 75, 210, 287
Civil Rights Act, 256
Clash, pipeline and adoption, 21
Climate change, 264
    of workplace, 58
Coalitions, 194
Coercive leader, 320, 322
Commitment, 307, 336
    generating expectations, 90
    network of, 122
    producing action, 90
    requests and promises, 307
    types of, 88
Common sense, 106, 289, 310, 336
Community, 17
Competence, grounding exercise, 143
Concerns, 27, 336
    behind assessments, 152
    definition, 56
    listening for, 56
    orienting, 56
    recurrent, 350
Conditioned tendencies, 96, 234, 337
    of group, 236
    retraining, 223, 226, 236
Conditions of satisfaction, 90
Constitution, US, 127
Contingency, 9, 10, 14, 17, 21, 51, 53, 54, 62, 70, 71, 254, 337
Control, 257, 325

Index

Context, 139
    conversation for, 92, 94
Conversations, 81, 83, 84, 337
    as communication, 87
    for message exchange, 84
    generating worlds, 99
    managing, 248
    missing, 116
    restless sea of, 17
    with machines, 97
Conversation for action, 92, 117
    comparison with OODA loop, 120
    conditions of satisfaction, 117
    failure modes, 119
    fractal universe, 123
    loop, 117
    universality, 123
    definition of, 83, 84
Conversation for context, 92, 94
Conversation for possibility, 92, 93
Conversation for relationship, 92, 94
Coordinator, 245
    controversy on surveillance, 297
    mail system, 297
Copernican revolution, 71
Copyright, 302
Courage, 331
Covey, Stephen, 64, 175, 252
    emotional bank account, 176
Customer service, 175, 302
Customer, 248, 249
    of promises, 249
Cyc project, 106, 310

D

Dashboards, 287
Data obsession, 286
Data, biases, 287
Declaration, 127
    authority to make, 128
    of Independence, 125
    speech act, 127
Decision-making, nonrational, 82
Declining requests, exercise, 237
Deepfakes, 302
Deepmind, 263
Defense Department, US, 69
Dehumanization of workers, 7
Denning, Dorothy, 327
    cell story, 327
Denning, Peter, 362
Descartes, René, 82
Detachment, 324
    outside observer, 324
DevOps
    development, 291
    model, 279
Diffusion of innovation, 74, 204
Digital meters, 287
Disruption, 210, 337
Domains of concerns, 350
Dreyfus hierarchy, 30, 43, 46, 223, 311, 337
Dreyfus, Hubert and Stuart, 30, 43
Dreyfus, Hubert, 39, 42, 43, 161, 317, 319, 325
Drucker, Peter, 273, 285
Drunk driving, 264
Dunham, Robert, 362

E

Ecosystem
    human, 41
    of community, 202
Edison, Thomas, 4, 243
Education, disruption, 211
Eight practices. pr2
    map, 16, 49-54, 344
    self-assessment, 348
    summary 344
Einstein, Albert, 1, 61, 99, 285, 301, 315
Embodied action, 311

Embodiment, *see embodying*
Embodying, 30, 221, 316, 338, 346
Emergence, 338
  of new practices, 12
Emotional balance, 230
Emotional fortitude, 96, 230, 238, 338
Emotional reactivity, 230
Emotions, 308
  definition of, 157
  eight basic, 158
Energy
  following attention, 227, 228
  in your head, 229
Envisioning, 132, 338, 345
Epicycles, of astronomy, 71
Epilog, 331
Equilibrium
  avalanche, 202
  disruptive change, 202
  incremental change, 202
  punctuated, 202
  social, 203
Equipment, 342
Ethics, 305
Eureka story, 3
  flaws, 5
Executing, 243, 346
  successfully, 246
Exercises, somatic, compilation, 354
Experience, somatic, 227
Expert systems, 42, 106, 223, 310
Experts Lament, 33, 36

F
Fabrication, 302
Fail fast and often, 169
Fakes, 302
Filter bubble, 103
Flores, Fernando, 28, 81, 83, 88, 99, 101, 116, 134, 148, 235, 245, 288, 297, 307, 350
  negative assessment exercise, 235
  world game, 101
Flores, Gloria, 56, 155, 165
Flow state, 316
Floyd, George, 70
Folk legend, 61
Ford, Henry, 4
Fulgor, 358
Funnel, 290

G
Game, 30, 40, 339, 359
  definition of, 40
  finite and infinite, 40, 315
  talent in, 41
  coordination, 289
Gates, Robert, 59
Generative AI, pr1, 11, 97, 106, 261, 263
Gettysburg address, 134
Gladwell, Malcolm, 318
Golf, 318
Gould, Stephen Jay, 202
GPS, 286
Granger, Kari, 104, 299
Gratitude, 332
  and appreciation, 240
Greene, Robert, 315
Grounding, 141
Grove, Andy, 211, 288

H
Hackathon, 290, 291
Hallucination, 302
Handler, Ruth, 255, 257
Hanna, Thomas, 226
Harari, Yuval Noah, 184
Heilmeier, George, 138
  catechism, 138
Hinton, Geoffrey, 299
Horizons of innovation, 357
Horne, Sabra, 8

Index

Huang, Jensen, 264, 301
Human centered design, 268, 328
Humility, 316

I

Identities, 146
  basis in assessments, 146
  personal, 146
  public, 146
Images, 302
Imagination, 310
  and language, 107
Importance, 252
Inference, first person, 312
  from unrepresented data, 310
  statistical, 310
  third-person, 312
Information theory, 84
Innovation cell, 74
Innovation definition, 17
  adoption aspect, 18
  community aspect, 17
  practices aspect, 18
  social space aspect, 17
Innovation leaders
  eight practices of, 13, 15
  practical philosophy, 322
  personal qualities, 13
Innovation schools, bibliography, 363
Innovation source
  generative, 362
  leadership, 362
  mystical, 362
  process, 362
Innovation
  and chaos theory, 20
  as a game, 44
  as social process, 81
  dark, 331
  definition of, pr1, 77
  disruptive, 75, 210
  early definition of, 2
  in-the-making, 20
  origins in conversations, 13
  ready-made, 19
  science view, 19
  six horizons, 357
  social, 2
  theater, 243
  unpredictability of, 20
Innovator's Way, book, pr2
Innovators, serial, 293
Intel Corp, 288
Intellectual property, 74
Interpretations, 85
Inventors, role of, 4
Involvement, 324
iPhone, 12, 255, 262
iPod, 261, 262

J

Jobs, reframer, 207
Jobs, Steve, 12, 207, 243, 255, 257, 261, 262
  as reframer, 207
Journalism, drafting-summarizing, 302
Joyce, James, 221
  Mr Duffy, 221

K

Khan Academy, 264
Khan, Sal, 264
Kaufman, Ron, 164, 201, 323
Key distinctions, 335
King, Martin Luther, 256, 257, 285
Kipling, Rudyard, 189
Knowledge, 43, 222
  performance, 311
  procedural, 311
  tacit, 43, 311
Kodak, 67, 210
Kotter, John, 47

KPI, 292
Kurzweil, Ray, 211, 300

L
Lamb, Cindi, 265
Language pr5, 300, 301, 305
    for coordinating action, 116
    host of worlds, 116
Lao Tzu, 201
Large Language Model (LLM), 107, 299
    as innovation leaders, 312
    augmentations for leadership, 313
    entering language, 305
    fine-tuning, 304
    inference of improbable, 313
    parameters, 303
    prompt, 303
    training, 303
    tweaking, 303
    banality of, 301
    basics, 303
    optimism toward, 301
    pessimism toward, 301
Larsen, Reif, 61
Latour, Bruno, 19, 285, 268, 298
Leading 47
Legacy,
    loss of name, 327
    of leader, 326
Lenat, Douglas, 106, 310
Leonard, George, 319
Life, art of, 320
Lightner, Candace, 264
Lincoln, Abraham, 134
Listening, 86
    active, 87
    deep, 57
    definition of, 55
    for listening, 86
    to the listening, 227
    with whole body, 233

    see also Resonance
Locality, power of, 328

M
Machines, 299
    marshalling forces, 312
Macintosh computer, 262
MADD, 264-265
Maintenance, of ships, 64
Making a mark, 327
Making sense, 310
Management
    agile, 75
    lean, 75
    network of commitments, 122
Mandela, Nelson, 155
Mandelbrot, Benoit, 124
Manifesto, 134
    Elements of, 136
    Example, 137
Map, 62
    as flowcharts, 67
    Micronesian Stick, 63
    of social space, 218
Marine Corps (US), 142, 247
Master, 39, 315,
    style of, 316
Mastery, 315
    as community assessment, 319
    Being in the World (film), 316
    common factors of masters, 317
    Mastery, in all domains, 316
Mattel toy company, 255
Mattis, James, 59
Measuring, 285
Mechanization, lure of, 332
Medical diagnosis, 301
Meditation, 239
Mental models, 288
Merit, 290
Mess, 168, 268

Index

mastering, 197
Metrics,
for adoption, 293
Metrics
   for organizations, 290
   input-output, 292
   key performance indicators, 292
   tools for guiding navigation, 298
Michelanglo, 315
Mind-body dualism, 82, 225
   Taylorized, 9
Mobilization, 255, 339, 346
   business, 259-260
   civilian, 259
   climate change example, 264
   community example, 266
   drunk driving example, 264
   essence of, 270
   example technology, 263
   in organizations, 274
   incentives, 270
   mastery of, 256
   metrics, 270
   military, 259
Model
   blindness of, 288
   directing metrics, 289
   mental, 288
Mood, 155, 160, 308, 359
   assessments of, 158
   cultivating, 164
   filter of interpretation, 158
   definition of, 157
   expansive, 157
   for teaching and learning, 168
   force for productivity, 162
   in the room, 157, 161
   listening for, 161
   navigating, 162
   navigation levels, 163-165
   of groups and eras, 157, 159
   of team life-cycle, 167
   orchestrating, 164
   restrictive, 157
   sensing and reading, 161
   shifting, 164
   situational, 159
   social, 261
   table of common, 160
Moore, Geoffey, 206, 277
Moore's Law, 203
Morality, 305
Morgan, JP, 27
Mothers Against Drunk Driving, 70, 265
Movement, social, 276, 278
Music, 302
Musk, Elon, 256, 257
Mystery, 340

N
NASA, 246, 256
   computational science, 31
National Science Foundation, 69
Natural disasters, 209
Navigating 41, 61, 62, 77, 340
Navy US, nuclear, 47
NBA, 40
NCAA, 40
Negative assessment, script, 149, 239
Netflix, 210
Network of commitments, 88, 122, 248
Neural network, 300
Neurons, artificial, 303
Newborn, Dave, 293
Nichols, Vincent, 155
Niebuhr, Reinhold, 331
Nietzsche, Friedrich, 181
Nonrational decision making, 82
NVIDIA, 301, 264

O
Objectivity, 325

Obviousness, background of, 310
Offer, 340, 345
Ontology, 288
OODA Loop, 115
Open spaces, 11
OpenAI, pr1, 263
Operation Iraqi Freedom, 195
Opinion polls, 140
Organization
    chart, 92
    civic, 278

P
Paradox, metrics v. outcomes, 286
Pasteur, Louis, 134
Patent office, 293
Patton, George, 243
Performance
    knowledge, 311
    reviews, 141
    skill, 222
Philharmonia Baroque Orchestra, 41
Pipeline model, pr2, 6, 7, 66, 290
    complexity, 70
    flaws, 70, 73
    loops organizing production, 122
    patches, 76
    US Department of Defense R&D, 66
    with feedback, 74
Plateaus, of skill, 319
Poetry, 302, 310
Polanyi, Michael, 43, 311
Power, 189
    and community, 190
    and resistance, 194
    and social networks, 198
    as illusion, 189
    as influence, 190
    as perception, 190
    kinds of, 192-193
    navigation of, 195

Power centers, 194
    alignment, 194
    coalitions, 194
Powerpoint, 247
Practices, 18, 222, 340
    adopted, 223
    embodied, 43
    leadership, 223
    of learning embodiment, 224
Prejudices, 325
Prime innovation pattern, 14, 135
Procedural memory, 311
Production
    line, 279
    story, 5
    new, 278
    story, flaws, 9
Productivity anomaly, 292
Programming, initial draft codes, 302
Prompt, 303

R
Reactions, in body, 95
Reactivity, emotional, 230
Readiness, 340
Reagan, Ronald, 182
Realities, objective and subjective, 103
Recurrences, 340
Reframing, 71, 76, 77, 207-209, 216
Reputation, 142
Research, basic and applied, 69
Resentment, 180
Resignation, in metrics, 293
Resistance, 54, 76, 201, 212
    as metaphorical friend, 204
    as phenomenon in language, 203
    bureaucratic, 273
    early signs, 204
    exercises of responses, 214
    forms, 212
    self, 214

Index

somatics of, 213
Resonance, 161, 166
    emotional, 309
Ressentiment, 181
Rheingold, Howard, 255
Rickover, Hyman, 47
Roberts, Nancy, 209
Robotics, 267
Rogers, Everett, 204, 277
Roosevelt, Franklin, 69
Rousse, B Scot, 43, 56, 357
Ruspoli, Tao, 44, 316
Russia, 102, 256

S

Sailors, measuring progress, 285
Sartre, Jean-Paul, 81
Schmidt, Eric, 1
Schon, Donald, 201, 273
Science, breakthroughs, 301
Scientific management, 2, 68
Scraping, 302, 305
Scrum model, 279
Seaport, 232
Search, for lost keys, 288
Searle, John, 87, 88, 116
Seba, Tony, 211
Sensibilities, somatic, 228
Sensing, 341, 345
Serenity, 316
Serenity prayer, 331
Servant leader, 320, 322
Service, care in action, 323, 324
Shannon, Claude, 84
Singularity, 211, 300
Skill, embodied, 43, 44
Skills profile, 293
Skills, hard and soft, 23
Skilling, 39, 44
Smith, Fred, 177
Social media, 103

Social movement, 257
Social network mapping, 198
Social space, 17, 341
    as game, 83
    as production system, 286
    map, 218
    structures of, 286
Sodol, Lee, 263
Software development, 279
Software engineering, 56
Somatics, 94, 95, 225-227
    four core practices, 226-237
    proactive response, 95
    reactive response, 96
SpaceX, 256
Speech act, 16, 83, 87, 91, 116
    assertion, 90
    assessment, 90
    declaration, 89
    promise (and offer), 89
    request, 89
Spider diagram, 293
Spiral model, 279
Stakeholder, 206
Starlink, 256
Startups, 276
Statistical inference, 304
Stochastic parrot, 305
Strozzi Heckler, Richard, 167, 221
Subcommunities, 207
Sustaining, 341, 346

T

Tacit knowledge, 310
Talent, thirst for, 41
Taxonomy of innovation models, 362
Taylor view, criticism of, 7
Taylor, Frederick, 2, 6, 7, 67, 68, 281
    criticism of, 7
Teachers, importance of, 238
Team, 244

moods for success, 166
mutual support, 244
shared promise, 244
startup conversations, 245
Technological way of being, 325
Technological progress, 5
Technology transfer, 66
Ten thousand hours, 318
Tesla, 256
Theater, innovation, 243
Theodore Roosevelt, 3 (and prolog)
Thrownness, 342
Thunberg, Greta. 264
Tools, 342
Top cover, 270
Touchpoints, 249
Transition, technology, 10
Troubles in Northern Ireland, 208
Truman, Harry, 58, 182
Trust, 171, 172, 175, 342
    and coaching, 185
    as assessment, 176
    as mood, 179
    as transaction, 174
    care, 177
    competence, 176
    from completing loops, 117
    in relationships, 178
    long time to earn, 183
    managing, 252, 253
    practices for, 172
    recovery when lost, 185
    sincerity, 176
    supportive practices, 181, 186
Trustworthiness, of LLMs, 302
Truth to power, 198
Turing, Alan, 299, 304
Turing test, 264, 304
Tzu, Lao, 320

U
Ueshiba, Morihei, 231
Ukraine, 102, 256
Uncertainty, fog of, 19, 62
Urgency, 252

V
Valley of death, 2, 10, 76, 286
Venture capital, 276
Vigilance, 288
Virtues, 331
Voices, 196-198

W
Walking in the neighborhood, 107, 110
Walking in the room, 128, 233
Walking, in various cities, 132
War, art of, 320
Water polo, 266
Waterfall model, 279
Waves, somatic, 233
Weber, Max, 273, 281
Wicked problem, 68, 268, 342
Wills, Garry, 255
Winograd, Terry, 246
Wisdom, 331
Workflows, 120
World of Warcraft, 28
World Wide Web, 206
World, 100, 307, 343
    bubble, 103
    conflicting wicked problems, 103
    constituted from conversations, 83
    reality of, 101
    social media, 103
World Game, 101
Wright brothers, 4

X
Xerox, 67
Xerox PARC, 67

ABOUT THE AUTHORS

Peter Denning's passion for ideas and experimentation was revealed as a teenager when he built a computer from pinball machine parts to solve linear equations, long before lines of code were being written for advanced computer chips. He invented the Working Set method for managing computer storage; it is used in all major operating systems today. He co-invented basic principles for computer systems to monitor access to data, which are the system foundations for cyber security today. He co-founded CSNET, the first non-government network to deploy the ARPANET protocols; it grew to 50,000 researchers and students at 120 universities and labs and stimulated the modern Internet. He co-founded Operational Analysis, a mathematical method for predicting performance of networks of computers. He founded and led a movement to reframe computing as a science based on timeless principles, leading to the modern acceptance of computer science as a foundational field with computational thinking as the core practice. He co-founded generative leadership, which applies language-action philosophy to teach skills for eliciting commitments, coordinating actions, and mobilizing people to innovations. He has published 13 books in these areas.

Todd Lyons works alongside Peter as his co-author, co-creator, and instructor of Innovation Leadership at NPS. For 30 years as an active US Marine, Todd recommended, guided, implemented, and executed more new ideas than most of us would imagine in a lifetime. As a Marine and Naval Attaché in the Middle East, he developed and established new practices and agreements to support United States efforts across the diplomatic, informational, military, and economic arenas. He is currently the vice president of the NPS Foundation and Alumni Association, where he creates new opportunities for NPS faculty and students to work in collaboration with industry to meet the challenges identified by senior DoD leadership. He bridges the divide between academia, industry, and the military to deliver capabilities at a pace the operational environment requires. He understands how bureaucracy works and how to make it work, even when it looks stuck to others.

Made in the USA
Middletown, DE
25 July 2024